My Farming Life

by

Ken Mewett

New Millennium

292 Kennington Road, London SE11 4LD

British Library in publication data.
A catalogue record for this book is
obtainable from The British Library.

Front cover photo:
1985. The author testing wheat at Colemans Farm

Printed and bound by Watkiss Studios Ltd.
Biggleswade, Beds.
Issued by New Millennium*
Set in 12 point Times New Roman Typeface
ISBN 1 85845 288 0
* An imprint of The Professional Authors' & Publishers' Association

ACKNOWLEDGEMENT

Thanks to Kay Miller for the work she put in
word processing this manuscript

FOREWORD

I have much pleasure in writing this foreword to Ken Mewett's book on his farming life.

Although my own background is totally different to Ken's, ou· farming lives are very similar. I have encountered so many of the difficulties he describes. How farming has changed from pushing dung up planks to the present day, when hardly anybody has to do any hard manual work. Now all the heavy lifting is done by machines.

I think that people engaged in the agriculture industry will find this book most interesting, and the general public will find it full of drama, tragedy and humour.

Peter Braden
April, 1999

My Farming Life

I was born on 15th November, 1926, a farmer's son. I have a sister who is fourteen months younger than me. My grandfather was a head game keeper on an estate at Guestling, near Hastings, in East Sussex, and my father was second to the oldest son of four in the family. He was the one who started the working of their early farming career.

His father and stepmother (his own mother died when my father was eleven years old) once told me he was the mainstay for a while, helping bring up an invalid brother and also a younger sister and brother. They moved from Brightlands Park where my father was born in 1886. His father ran the pack of beagles at Brightlands Park in Sussex, and when he was a young man, the gentleman owner, my grandfather's employer, wanted him to go to France with the pack of beagles, but he declined, for what reason I do not know. Perhaps it was the fear of going by boat across the Channel. To this day I have still got the hunting horn used for the pack of beagles.

The family eventually moved to Eastways Farm, near Hastings ~ a larger house, small amount of ground, where my grandfather carried out his head game keeper duties. They used to bring up many pheasants and also they had a few poachers in those days.

My father told me he used to shoot rabbits sitting out in the summer with a 20 bore shot gun, which, by the way, I still have. He was a pretty good shot, much better than me.

As far as I can remember the rabbits used to be cooked for the young pheasants, something to do with protein. Of course in those days rabbits were very plentiful.

I remember my father telling me that his father was losing too many pheasant chicks in a big wire netting run, and he discovered the culprit was a sparrow hawk. So he waited, and being a very quick and excellent shot, when the sparrow hawk dived down, and, of course, that was the last time it ever dived into a run.

When the pheasants were roosting and in full growth, my grandfather used to put a thin wire across a ride or pathway in a wood, where he thought poachers would be coming through. Attached to the wire was a little trigger onto an iron rod, which held an iron encasement with a 12 bore cartridge full of powder inside, and when the wire was walked into, the trigger was pulled, firing the cartridge and making a very loud noise, giving the alarm that someone was after the pheasants. Myself, I don't think it much of a job poking about in the dark after poachers. In those days many wealthy gentlemen, and titled ones, used to come to this estate to shoot. When the stands were allotted where they were going to shoot from, each shooter had two guns and a loader. The loader was a man who had to load both shot guns, then, as soon as the first gun was fired, they had to have the second gun to hand for the gentleman to fire, generally at oncoming birds. The tale was, the host was such a quick shot, that before the last bird was shot and hit the ground, with the first gun, he was handed the second loaded gun and he had shot another bird. One must remember that there were quite a few birds coming over the guns at a time, but still that is extraordinarily quick shooting.

My father told me that one gentleman had the best guns and the best cartridges of that time, and he could hardly hit a barn, but one day a pheasant came so close, he swung the gun up and being so close, nearly shot it all to pieces. He was so delighted and nearly went mad. When my grandfather set the beaters going in the wood, not before the guns were at their right stands, of course, he would walk behind the beaters and shoot birds that came back over them. He was such a good shot, that if they were in range, very few ever got away. So at the end of the day the gentleman shooters used to come to him and say, "Mewett, how do you shoot like that?" Of course his answer was, "Well sirs, I shoot where they are going and you shoot where they have been," meaning really instead of keeping the gun moving through the bird when pulling the trigger, they stopped the gun, then that was a case of shooting where the bird had been.

Eventually my grandfather, being a widower, met the house keeper of Lockhurst Hall and, in time, married her, so becoming my father's stepmother. I remember him saying he had his best Sunday suit on, I assume after going to church, and he and one or two other boys went bird nesting, climbing a tree to get at a nest, and he tore his Sunday suit. When he got home, my goodness, he was severely reprimanded! As far as I can make out, his stepmother was not beyond using a copper bat; for those who don't know, it is a small round stick, about 1½ inches thick, about 2½ft. long, used to stir the week's washing in the copper, which held a few gallons of water and being heated with a wood faggot and lit underneath, and fed with more wood to get it to boiling point, was somewhat different to the washing machines of today.

As I said, Eastways Farm had a few acres belonging to the house where the Mewett family lived. My father left school when he was 13 years old. At the start of their farming career my father was still in his teens. They put up a galvanised tin shed, purchased six in-calf heifers, and it was my father's job to milk these heifers by hand, as in those days there were no milking machines. He mentioned one or two of the heifers did kick for a start as their udders were pretty tender after calving, but nowadays one would not be allowed to milk cows in a tin shed! Then, after milking some of the heifers, the milk was put into two five gallon churns and, with the yokes over his shoulders, he had to carry the milk across two small fields to the neighbouring farm, so that the milk could be taken to the dairy in the

3

nearest town. It must have been a very tiring day for a young chap, getting up at four o'clock every morning, seven days a week, with other chores to do.

Eventually, the Mewett's rented a small farm called Bankhurst, about 60 acres, where there was a brick cowshed and a stable for two or three horses. The landlord was the gentleman from Lockhurst Hall, and the cow numbers got up to 26. They also had Kent breeding ewes, putting on them a Southdown ram, 40 to a ram, and at the other end of the village of Eastfield, about 2 ½ miles away from High Bankhurst Farm, they rented another 60 acres where they kept sheep and Sussex bullocks, yarding the bullocks in the winter, and my father had to bicycle twice a day to feed them in the yard.. The power in those days was horses mostly, except traction engines for thrashing. Of course, some parts of the country had them for ploughing. One of these great monsters started at each end of the field with a chap sitting on a four or five furrow plough being winched from one end of the fields to the other, but they had to be bigger fields than those around here.

On these two particular farms they used a balance plough or, as it was called, a one way plough, it had one wing and share in the ground and one sticking up on the top of the frame of the plough When one got to the end of the field, you pushed the handles up and they clipped You turned the two horses round into the same furrow, pulled the handles down, and the wing and share that was sticking up on the frame was now in the ground, ploughing and turning the furrow the same way as the previous one. With horses one would plough about one acre a day; nowadays with a tractor and four furrow plough, ten acres for an eight hour day.

In 1912 a further farm was rented from the Estate of my grandfather's employer, Sir Hylton Brise. The farm's name, Eighteen Pound, 55 acres in all, was taken over on 6th April, 1912 by Henry Mewett of Eastways Farm in the parish of

Gore in the County of Sussex, the rent being £55 per annum, the farm house not included. The farm was only about half a mile up the road from Eastways Farm.

My father's youngest brother, Harry, married the district nurse at the time, on 21st September, 1920. He met her as she had to come to dress my grandfather's wound after a serious operation, about two or three times a week. After they married they went to live at Eightpounds Farm House.

My mother was a friend of the district nurse, and she was invited down to the Farm House one weekend, and on the Sunday morning, my mother's friend said to her, "You better come down to the farm yard to meet my brother-in-law" and they arrived and there was my father with a pen of sheep, cutting maggots out of a backside of a sheep and putting Jeyes Fluid on it. My mother ran that tale many times over the years.

Then, of course, the 1914-18 war came. Besides having a breeding flock of ewes, milking cows, bullocks, and some arable, they bought lambs in the autumn, mostly Kent and Kent half-breeds, put them out to keep on several different farms in different parishes. Generally they were purchased from Northiam or Tenterden in those days, and were sold in the spring. Through the war years the Mewett's made a lot of money out of them, but nearly everything made money then as there was a war on.

The family were able to buy two private houses in the nearby town, purposely so that my grandmother could live off the rent when she was older. They also owned four cottages in the village of Eastfield, later condemned just before the second World War.

My father graduated from a bicycle to a motor bike, then a motor bike and side car, then on to one of the Ford pick-ups in those days, to a Morris Oxford car. With the Ford pick-up he used to go into the nearest town to collect cake for the dairy cows.

I remember him telling me when he had his motor bike, coming down the road from the farm lane there was a very sharp bend before one got to a small bridge where the stream flowed under to divide parishes of Gore and Eastfield. No doubt he was coming too fast, like most young men with motorcycles, so fast in fact, he could not make the bend, and just went flying up the bank and landed in the hedge. He never broke any bones, but had a few scratches, and one or two thorns that hurt a bit, and, of course, a little blood about the place from the scratches, but it taught him a lesson; he took the corner slower in the future!

A tale my father told was in the 1914-18 war time, he had just purchased a new trilby hat - he always wore a trilby hat - so this new hat was his best one. He had never paid so much for a trilby hat, 2 guineas it cost, and that was a lot of money in those days. This particular evening, it was quite a dark evening, he went sailing along all dressed up with his new trilby hat on, no doubt it was on a Sunday, as he said to me once, he seemed to be always working. As he was sailing along on his motor cycle, the wind seemed to get stronger, and all of a sudden his hat blew off. He stopped and searched about, but he never found it - so goodbye to two guineas! I just wonder what his stepmother thought of that, or said; as he was older she could not very well hit him with a copper bat.

When he purchased a motorcycle and sidecar he was able to take his father about a bit between the farms, as his father was more used to riding a pony, and didn't want to drive a machine.

While I am on the subject of transport, as my father's invalid brother, could not walk, they got him a biggish basket affair which he sat in, two wheels over which he sat, and a small one that swivelled about for turning, and was pulled by a donkey, which his brother could handle.

Mother, father and sheepdog at
Bankhurst farm in 1926

My grandfather holding his pony, circa 1916

In October 1921, my grandfather died aged 65 years old. He only survived two years after the serious operation he had. I remember my father telling me, one summer his father came in for his tea - they were in the process of haying - he had been using the hay rake, sitting on the iron seat, pulled by a horse, of course, and as he walked into the house he said "My golly, that job shakes your guts up." Then after my grandfather died, my father and his youngest brother went into partnership.

As I mentioned before, my father's youngest brother married the district nurse on 21st September, 1920, and lived at Eightpounder Farm House. Most times he had to walk through the fields to Bankhurst Farm, about one and a half miles, each day.

In September 1925, my father married my mother, and they had my father's crippled brother live with them, and about that time Sir Hilton Brise was drowned at sea. The estate was then sold off.

My father bought, on mortgage, High Bankhurst Farm, and the farm the other side of the stream that divided the two parishes of Gore and Eastfield. My father's young brother bought it and lived there after moving from Eightpounder. That wasn't such a long walk between the two farms. The farm's name was Bankhurst. About half the cows went to Bankhurst Farm; the two brothers used to help each other with haying and harvesting. This was in 1929. As my mother and father had his invalid brother to live with them, my Uncle and Aunt had his stepmother to live with them.

My mother used to make dandelion wine in a big earthenware vessel, which must have held four gallon of liquid, and at a special period she would bottle it off. I can remember all of a sudden a big pop came from the larder where these bottles were stored, and, of course, one of the bottles had its cork blown off. It was lovely wine, rather potent.

8

One hot summer evening, my uncle had been helping my father haying, and just before he walked home to his farm, my mother asked him if he would like a glass of dandelion wine. "Yes please Flo." Knowing my mother, if she gave anyone drink or food, there were no half measures about it, so out came a glass tumbler full right up with wine. He started to drink it and said: "My goodness, this is good, thank you." The next morning when he came haying again at High Bankhurst where my father and mother lived, as soon as he saw her, he said "Flo, my god, what did you put in that wine? Every time I went to walk, the ground came up to meet me!" They all had a good laugh about it, and the tale was told many times.

I was also told that, when everyone was carting and stacking hay at High Bankhurst Farm, and I was playing round about - I was three years of age at the time - wondering where I was, someone would say "Where is Ken?" I would appear all of a sudden, stand up straight, point to my chest, and say "Dare tis," meaning I am here.

There is something I can remember to this day: it was at High Bankhurst, where I was born, I was only three or four years of age at the time, and I had just been bought a new straw hat with a blue ribbon around it. In those days, very often there was a pond adjacent to the cowshed and stables. At the edge of the pond there was a sunken flatter piece of ground where by four gallon buckets were dipped and carried to the cowshed and stables to water both cows and horses. My father and uncle were building a hay stack, not far away, and I got to the edge of the pond, where it was flatter and was watching the haying proceedings going on, and all of a sudden I spotted my reflection in the water of the pond. It was a beautiful July day, the sun was shimmering on the water, so I got down on my knees to get closer to my reflection - wonder I did not fall in - but I got my face so close to the water my lovely straw hat fell into the water. I was very upset as the hat drifted away from me, and sank out of sight. So far as I remember no one ever got it back.

High Bankhurst Farm House was very nice, but in those days it had solid fuel fires, candles and oil lamps for lighting, water from a well, with the toilet, called a privy, about twenty yards away. Of course, in those days there was a poe under each bed. As one can guess, in the winter milking by hand and attending horses was all carried out by paraffin lamps, or storm lanterns, as they were called.

I could never understand where High Bankhurst got its name from, as it was at a much lower level than Bankhurst Farm, which was on a hill.

Just along the lane from us, at High Bankhurst, was Lodgers Farm, a dairy farm, and also they retailed milk into the nearest town. There were four children, two boys and two girls, and they had a Shetland pony to ride. Although I was shy, - and I mean shy! my sister Olive and I would go along and play. Well, one day they let me ride this pony. One held the pony, they gave me a heave up on it, and the eldest brother sat down on a four foot chicken coop; the other two got seated on small chicken coops, and that left the youngest one holding the pony. Then they shouted to the one holding the pony, "Let go!" Away went the pony. They all knew what was going to happen, but I jolly well did not, and what happened was, I just slipped under the pony's belly, and really hit the ground. Unknown to me they had loosened the girth on the saddle, but the eldest brother, sitting on the tallest chicken coop, laughed so much he fell off. I think he hurt himself more than I did but, by golly, it shook me up.

When I was about five years old, I used to go to Sunday school and to the local Council School which was Eastfield.

When going to Eastfield School, as my father had to take his milk up to the village, I used to be taken by car with the

10

milk in the morning and generally walked back in the afternoon.

On this particular afternoon, I was walking home from school on my own, down the country road to High Bankhurst Farm. Before you got to the farm about four hundred yards, the road was lined either side with woodland. Just as I was walking between the two woods, a thunder storm came up and there was a terrific clap of thunder. It was bad enough for a five year old boy, who was frightened of thunder, but not realising that on one side of the road in that particular wood, the farmer kept sows and their piglets, just as the clap of thunder came, I suppose the sow was lying down with her piglets right near the edge of the wood. The thunder made such a noise that the sow jumped up squealing, with the piglets running after her. Well, what with that and the noise of the thunder, I nearly had a heart attack, and messed my trousers at the same time. As I have said before, I was very shy, and when at school I never did put my hand up to go to the toilet, always held on till play time.

When I was in standard one, in those days that is how they defined grades at school, the same as Arithmetic is called Maths now, in council schools anyway. It was in the summer, a beautiful afternoon, and the lady teacher from Standard One had us sitting on the grass joining the Tarmac play ground. She was telling us a story, and I wanted to go to the toilet so badly, but being so shy, I could not bring myself to put my hand up and ask to go to the toilet. So you can imagine what eventually happened - I messed my trousers, and for about ten minutes I sat there, feeling terribly embarrassed, until we were dismissed to go home. I had to walk home, and at that time the younger children from Lodgers Farm walked with me, and I, being so upset, was crying all the way home. They kept asking me "What is the matter?" but I would not tell them.

On another occasion I came home from school, I remember in that same year, and I just got home, approaching the farm house, when I saw a car parked in front of the house that I had never seen before. Immediately I got all embarrassed, for I knew I would have to meet someone I did not know. As soon as I got in through the back door, my mother was waiting in the kitchen ready with flannel and towel in hands. "Now, Ken," she said "Let's wash your hands and face and come and meet Mr. and Mrs. Eldridge who are in the sitting room." She took my hand and led me into the sitting room to meet them. "Now, say hello to Mr. and Mrs. Eldridge," my mother said quietly, and with that I pulled her skirt with one hand, got round behind her, and with my other hand pulled the other side of her around behind her, stuck my head into her backside and howled and howled, so that finished that meeting!

In those days we used to have a traction engine to drive the thresher. The owner of the thresher and engine used to go round to the different farms and one had to get coal in ready just before they arrived. I remember one winter morning, my sister and I had just got up and we rubbed the condensation from the window of the sitting room to see out as we heard a noise, and there was the steam engine. It just got up steam enough to set the pulley wheel going to drive the thresher - all very exciting to four and five-year-old's. This was about 1931-32 when the depression was hitting hard, and farming was no exception. I remember my father telling me that about 1922 things started to be depressed. The lambs that they had out to keep on different farms lost their value by £500 over night, and that was a lot of money at the time. There were no guaranteed price structures after the 1914-18 war, as there were after the 1939-45 war. The government of the day seemed to be hell bent on importing food. But when the first world war did come, there were more and more fields being ploughed up to produce more food. Imports did not get through very well, we being an island with a sea all around us. Apparently the Germans had a field day at times sinking shipping. The financial side of farming seemed to get worse, but being children, we did not understand the seriousness of the situation, and to us it was a lovely world. My mother's mother came to stay sometimes, and one highlight was when our mother was cooking breakfast, she would say to us, "Breakfast is nearly ready. Go and call granny," and we would bound up the stairs, all excited, as we knew what would happen. We would knock on gran's bedroom door, and say "Breakfast is ready," and the answer was "I won't be a minute, dears, I am just putting my combinations on"!

As I have mentioned, my father had to take the milk he produced up to the village of Eastfield to catch the lorry that collected from each farm in that area, as we were not on that particular route. The reason for this was, that the farmer at Lodgers Farm, only just about four hundred yards further down the lane from where we lived, who used to buy our milk to bottle and take it into the nearest town, stopped paying my father for a period, although he was a friend, and used to go to school with him. It certainly could not go on, as far as I can make out, and he never did pay all the money back, His ploy, was: "One cannot get blood out of a stone."

Then in or about 1933, the old manager of Lloyds Bank let my father borrow money as the Mewett family had started from nothing really in farming, and, of course, were very successful, especially in the 1914-18 war years, so he knew their business very well. The old manager became retiring age, and a new manager took over. I suppose you would call them wiz-kids nowadays. Well, he called in the loan my father had, and that forced my father to sell his farm, High Bankhurst, of about sixty acres, in April 1934 for £1,600. That was about the time the Milk Marketing Board came into being. I remember my father saying that before the Milk Marketing Board came into being, the dairy that one made a contract with for forty gallons a day, say, when the spring came and the cows were turned out of the sheds after being in them all winter, and being out on grass, of course the milk yield went up by a few gallons. As soon as the bank holiday came, the dairies would take the extra milk, but after the holiday there were a few gallons they would not take. Therefore, one kept a pig or two for the surplus milk, and what the pigs could not consume, the rest went down the drain - terrible state of affairs.

Another thorn in the side of farmers of that period, 1920-30s, was the Church of England, who put on farm land a charge one had to pay called Tithe. I came across a charge on 10th September, 1923 for 102.772 acres for £33.19s.3d. per annum. As I see it, just as the depression was coming into being, that was quite a bit of money. Just before my father sold High Bankhurst, he rented a seventy five acre farm at the far end of Eastfield called Southways, the land only being divided by a road from the sixty acres he already rented of Coombe Barn Farm.

Around 29th or 30th September, 1933, we moved to Southways Farm, a very large old farm house. The kitchen chimney was enormous and one could look right up it, and at the sides of the chimney there were iron pegs for chimney sweep boys to climb up. I think the house was about four hundred years old.

The fire place itself was about seven or eight foot wide, where my mother had a concrete block made about three foot six inches wide and the same in length and about a foot high, and on that she stood her big double doored oven, solid fuel, of course, lit every morning with chopped faggot wood, and sometimes a little paraffin if the wood was damp. I may add my mother was an excellent cook. Just about four or five yards away in the brick yard was the wood shed

14

Myself with my mother and baby sister
at Bankhurst farm in 1938

My father on his tractor at Southways farm
before the war

15

where the faggots were kept, and that shed, the size being big enough to hold two tons of coal at a time. In the same brick yard which had a fence around it with an entrance gate, was a well, with a pump, quite a large one too, where we filled buckets to take into the kitchen for drinking and, of course, washing. In the corner of the kitchen was the copper, to put the week's washing in, and lit with faggots. Of course, the reason for the water in buckets was there was no piped water laid on.

The one thing we did have there was a proper flush lavatory as we called them, the water coming from a big tank in the roof, filled by rain water. Well, when it was a dry period there was no water to flush the lavatory down, so the back-up was about a thousand gallon tank just outside the backdoor, which was filled by rain water coming off the large house roofs, dip the bucket in, and away through the back door, up the passage, into the lavatory, which was halfway up the long passage, flush it down, fill another bucket and stand in the lavatory room, which was quite big, for using next time. Of course, it ran into a cesspool. It was very good in that period really, as many farms and cottages had holes dug out and nice seats built over them, or buckets in a brick and tiled lavatory.

In the 1930s, a law came in, for hygiene, the brick floor in the cowsheds the bricks had to be taken up and all floors and gutters concreted; so that was done. This particular cowshed was for about 20 to 24 cows.

At the same time as being concreted, a brick dairy shed had to be joined onto the cowshed, for the pails and churns. Also, there was a well with a biggish hand pump in the farm yard, which was covered by a galvanised shed so one would not get wet when pumping water to the cowshed. The pipe led from the pump to the cowshed up to a header tank above the cows, connected to water bowls between every two cows, and the distance from pump to header tank must have been two hundred and fifty yards. I still visualise the herdsman pumping water every afternoon in the winter.

The manure from the cows in the winter and summer was wheeled from the shed along planks about forty yards in length, until one came to quite a drop in the ground where you tipped the barrow up, and as the mound all built up, you put another plank on the heap so you could wheel the barrow full along the end of the heap, and that is how the heap was made longer!

Coming from the cowshed, a matter of about five or six yards, you entered the big Sussex barn where flakes of hay were kept and cow cake, also flaked maize for the cows. In the barn there was a 5 hp petrol engine on a block that drove an oat and barley crusher. Always oats went through it. My father's youngest brother used to bring his oats with horse and cart to be crushed.

On the opposite end of the engine was where the saw bench was pulled around to saw the wood in the winter, mostly for the big dining room.

Attached to the barn and cowshed was a yard where the bull was kept, always a Sussex bull, and of course the cows were Shorthorns in those days.

So the barn was made up of one wall, the cowshed wall, another and the barn wall, on the south side was a wall about five feet high. The yard floor itself was lower, but against the inside wall was a long manger to feed the bull and any dry cows or heifers that might be in with him, and west side was the hovel, or the roofed piece, where the animals could lay down on straw, but the open part generally had hedge brushings and bracken for the floor. It was all adjacent to the hay stacks. The milk churns, which were five gallon ones, were taken on wheels forming a frame on a small axle, the frame being about the height of an average mans, waist. It had about four cross bars with an iron hook or two on them, and the frame continued forward like shafts of a horse cart, which one got between to pull, the only difference was it had a bar in front holding the shafts together. It helped pull the weight, as it was against your stomach. This had to be pulled down to the end of the lane, to be picked up by lorry twice a day, about 7.30 am. and then by 2.30 to 2.45 pm. in the afternoon.

The flock of Kent ewes were kept at Coombe Barn Farm, just the other side of the road to the ground of Southways Farm.

All haying was done with horses, mowing, turning and carting by wagons, so there used to be a carter or horseman as one called him.

My mother used to keep quite a lot of chickens in about an eighth of an acre, with six foot small mesh netting surrounding the run with large coops to roost and lay eggs in; a few ducks were kept, Aylesburys and Carky Cambells; the chickens were mostly Rhode Island Reds, with a few Light Sussex.

That reminds me; just before Christmas, the one at Bankhurst Farm, my mother had about twenty Light Sussex cockerels fattening for Christmas. About a week before they were going to be killed, she went out to feed them, and before her very eyes was a terrible sight - cockerels were laying about everywhere, some dead, some maimed and feathers everywhere. My mother was so upset she was in tears. My father reckoned two foxes had burrowed under the netting, got in. You may or may not know, they only take one chicken away but they generally kill and maim the rest of them.

It happened either the same morning or the next morning, the local hunt met at a pub at Eastfield. My father was a very even tempered man, but as my mother was so upset, it upset my father, so he got hold of a couple of these dead cockerels, got in his car - I went with him - and drove up to Eastways village at the pub where the hunt was meeting. I can see now, the huntsmen with their scarlet coats, the ladies and gentlemen with their smart gear on. My father got out of the car, got hold of the dead cockerels, went over to the master of the hunt, in front of the whole meeting, held them up in the air and said, "Look what these damned foxes have done." It was totally out of character for my father.

Going back to Southways Farm, as the situation was pretty bad financially in the 1930s, soon after we moved to Southways, my mother, thought she would take in guests for holidays for extra income. She started by going to different big house sales and bought different pieces of furniture, to get Southways big farm house rooms better equipped for the job in hand, as there were four rooms downstairs, four rooms up from the first flight of stairs, and four rooms at the top of the second flight of stairs, which were called attics, having windows protruding from the roof; quite big they were. My sister and myself and my parents slept up in the top rooms.

We generally had visitors to stay from around south London, some a week, some a fortnight. As I have said, my mother was an excellent cook, and also, having been in service before marrying, she knew how to present the food on big plates. These visitors started coming for Easter weekends, Whitsun weekends, then we had some at Christmas time.

As it went off well, and once they came to stay, they always wanted to come back again, so it was a good thing that from the start of this project my mother employed a girl that had just left school, for ten shillings per week - Flossy, her name was - until she left to get married. After her there was the daughter of a lady who took washing down in the village, and her name was Ivy. My mother and these girls used to have a laugh at times; jolly good thing it was, as they both had to work pretty hard. When I think back, I don't know how my mother did it at times. Oh, I forgot to mention that there was no electricity; it was all paraffin lamps and, of course, candles. So I was going up those two flights of stairs to bed with a candle, afraid of the dark, until I was thirteen years of age. As well as being dark, in the winter it was damned cold. Once you got in bed you did not want to get out. If by any chance my sister or myself became ill, and had to stay in bed, the fire would be lit in the bedroom, and if very cold, a Valor paraffin heater would be lit and brought in the room. What a performance to what it is today, with gas or oil central heating! It was about every year around November I developed bronchitis until after I was seven years old, then I would be put into one of the best bedrooms, where there was only one flight of stairs up to them, the fire would be lit, and also at night the paraffin Valor stove would come into operation, so I was nice and warm, with hot water bottle at night if my mother thought it was necessary. My sister and I had wonderful parents. Of course I was not keen on being in bed, but the worst thing I can remember was the district nurse coming each morning to put Kaolin poultice on my chest. She was very gentle, but golly it was jolly hot! Made me wince a bit, but it was the best thing that could have been done. The doctor at the time told my mother that I would either grow out of it after I was seven, or have it the rest of my life. Well, I am seventy now, and touch wood, I have not had it since that time!

A lot of things happened when I was seven years old. I had to have my tonsils and adenoids out, as I used to talk nearly through my nose, but after the operation I was quite alright, thank goodness. The best thing about that incident was my parents bought me a biggish tin aeroplane, with a battery that worked lights on the wings and tail piece. It was a lovely model, and I was so delighted with that plane. I have always been tall, I was well over the average height when I was seven, and remember in the local hospital they put me in what looked like a big cot with sides to it, and I had a job to stretch my legs out in it. My mother remarked on it the first time she saw me on her first visit, but I survived. I can't remember whether they put me in a bigger one or not. The highlight of the operation to my mind was the lovely model of a plane.

As I mentioned earlier, my mother started taking in paying guests. She was the best customer at the local butcher's shop in the village. Those days they came up twice a week to the farm for orders with a van, and delivered the next day. That is how we lived so well, food wise, and, of course, the meat was beautifully cooked. I remember coming home from school, which was about one mile away, at lunch time - one had from 12.00 noon until 1.30 pm. to get back to school again - and after our first course, the second course was suet pudding, made in a cloth, at least once or twice per week, sometimes plain suet pudding eaten with golden syrup, or jam roly poly, sometimes the pudding had sultanas and currents in it, generally called spotted dick.

Each year my mother made quite a few pounds of jam to last throughout the year, as we had jam on the table nearly every tea time. My goodness, it was good! ! I have heard my father say; "My goodness, you children of today are spoilt! - you have bread and butter with jam. When I was a boy you either had bread and butter or bread and jam; you were not allowed both." Apparently it was a true fact, and of course, some families were living like that then, very often they could not afford butter so had to have margarine, and very likely did not have both on their bread, so we were very fortunate, especially living on a mixed farm; we had eggs, milk and chicken meat, and also at that time there were enormous numbers of rabbits about, and my father, being an excellent shot, we were able to have rabbit stew and pie. Sometimes the rabbits were netted with a ferret put down the hole, after netting each hole in the burrow. If there was a rabbit caught in the net, one got hold of it, got it out of the net, held it up by its hind legs, opened your hand, and hit it with force on the neck, behind the head; a very quick death, it broke its neck. Sometimes one missed a hole, called a pop hole. very small it was. As there was no net over it, away the rabbit went, but if my father had his gun with him, it certainly did not go far, otherwise it was the rabbit's lucky day! The gun my father used was a thirty inch double barrel B.S.A. pistol grip, twelve bore shot gun. I thought it was heavy, but father used it as though it was another arm to him. He used to go rough shooting on Saturday afternoons in the winter, taking the dog Sometimes the dog would push out a rabbit from a seat, and tear across the field like a train. Sometimes it was forty yards distance, and father was up with the gun, lent his body forward, kept the gun swinging, then aim ahead of the rabbit, pulled the trigger, still swinging the gun through, the rabbit just ahead, and it would do a somersault or two, after the speed it was going, and just lay there dead. He always shot them through the head, I can't remember him shooting them in the backside.

From about eight years old, I used to walk miles, behind him of course, as it was safer, and I was told in no uncertain manner if I did not I could not come. The excursions were on Saturday afternoons in the winter. It was such a joy to me to see him shoot those rabbits, but it did not matter whether rabbits or any birds, they were always shot up front.

I remember when I was about twelve years old, it was the Saturday before I went back to school after the Christmas holiday, and I asked my father if he was going shooting that afternoon. He said he was not, and I got so upset as I loved watching him shoot these rabbits tearing across the field. I started crying, so my mother persuaded him by saying to him, "Go on, Perce," (that was his name) "as it is his last day of his holiday before going back to school." My father gave in, and I enjoyed a lovely afternoon.

Going back to my mother's work in this paying guest project, all hot water had to be boiled on the cooking range, two big iron kettles, must have held one and a half gallons each, and then there were two smaller enamel kettles on a small paraffin cooking stove that stood on the top of the wash copper. The system worked like this for visitors - 8.00 am. hot water was carried up in gallon enamel jugs for the wash stands, as well as a tray of tea to each bedroom, generally three rooms. Then breakfast was cooked and ready for 9.00 am.; about five minutes before that the gong was sounded to remind them breakfast was being served, then afterwards there was the washing up and drying - remember there were no dish washers in those days.

At 1.00 pm., lunch. If anyone was going out and would not be back at that time, sandwiches were made if they wanted them, then, after washing up again. I can see my mother now in my mind as though it was yesterday. She used to suffer as she called it with sciatica, so after the washing up was done, she would take two Aspros and rest for half an hour. We always said she must have been like a chemist shop inside her. Then it was tea at 4.00 pm., then there was a lovely cooked dinner at 8.00 pm. I remember some of it now, mashed potatoes piled up to a point and lovely lamb cutlets stood upright all around it and sometimes her lovely beef steak and kidney pudding. One gentleman said to my mother "Mrs. Mewett; I will never go any where else to stay, as I could not bear to miss your suet steak and kidney puddings." He never drove so his two friends used to drive him when staying. It got that they came at Easter, Whitsun, holidays and Christmas. He had a daughter at boarding school, and she was staying one Christmas with them, and her father gave her the biggest box of chocolates I have ever seen, and she was eating, and would not have offered one of them, if it had not been for her father's friends saying, "You must offer them around," so I wondered what sort of manners they taught at those boarding schools.

There was another thing about visitors at Christmas: my sister and I had some lovely presents extra, which, as a result, my father would say, "You children of today have too many presents. When I was a boy I only had a stocking (not a pillow case!) and in it would be a few sweets, nuts, an orange and apple, and one toy." Apparently that was true, so we were very fortunate.

Going back to my school days, all I thought about was farming. I would not read much, no more than I had to. My sister, on the other hand, could read before she went to school at five years old. When the eleven plus exam came, as my sister was only two or three points short of passing it, my parents paid for her to go to Brye Grammar School, which was ten miles away. She used to catch the bus at the end of Southways Farm Lane.

When the second world war continued into its second year of being, the pupils of Brye Grammar School were evacuated to Bedfordshire, so my sister was there until she was sixteen years of age. The local garage used to run a taxi on a Sunday for different families' mothers to go to visit their children. As far as I can remember my mother went about once a month. When my sister left school, she trained as a children's nurse, eventually getting a post as a nanny, and went on to one or two others until she married. As I have said, I was much slower at school than my sister. Well, years after, when I was in my forties, my mother told my wife and I that when I was going to school, I suppose it was when I was half way through my schooling, she went to see the head governess of the school, which was a council school. As soon as she met the governess, Mrs. Hind her name was, her husband was head master of the same school, she said: "What can I do for you Mrs. Mewett?" With that my mother said: "I am worried about Ken. Olive, his sister, could read

24

before she went to school and she is streets ahead of Ken in her school work." Mrs. Hind's answer was, "But Ken plods along quite well. Now Mrs. Mewett, you have heard of Winston Churchill, when at school and look where he is going." So apparently my mother felt better.

The war started when I was thirteen years old, and like a lot of other farmers, my father had to plough up more pasture, and he planted wheat and oats. At that time he purchased an old Fordson tractor. It had cleat iron wheels, no mud guards, and started on petrol, and as soon as it warmed up you switched over to paraffin. My goodness, you would not be allowed to drive it like that nowadays, well, employees at any rate. He also purchased an old plough that took care of the ploughing, then some sort of conversion that fitted between the horse shafts of the wagons, so the tractor could pull them. Also, the mower had the similar sort of thing so the tractor could pull it, being a horse mowing machine really. When mowing, I sometimes sat on the seat, so that when I came to the end of the run at the corners of the field, I had to pull the lever to lift the bed of the mowing machine where the mowing knife actually ran, to get out of the un-mown grass, turn round on the corner, and as the mower was coming up to the uncut grass, let the bed down again. Away I went, cutting another four foot of grass down, which was called a swath, hence when the grass was eventually turned, the piece of machinery that turned it was called a swath turner. When the grass was becoming drier, at the hay stage, one would row it up with the turner, then in those days pitch it loose onto the wagons, generally with half pitch prongs. One soon used to get the knack of getting a nice pitch fork full by golly! A few hay seeds used to get down your back, especially when making the roof of the stack where there was always a pitch hole. You just imagine, as the chap on the wagon kept pitching on to the stack, depleting the hay until he got to the bottom of the

25

wagon, you had to have the pitch hole situated as far as the pitcher up the wagon could reach. The man in the pitch hole pitched the hay up to the stacker, and there seemed to be more hay seeds go down your back. Mixed with sweat as well it was rather irritable.

Then the cereals would be cut by binders and the sheaves stacked in sixes called, in Sussex, shocks - other places, stooks - and the binder was converted on the shaft for tractor pulling.

The sheaves used to stay out about a week or ten days to dry before being carted, and if it was rainy weather conditions, I have know the shocks to stick together, and it was quite a job to pull them apart sometimes, it certainly affected the quality of the grain. The corn sheaves were much better to handle for pitching and loading, except for the loader, when there were several thistles in them. I remember when I was loading one day, just before finishing the load, the pitcher was stretching up with the sheaf on the edge of the load, as I went to grab hold of it, he plunged the sheaf up, the result being the fork met my hand, and by golly that did hurt! I was more careful after that, but, of course, he should not have shoved the fork up as I was getting hold of it. I was certainly taught that when I was the pitcher.

Going back to the dairy herd, I remember my father putting five or six young heifers, their age four or five months old, in to what we called the platt, a small pasture about two acres. Along the far end there were big oak trees, and he always turned them out there over the years, and then one morning they were all in a pretty bad way. He called the vet, and he diagnosed acorn poisoning. He did what he could for them, but two of them died. Apparently there was a glut of acorns that particular year.

As I said before, we had several chicken on the farm, and a few ducks. My mother used to hatch a few chicken and ducks under four or five broody hens. I remember the family came back from shopping in the nearest town - it was the time when the chicks and duckling were about a week or two old. We used to keep four or five cats and they used to hunt at night and come indoors in the daytime. These hens were in small individual coops with their chicks and ducklings. As my mother went to look at them, to see if they were alright, our ginger cat had killed a chick and was running away with another one. Well, my mother was so upset she burst into tears, told my father what had happened, and with that he went and got his gun and shot the ginger cat straight away and buried it.

Just before the outbreak of war, my mother was approached by a lady from the suburbs of London, as she was recommended for looking after her visitors very well. For instance, another guest house in the village was full, and the family that generally stayed there was recommended to go to Mrs. Mewett of Southways Farm. Well, my mother took them in for a week. The father of the family was a big man. It came to breakfast time - my mother never messed about with one fried or one of anything - of course, with her breakfasts it was two eggs, two sausages, two fried breads and toast and marmalade as well. The first of my mother's breakfasts they had, the father of the family said; "Mrs. Mewett, do you realise at the other guest house I had just one egg, one sausage and a piece of fried bread - fancy, a man of my size! " That made my mother feel good.

Anyway, going back to the lady approaching my mother, it was her bank manager husband who had a serious nervous breakdown, and the doctors advised a good quiet place in the country to recuperate. So he came and stayed with us. He was very nice, and a quiet man. He used to play darts with us, and also went for walks on his own quite a lot. My mother used to ask him if he would be back for one o'clock lunch when he went on his walks, and he was always on

27

time. Then one day he was rather late for his lunch, and it worried my mother. When he did arrive back, he was hobbling on one leg. Of course my mother asked him what he had done, and his answer was, "Oh, Mrs. Mewett, I have sprained my ankle." Well, she said the ankle was swelling half the size again, so she put cold compresses on it for a day or two, and it gradually went down. It stopped his walking for four or five days. He started walking again, then one lunch time he did not come back to lunch. Tea time came, and it was the time of year when it was getting dark at tea time. After tea time, as we knew he walked down towards and passing a wood, it was so worrying that my father got the car out and my mother, my sister and I got in. As you could get to the wood by road and then down a farm lane, we drove all the way to the entrance to this wood, armed with two storm lanterns alight, as it was pitch dark. We walked along the side of the wood, shouting at the top of our voices: "Mr. Cowl, where are you?" for that was his name, but of course to no avail. So, before we went back home, we drove down to the phone box in the village, as we never had a phone in those days, and my mother phoned his wife and told her of the situation, and home to bed we went.

The next morning, after milking and breakfast, Claude, my father's cowman, said he used to see Mr. Cowl go into the wood, so down to the wood they went, searching through it, and Claude shouted to my father "I have found him" and the poor devil was hanging from a tree, dead. With that, they called the village policeman, and carried the body up to my father's granary. While the policeman was searching him, all he found was one and a half pence in his pockets. Apparently his wife kept him so short of money; I won't repeat what the policeman said about it. Actually the poor man used to go to the village sweet shop and post office, buy a few sweets, and as he never had any money, he booked

With my father, my mother and little sister
at Southways farm in 1934

Holding the cart horse at Southways farm in 1936

it to my mother's account. As the post mistress knew my mother well, she never took much notice, but what a terrible situation for the poor man.

He had ended his life with one of the farm wagon ropes. Father and mother always said that the first time he tried to hang himself he failed. That was the day he sprained his ankle, slipped off the branch, I suppose. No doubt he was determined to do it. We all felt very shocked by the incident.

As I mentioned, Southways was a very big house, and I can remember honey bees being in walls - one could see them enter the house, just under the eaves of the roof. No doubt there had been bees there for years. Sometimes they would swarm at a particular time. One summer they did just that. It was the biggest swarm of bees I have ever seen then or since. They were hanging onto one of the apple trees, about ten yards away from the front of the house. It measured about two feet and a half wide and about one and a half feet deep. They hung in the shape of a half moon, and there must have been thousands and thousands of them.

As I said before, at the beginning of the war, I helped my father on the farm, and I used to keep a book and put down the hours I had helped harvesting or haying; a few hours kept adding up. I had always wanted an air gun which fired lead pellets. I suppose I kept asking for this gun, so in lieu of the money, I was presented with this lovely air gun. I think it was called a Diana, very shiny, and you had to pull on the barrel to open the breach, put the pellet in and close it up again, then it was ready to fire. I used to shoot at sparrows mostly, as there were so many in those days, all along the hedgerows of the corn fields, just on the headlands, as we called it. In the summer, when the ears were getting riper, these sparrows certainly used to slaughter them. My shooting then with this air gun was a much bigger percentage of misses to kills. However, I was very proud of that gun.

Dad's two carthorses. Myself and sister on right,
two cousins on the left, circa 1935

With my sheepdog puppy at Southways in 1937

Anyway, while we are on the subject of guns, when I was thirteen years old, my grandmother on my mother's side, came to stay for a while. Well, there was an old Damascus barrelled twelve bore shot gun of my late grandfather's, on my father's side, that used to stand behind my father's bureau with his twelve bore. There was room for them as the bureau was placed across the corner of the room, ideal to keep the guns out of reach of my sister and me when we were younger.

Well, this particular gun was given to my grandfather many years before, by a well off gentleman. It had an under lever to open the breach, and was a hammer gun. It had been used so much, it was getting very thin on the end of the barrels. As I was very tall then, about five feet eleven, I could reach over and lift the gun out. First I would scrub it then kept cleaning it - my father knew this, I may add.

Then came the time my father and mother went out for the afternoon and as only my grandmother was there, I thought I would take the gun. I knew where the twelve bore cartridges were kept, so I put about half a dozen in my pocket, thinking, as I had seen my father shoot dead many rabbits running across the field at great speed, that it was easy.

Away I sneaked out, put two cartridges in the breach, as it was a double barrelled side by side shot gun, and pulled the hammers back so it was ready to fire. I came to part of the field near the hedge where there was a lot of dead bracken - in those days there used to be a lot of bracken about growing along the side of some fields - and I proceeded to walk and stamp through this bracken in the hope of putting a rabbit out. All of a sudden a rabbit bolted out, ran straight away from me, and I remembered my father saying if that happens, aim over the top of its ears and fire. Well, I lifted the gun up, aiming over the top of the ears of the rabbit, but I took longer to pull the trigger and the rabbit was a hell of a way off by then. I fired and the rabbit bowled over and

32

over and laid on its back kicking. My goodness, I was so proud of myself, and felt I was walking on air when I strode down to get this first rabbit I had shot. As I went to pick it up, it jumped up and ran away. I was so flabbergasted it was a second or two before I could aim again. I shot at it, but all I did was knock a bit of flick out of it. So that was the end of my first excursion of shooting with a shot gun. As you can imagine, my grandmother was so worried she told my mother and father as soon as they walked in the door. I was moderately reprimanded, I suppose for the sake of my grandmother, but after that I occasionally went with my old school friend, Jack, ferreting on the farm, and took it then.

Jack was one year older than myself. He left school at fourteen years old. I just had one more year to go before I left, but before he left school, he used to come up to Southways Farm every weekend, well, most weekends. Then the war had started in September 1939. Jack wanted to go into the Navy, but had to wait until he reached the age of fifteen. As Jack's father worked for the local coal merchant delivering bags of coal, he was employed to work on the coal round until he was fifteen years old. In the meantime, as he was earning money working on a regular basis, when he came up to the farm on a Saturday afternoon, he used to bring a packet of fifteen Tenner cigarettes with him, and out of sight of my parents, we used to smoke them. As there was a shortage of petrol, eventually my father left his car in the garage and never used it, and I remember sometimes we used to get in the car and have a smoke. Once we were getting out of the car, after a smoking session, and my father caught us and said, "What are you lads doing?" to which we replied "Nothing! !," but my father must have smelt the smoke. As I said earlier, I had wonderful parents.

Jack joined the Navy and went through all the war as a telegraphist. After the war he joined the postal service, went on the post rounds, then worked behind the counter, eventually becoming relief manager. Sadly he died of a heart attack when he was about fifty-two. Jack and myself were the tallest boys in the school.

In 1940, when the Germans were bombing London badly, evacuees were billeted out to different homes in East Sussex, and my mother took five boys in. Three of them came from the slums of the east end. The youngest of the three was six years of age, and he could not pronounce some simple words - no doubt it was not his fault.

Well, the first night they were with us, they all three slept in the same room (don't forget they had poes in the room), my mother went to make the beds in the morning, and as she walked into the room she thought: "There is a funny smell here," She looked about and, to put it plainly, they had shit right in the corner of the room! My mother could not believe it, but she soon taught them differently. Now the other two were different; one's father drove his own taxi, the other boy's father had a sweet and tobacco shop. Of course, these families were much better off, no doubt, and they went to better schools! Now the one whose father owned a tobacco and sweet shop - the family had to flee Czechoslovakia just before the war - was very polite and well mannered. One day he was sitting round the table with us, accompanied by myself, my sister, who was about twelve years old, the four other boys and my mother and father. My mother was at the time serving some food on the plates around the table. Well, this young Czech boy looked up at my mother and said "Mrs. Mewett, it would be the most beautiful thing in this world if you would allow me to sleep with Olive," (that was my sister, of course). I used to be so shy in those days, I was so embarrassed I did not know how to sit there. I can still see the look on my mother's face; it was with horror she said: "Certainly not. How dare you! " and with that my sister burst into tears and cried her eyes

34

out. I suppose the sexual side of life was looked at in a more casual way in his country, and was more open.

For a short time, at the beginning of the war, a Mrs. Syvier and her daughters stayed permanently, to get away from the London area. Her husband was a bank manager; previously to that they had always come to Southways for their holidays. Before she was married, nursing was her profession.

My sister and I used to have our upsets, as do most children. The trouble was, my sister had a ploy. Even when I had not smacked her when we had a disagreement, because when she did get into a temper, not only did I have to guard against her fists, it was her kicking as well, and, of course, with that I did used to get a smack in. The ploy was, when she did not win the argument, she would run to my mother and say, "Ken has hit me!" and with that my mother was after me, although I had not touched her.

Well, Mrs.Syvier, while she was staying permanently, noticed this, and one day she told my mother, "You know, Mrs.Mewett, Olive, if she cannot get her way in an argument, she will come running to you and say, "Ken has hit me," but of course very often he had done no such thing." My mother was more lenient with me, not to say both my father and mother were quite lenient. We both got reprimanded, but it had to be something quite bad before we were smacked through our childhood years!

Also around 1940 there was a scare of being invaded by the Germans. The evacuees went away from the south coast as we were about three and a half miles as the crow flies from the sea. That was the time that Brye Grammar School was evacuated to Bedfordshire and my sister went with them. Hence the local garage owner ran a taxi on Sundays for parents to periodically visit their children in Bedford. From then on, there were no more fights between my sister and me and we have got on very well ever since.

There were a band of men called the Home Guard, which my father belonged to. When they were first formed there were very few rifles for them, so some took their shot guns on duty. One dark night my father and another chap or two, my father with his shotgun, heard something coming down the road. There they were, guns at the ready to stop whoever it was, and to their amazement, when they shone a torch at the object, and to say, "Who goes there?" the object was a calf! It had broken loose from some farm. That incident was talked and laughed about for weeks. Thank God it was only a calf, or most likely I would not be writing here today.

Then there were the dog fights, as we called them, when our fighter planes intercepted the bomber and fighter places the Germans sent to bomb London by daylight. I remember one particular day, three or four of our fighters forced this bomber to land. It crash landed, of course, but very skilfully as we could see after we had walked through the fields; immediately the military were cordoning it off as we got there. Afterwards we heard it was a newer type of plane called a Dornier 17.

Then one night, I suppose very early morning, we were awoken by a terrific explosion, As I have said before, Southways was a very big house, and as the explosion came, it shook the house as though it was a pack of cards, or like one getting hold of it with both hands and giving it a good shake. It was very frightening, but the old house put up with it. This explosion was a very big parachute mine, which fell half a mile from the house. It made a terrific crater near a pylon, snapping one or two power lines.

Then came the day that altered my farming life. I had just left school at the age of fourteen. My father and mother decided to finish farming themselves, and go to work for someone else.

So, on Saturday, 11 January, 1941 at 12.00 noon sharp, the auction was held. On the front of the catalogue it is printed Live and Dead Farming Stock, Valuable Dairy Herd of 11 Cows, 1 Sussex Bull, 2 Yearling Heifers, 1 Roan Percheron Gelding, 60 Laying Hens and Chicken, Implements, Harnesses, Carts, Wagons and General Farm Tackling, also Surplus Household Furniture.

When I look at this catalogue, I very often wonder how we got so low in the number of cows and chickens, and a day or two before the sale, the jolly horse died. As one must say, things were not going at all well, and the total of the sale was £623.5s. 6d.

I remember, after the sale, my father had already agreed to work for a farmer. His name was Mr. Rankham of Frankham Farm, in the Village of Burash. I often wonder how my father felt going to work for a man, to whom he had previously put sheep out to keep for many years on the farm. It must have been awful. Of course, I was going with my mother and father as well, and working on the same farm. My sister was in Bedfordshire with Brye Grammar School. My father and I were standing outside Southways Farm House - I think I mentioned previously I was very shy and never said a lot - but at this particular time, as the war agriculture committee came into being, and were ploughing up pasture land for the war effort, growing other crops, then a particular government man came round, and if they thought a particular piece of land should be ploughed up, one had to do it by law. While we were standing outside Southways Farm House, I said to my father, "What about buying a tractor and plough, and start ploughing for different farmers, as so many acres have to be ploughed up?," but his answer was "Where are we going to live?," so that ended that conversation. Straight away it shot through my mind, I shall never have a farm of my own, but one day I shall manage a farm for someone else, which I eventually did, but, by golly, it took me a long time, fourteen years to be exact, to get my foot on the first rung of the management ladder. I had no qualifications, only practical experience as I went up through the different phases of my farming life.

I may add that, just before the war my parents enquired about me going into the Sussex Agriculture School, as it was called then, but now it is a college.

They were informed that I had to be fifteen years old before they accepted me. Well, the war came, my father finished his own farming, and I went with him to work for Mr. Rankham, so that was the end of that episode.

Then came the day we arrived at Frankham Farm cottage, and the one thing I noticed that I did not really like was a bucket lavatory, and after coming from a flush lavatory, it was quite a shock for a boy of fourteen years old.

My father went to the farm in the capacity of working foreman; my mother went to work in the farm house for Mrs. Rankham, who was very nice, and as a boy of fourteen, I thought she was lovely. Her husband was very nice as well. I always remember he very often had a pipe in his mouth, and always smoked Tom Long tobacco. I overheard my mother tell my father that Mr. Rankham slept in bed naked! Well, in those times it seemed very unusual, out of the ordinary! When I think of it now, my goodness, I don't blame him, especially the lovely wife he had to go to bed with. But as a family, my father slept in a shirt, myself in pyjamas, and my mother and sister in night dresses.

Just down the road from us was Burash Place, and the further end of the farm on the west side was Southall Hall, both with French Canadian soldiers in them, billeted for the purpose I suppose ready to go by sea from the south coast across the Channel. It wasn't far through the wood from Southall, where we grew wheat that year, and we stacked it there with the help of four or five of those soldiers. They were strong and soon learned how to do the job of pitching and carrying, but, by golly, one had to look out what they were doing with forks! I remember two were on the stack pitching to the stacker, and when finished for the day, instead of getting down the ladder with the fork, they threw it, prongs first, down on the ground. They certainly had to be told not to do that! They could have injured or killed someone. But these chaps were very willing, and I jolly well soon heard language I had never heard before, and then saw in the wood dividing the Hall from the field, French letters, condoms in today's terminology, hanging about where they had been thrown! Well, I must admit I had seen eight or ten girls waiting for these chaps when they came off duty. It was all very embarrassing to me in those days, but when I think of it now, I do hope they had a passionate time, for no doubt half of them would never survive the war.

Now, back to farming. We were milking cows in the cowshed, and up at the end of the shed, nearest the drive, inside of course, there was a hundred gallon paraffin tank, where we used to get paraffin to fill the two tractors up. Just fancy the hue and cry there would be now-a-days; well, it would not be allowed now.

Now, we are on the subject of milk: just before I was sixty years of age I had the occasion to speak to a Women's Guild about the farming scene, and nearing the end, a question came up about why we could not get lovely milk now like it was produced before the Second World War. My answer was that I am glad I am old enough to tell you. First, I had five years hand milking myself, and if you saw what I saw go into the milk buckets, you would not drink a drop of milk from that day till this day! We have the most hygienic milk that has ever been produced, besides all cows are tuberculin tested and brucellosis tested, and both are a thing of the past, thank goodness.

For at one time, abortion and tuberculosis were prevalent, and in the early days and up to the end and after the Second World War, the tuberculosis sanatoriums were full. After the war the scheme came in for testing all cows for tuberculosis and after a few years it soon put these sanatoriums into, I suppose one calls it, liquidation.

Another question from these particular ladies was the subject of eggs. Why cannot we have eggs fresh from around the farm yard where they can lay their eggs anywhere rather than battery hen houses?! Well, the answer to that one is, first, instead of paying fifty pence for a dozen eggs, you would have to pay one pound a dozen.

The other thing is, when collecting these eggs, some would be in the proper nest boxes, but others would be on the edge of hay stacks or corn stacks, and consequently one or two nests would be missed and one would find half a dozen eggs in them, well they certainly were not fresh.

In nineteen fifty-six, I worked on a farm which had a lovely four hundred brick built battery house, one chicken to a cage, food, water, and grit, moving very slowly by electricity in front of the cages, twenty four hours a day. All the food was mixed by hand, including grass meal in it, and they could not have been looked after better, with scrapers going underneath the cages twenty four hours a day; now these eggs were fresh.

The other question was, the brown eggs - they are the best? Well, I explained this is not quite true; it is all psychological. There is no difference in the quality of the egg at all. I remember while I was there on that farm, we used to send a dozen eggs, the colour being a whitey pink, to the local Christmas fat stock show and very often we got the first prize. One thing about it was those chicken did not go scratching and eating different things from the dung lump that came from the cowshed, where sometimes cows aborted, and of course the juices were all in the dung that were cleared out of the gutters and wheeled by barrow on to the dung lumps, so to my mind, the egg from the battery house was more hygienic than the egg from the stack yard, also fresher.

Now, going back to Frankham Farm, and the field I mentioned, the far west of the farm there was a corn field where we carried wheat sheaves and stacked them; that particular field was the first field I ploughed on the farm, and for that matter the first tractor I had ever driven.

The tractor was a Fordson, spade lug wheels, orangy-yellow in colour. I believe they were the first Fordson type tractors to arrive in this country at the beginning of the war.

I know when Mr. Rankham let me drive this tractor I was pulling wagons of hay through narrow gateways in those days, I was lucky not to hit a gate post. Apparently, years after my mother told me at the time, I was left on my own to drive this tractor. She said to Mr. Rankham, she thought I was too young to drive with these big wagons of hay, especially through gateways. His reply was, "Don't worry Mrs. Mewett, he will be quite alright." He must have had faith in me as just before, in February I believe it was, he sent me to plough this West field with a new cockshut two furrow plough - I was proud of this tractor to plough. My goodness, it was frosty in the mornings, and in those days one had to swing the starting handle very vigorously to get the engine to start, and then you had to be careful it did not kick back. Thank goodness I was strong. Every night when one got back to the farm, one had to let the water out of the radiator for fear of freezing.

Proceeding with ploughing that West field, when one got there first thing in the morning, hitched up to the plough, there was usually trouble with the tripping mechanism as it had frozen - a few minutes with a screw driver used to generally knock the frozen mud off - and away we would go again.

The adjoining field belonged to the neighbouring farm and was a hop garden. Whilst working in West field, I looked

41

through the hedge one day and saw a lovely new Case rowcrop tractor - it was orange in colour, and it had been left there for an hour or two with no one attending it. I could not resist getting through the hedge and having a good look at it. To me it was magnificent, because it was new I suppose, it seemed more so.

Mr. Frankham decided to grow Arron Banner potatoes, and we planted thirty acres of them. I used to be the chap to pull out the rows with my tractor with a three row potato earther. All was planted and fertilised by hand, with four or five women from the village, and staff of the farm.

Then came the time to earth these potatoes up. I liked that job very much, and was very proud it see the rows so straight.

By the way, the main tractor driver drove a green spade-lugged Fordson tractor, it being a year or two younger than the one I drove. This driver was a married man from the village, and I got on with him very well, but by golly didn't he used to pull my leg, knowing I was so shy, the devil! But we had some laughs.

There was a carter there who looked after the two horses. He had been in the 1914-18 war, and knowing I was so shy, he blurted out one day, "When I was in the army in France, oh! there were some lovely French girls around the area I was in," and one particular one he fancied a lot, and she seemed to fancy him. With this in mind he asked to have sex with her, and being a sensible girl, she said, "You must show me your penis first as I do not want any of the diseases genitals get," and with that he showed her his penis, and as it was quite healthy, she was very happy to have sex with him, and he said it was so lovely. Well, to tell me all that - I was so embarrassed I did not know how to stand there! It certainly got me thinking about different things!

In the farm yard we had about a dozen young pullets in a little chicken house. It had slats inside so that the dung droppings could fall through and it was raised off the ground with four feet to about ten inches, and it had a sliding door to let them in and out. One morning I let them out and I could hardly believe what I saw - there were two or three of these pullets with only one leg. The rats, or rat, had got under the slats and had managed to pull these legs through the slats and had bitten them off. I had never seen that before, and was so horrified I didn't want to see that again. Thank goodness I never did.

There was a pointed roof shed opened front and back, where we kept the tractor I drove, also several bags of potatoes ready to go on the lorry next day. I came first thing in the morning at 7.00 am. to start the tractor, and to my amazement the cows had got out, got into this shed, made holes in the potato sacks and made short work of some of these potatoes. By golly, didn't some of these cows scour! It was lucky it didn't give one or two blout. They happened to be disturbed in time for milking. It was generally weekends I had to help hand milk.

On the same farm, Mr. Frankham's brother-in-law, a Mr. Toy, a very nice man, used to rent a very big sort of granary where he used to bring up hundreds of chicks, and when old enough, they would be put in these different arks he had on different fields all over the farm. He employed a man to attend them every day, also worked himself, as they had to be fed, watered, and eggs collected. No doubt the public who could afford these eggs would go mad after them as, of course, they were free range, exactly in the sense of the word, also fresh as they were collected every day. These arks were on runners so they could be moved.

My father and I went shooting on a Saturday afternoon off, and I carried the old twelve bore I mentioned earlier, being the first time I had shot with a shotgun. This particular afternoon, we went into a (hosser bed) wood full of willow trees. I was tramping through the rough undergrowth, and to my surprise a dog fox jumped up looked at me, and in an instant I raised the gun and shot. I was so close, the shot made a hole in its head. This episode happened on my fifteenth birthday. By golly, I felt like walking on air! When Mr. Toy got to hear about it, he came to me pleased as punch, and said, "Very well done," and gave me ten shillings. That was a lot of money to me in 1941.

How my father did it I do not know, but he skinned this fox. It was a very fine specimen, but they do smell!, especially when skinning them. He dried it and gave it to a lady near London that my mother and father knew from the time when my mother took visitors in at Southways.

Another crop Mr. Frankham tried was tomatoes. There were some old buildings very near the farm house, just the walls remained, so they were very open to the sun light. I suppose these were about a hundred of these plants, planted close to the walls with canes for each one to be tied to. They grew so well, a finer lot you could not have wished to see, looking so healthy. Then all of a sudden they developed some kind of mildew, and it affected the whole lot and ruined them. It must have been a great blow to Mr. Frankham, but he seemed to be a man who covered up his disappointment and carried on regardless. I suppose, as long as he could smoke his Tom Long tobacco, coupled with some good shooting with his twelve bore Belgian shot gun, he was happy.

I remember sometimes on an odd Saturday afternoon in winter, he used to have a friend, a Russian gentleman, come with his gun to do a bit of rough shooting. Sometimes they got me to go with them, so that I could do a bit of beating in the hedges or rough brambles. I used to like that, especially when Mr. Frankham had a shot, as he was very good at shooting. It was very tiring walking all around the farm, but I did have a reward from the Russian gentleman, a nice two

44

and sixpenny piece. I enjoyed the afternoon, and being paid for it was marvellous.

The Russian gentleman had a very nice daughter, and Mr. Frankham was teaching her to drive - as far as I can remember the car was a medium sized Armstrong Sidley. Mr. Frankham was a handsome man and had a nice personality. One day I overheard my father say to my mother, "That Russian girl is very young and nice; I hope Mr. Frankham is teaching her just driving and nothing else."

The other crop that was grown on the farm was linseed. We used to cut it with a grass mower, which had the usual knife, the four foot bed as it was called, or cutter bar. The knife was sharpened with a file, the knife being screw clamped to an iron frame, about waist high. Golly, you used to have to have the knife very sharp for that crop, as the stalks were so tough.

But when I look back I learnt a lot on that farm. I was lucky that Mr. Frankham had confidence in me, the few months I was working for him.

Going back now to September 1929, when my father and his younger brother dissolved partnership, his brother purchased Bankhurst Farm in the parish of Eastfield, the total acreage being 68 acres, 3 roods, 1 perch for £2,000.

As far as I can see, from papers I have to hand, my father purchased the adjoining farm named High Bankhurst, where, of course, I was born, for £1,600, acreage being 49 acres, 04 roods, 15 perch., on the same date September 1929. Tithe for the two farms was £49. 10s. 00d. My uncle and aunty lived at Bankhurst Farm, also a daughter of my aunty's sister came to live with them, and was looked after when she was five years old.

They farmed with about 16 cows, 4 heifers, 40 Kent ewes, crops 9 acres of wheat, 4 acres of spring oats and 4 acres of roots and kale, with chickens, and two horses to do the work.

Now, early in 1942, my aunty from Bankhurst Farm paid us a visit to Frankham Farm. Previously she had written a letter to my father and mother, just before her visit. Apparently my uncle's cowman was leaving them, and they wanted me to go and live with them and take the job on in place of this cowman, which was milking seven days a week, getting up at 5.15 am. every morning - I really mean 5.15 am. every morning, as my aunty used to wake me at that time, and I took the milk pails out to the cowshed by 5.30 am.

My father said yes: as there was a war on, and I would be looked after well, and he thought it was the right thing to do, so off I went to work for my uncle for the sum of twenty three shillings a week, and my board.

When I look back, the work was done by horses, and not a tractor, although I loved horses, but at that time mechanisation was coming on farms so fast, a revolution really, and I had to change my ideas about horses working on farms. I soon got used to ploughing etc. with horses, but I must admit I missed working with the tractor, as it seemed I went back a step instead of forward.

This is the time when I ploughed with a new balance plough, or one way plough as they call it today.

One of the horses had canker of the heel; a lovely horse she was, but had to be put down. Another horse was purchased in her place, a gelding called Laddie, and he was a character. When ploughing with the balance plough, when one got to the headland, the two horses were stopped, then turned around, and while one was turning around the spread bats to keep the chains apart while the horse was pulling - if the spread bar touched Laddie's heels, he used to put his ears back and show his teeth. He was very annoyed if one was near his head, I think he would have tried to bite you. As soon as one had got the other plough board and share down on the ground, and as it was one way ploughing, the horse that had been pulling on the level ground when turned around had to pull walking in the furrow. One got the plough set well, one did not hold the handles, you just held the mould board that was sticking up from the frame of the plough which had previously been turning the furrow when ploughing up the opposite way.

No wonder I was fit and lean in those days, but of course very young. One walked when ploughing, harrowing, drilling, rolling, dredging and horse hoeing. The only way one got to ride was mowing, bindering, hay raking and swath turning. I remember going down to the stable and taking some Brasso, and cleaned the brasses of the harness. They wanted some cleaning as they had not been touched for some time. It was light evenings before haying and if we were not hoeing kale and mangels, I went down to the stable. One evening I was cleaning a pair of brass hames, and by golly, they did take me a long time to clean. When I was cleaning these hames, my uncle came down to the stable to see what I was doing, looked through the open window, realised I was intent on cleaning these hames, and said, "Oh, I see!" and went away again. I suppose he thought, "my goodness, rather him than me! "

There was one thing I enjoyed and that was in the winter on a Saturday afternoon, if the weather was fine, bearing in mind we used to hand milk the herd of cows starting at one o'clock, and transporting the milk down the end of the lane with the same sort of wheels and frame my father used to use for transporting his milk to the end of the farm lane, we would come back from that chore, get the shotguns out, my uncle with his twelve bore hammer gun, and I used to use my grandfather's double barrelled hammer, with under lever, twenty bore shotgun that he had made for him. It left us with about one hour and a quarter's rough shooting in the height of winter, then, when we came back, the cows used to have hay put round to them before we went in to tea.

Then after tea every evening I used to go out to the cowshed, where in this particular shed there was a well and pump.

Then my work started again, pumping water into these four gallon buckets, carrying them one in each hand to water the line of cows, as there were no drinking bowls.

As I mentioned earlier, I was slower at school than my sister, bless her. Well, one of my distant aunts on my father's side heard about this predicament, and sent me a book entitled arithmetic. Of course it would be maths nowadays. Decimals and fractions were my weak points. As I had no night school to go to, after I had watered these cows, I used to set about these decimal and fraction problems. I may add this arithmetic book had all the problems in the front, and the answers in the back.

I religiously tackled the problems, before I looked at the answers. I seemed to get so tired and I was in bed by ten past nine, as I had to be up at five fifteen in the morning, but that is how I mastered them, just determination!

In a very dry summer, there was a big pond the cows used to drink from. It was fenced off each side, and the front where the cows drank was concreted, so when the cows started to get down on their knees to drink my uncle would get a tank down there adjacent to the pond and fill it with water bucketed from the pond. There were also a few fish in the pond. When I was going to school with one or two of my school friends I remember, we had a go at fishing with bent pins and hazel sticks, but we never caught anything. We may have had a bite, but they got away.

At the beginning of April was time for drilling kale and mangels and just a few swedes, About the third week in March we were sowing spring oats. Of course before sowing we had to get a pretty good tilth, by harrowing and rolling; we tried to get the rows as straight as possible and we succeeded pretty well.

As soon as the roots and kale were showing up the rows, the next job was hand hoeing, then came thinning out, both a back-aching experience for a young chap of fifteen and sixteen years of age. Also, we had a row or two of potatoes across the field. When the plants got a bit bigger, we went between the rows with a horse drawn hoe or shim, to kill the rubbish seedlings.

Then came the grass cutting for hay. There were one or two dry summers and there were parts of the grass field where the grass was so thin it hardly stood up to the knife, and by golly, didn't those mower knives want more sharpening, owing to the grass being tougher.

Then came the picking up of hay. I remember we loaded a four wheel Sussex wagon as much as was safe. One horse was in the shafts, and one horse pulling the shafts by chain harness, which we called the chain horse. At this particular time, I was coming through the gateway with this load, holding the chain horse's bridle, walking a pace backwards, watching to see we did not hit the gatepost, and one must remember that these horses were putting great weight on their hooves, pulling the load; as I was walking backwards, I was half running in front of the chain horse, and the inevitable happened, he trod on my left toes. I thought at the time he had broken them, and momentarily it pulled my leg as well. To this day I have got two flattened middle toes on my left foot. It taught me a lesson though, although a painful one, but I still loved horses, and to this day if a riding horse passes by me and I am close enough, I always pass the time of day with the rider, and ask permission to stroke the horse's face, especially the nose, it is like velvet.

When I left Mr. Rankham's employ, and went to work for my uncle, Mr. Rankham told my mother I should go to a farm where they had tractors working. No doubt he was right, as really, I was taking a step backwards. I soon realised that, although I loved horses, I had to change my ideas to

49

mechanisation, as of course machinery in farming was replacing the horses at a very fast rate.

Now, as I mentioned, my uncle had forty Kent ewes with a Southdown ram put on them, breeding the half-bred lamb; then came the day we penned the ewes and their lambs up.

Next to the pen, on two or three bricks, was a drum with holes knocked in it, making a brazier - we would start a fire in it with wood, paper and coal, get it going well, so the coals were red hot. Very near to the brazier a post was knocked into the ground with a six inch square top to it, also the tools for the job in hand which were two one foot long iron rods with a sharp two inch iron blade on one end, and a nice round wooden handle to hold at the other end. These irons were put in the brazier. I was the one who had to hold the lamb, with its back and front leg held together on either side, holding it tight against my chest so it could not struggle, placing its backside on top of the six inch post, whereby my uncle used to get one of the hot irons out of the brazier, hold the tail across the top of the six inch post, and cut right through the lamb's tail. The best of that was one could cauterize if there was a spurt of blood anywhere after cutting the tail off, rather than cut the tail off with a pocket knife, which some farmers practised. Then, if a ram lamb came to have his tail cut off, I had to hold him in the same position, whereby my uncle would pick up his pocket knife, cut the tip of the scrotum off, and then get special flat clawed pinchers and pull the testicles out. I certainly was not keen on that job - they were quite big lambs!

What a lovely job, the rubber rings do in these times, and more humane, as long as they are put on the first day or within two or three days. Just before the haying came the shearing. We used to have a man come to shear the sheep, and I was the one to turn the handle of the shearing machine, to work the clippers. One had to turn the handle at a steady revolution trying to keep the same revolutions per minute.

The shearer told me I was doing alright so I felt quite good about the whole job.

I must say something about the harvest. When it was time to start cutting, it was done by a binder, a Massey Harris make. The cut corn fell onto the canvas, travelled up to a knotter; when there was enough for a sheaf, a needle came up threaded with string, bound it around the sheaf amount, tied a knot, and two arms came round and deposited the sheaf on the ground. I know one year we had such long strawed winter oats, they flopped over the width of the canvas, and being a foot more in length, it was my job to walk behind with a thick stick to push the mass of straw up the canvas. If one did not treat it like that, it just got blocked up.

Then, the next job was standing the sheaves up in about sixes or sometimes eights to harvest, before carrying and stacking. When finishing off cutting a field, as it got smaller, there was a little sport, shooting or catching rabbits; an odd time or two one would come across a rabbit hole in the stubble, and I have known two or three rabbits to be pulled out of it, eventually giving someone a lovely rabbit stew.

Then after harvest, about September time, after cutting and carting red clover, came the swapping or brush hooking, the tool we used for cutting the bracken, grass, and siding the hedge around the outside of the arable fields.

I may add we had to cut by hand around the outside of the field or headland as we called it, a width of about six feet so that the two horses could not trample down the corn when starting the cutting with the binder machine.

But going back to September, swapping or brush hooking around the outside of the arable field. There were one, or two years of that date, the sweat poured off one cutting this bracken, grass, and siding the hedge. It was what they called an Indian summer, it was so hot.

51

Then about November time it was time to pull mangels; pull the mangel up, cut the leaves off about two inches above the mangel itself so that it did not bleed as we used to say, meaning if one cut the crown the juices used to run, and if that happened they did not keep so well in the clamp. After cutting the leaves off one made a lump of about two barrow loads, so there were these roots in lumps all across the field, and each night before we went home, each lump was covered up with the leaves in case of white frost.

Then came the time to cart these mangels to the big clamp adjacent to the cowshed.

As I have said, we had two horses, and we used to cart these roots with two- wheeled dung carts, one horse to a cart, using long reins to guide the horse, so that one could walk a little way back from the horse on the side really, because sometimes there was a lot of mud flying about when wet weather came along. I had one horse and cart, and Fred had the other horse and cart.

Fred had been working for my uncle for some years, and he was a good friend to me. Fred lived in an extension joining on from the stables, about one hundred and fifty yards down through the field from the farm house, the only accommodation for an employee on the farm. The only water supply was a spring, about fifty yards away, where there was a cutting in the field that made a path and at the end a little wooden gate, stopping cows or sheep from entering the spring water.

Now, I have mentioned the spring and the short path of about four or five yards down to the little gate protecting the spring from animals.

Of course, in the summer the cows were out on the pasture and the bull ran with them. So at each milking, when I used to get cows in, the bull was in amongst them, to be chained up in the shed.

52

Well, there came the time we had a new bull, an eighteen month old roan shorthorn.

My father and mother came to stay one weekend. I remember my uncle, father and myself going on the Sunday afternoon to look at the cows, and as we went through the gate leading from the cowshed where there was an extension of concrete so that the cows could not stodge in the mud before coming in for milking, there stood this new bull and two or three cows.

As soon as we all three got near them, to show my father this new shorthorn bull, the bull started scraping the ground, putting his head down and snorting. As soon as that happened my father said to me, "You had better carry a strong stick with you when fetching the cows in," but being about seventeen years old at the time, I never thought any more of it. Then one afternoon, about twelve fifty five, I was driving the cows and bull up to the shed, and this bull used to turn round, and scrape the ground with his head down, and snorting. Well, I had no fear of him and went up to him and used to shout, "Get on you old bounder," and I may add I have a very loud voice, and always he would turn and run off with the cows!

This particular afternoon the same procedure happened, but this time as I got about six feet from him, I could see he meant to knock me down. In a split second I tried to run backwards, not knowing where I was, but his head hit my shins and over I went, as of course, in those days, cows and bulls had horns!

As I hit the ground, it shot through my mind, as he was at me, he is going to gore my stomach. Remember we are talking about split seconds. All I could do was to roll away from him, which I did, and to my surprise I had rolled down this bank onto the path that led to the gate of the spring, and as soon as I realised where I was, I was over that gate like lightning!

Around the spring was a fence, trees and brambles, with about a fifteen foot drop, so the bull was standing that height above me, hardly seeing me for trees and bushes. I think he wondered where I was, and by golly, he sure was roaring, but after two or three minutes, which felt like a lifetime to me, he went off up to the cowshed with the cows.

When I told my uncle what had happened, the bull was destroyed the next day. When I undressed to go to bed that night, I looked down at my left groin, because I knew that is where he had hit me, and there was a graze about six inches long down that particular part.

I had a very lucky escape. After that experience I always kept my eye on a bull very closely, but not letting myself be afraid of them, I think that would have been fatal.

When going out to the cowshed first thing in the morning in the winter, we carried a paraffin storm lantern, for that is how we saw to milk the cows, or any other job that time of the morning. My first job was to feed the cows with a small amount of hay, which was stacked in flakes in a divided part of the cowshed.

It was the time we had several soldiers camped around Bankhurst Farm buildings on manoeuvres, I went to get the first fork full of hay and to my surprise there was an army chap sleeping on top of the flakes of hay. I had to shake him a couple of times before he woke up, and when he did, he apologised and moved off to somewhere else. With all these manoeuvres going on around the farm, apparently some of the army men made a biggish hole in the hedge. As soon as my uncle found this out, he got pretty upset about it, and went to see the commanding officer! My uncle started getting pretty temperamental about it, but with that the commanding officer apologised, saying these things do happen, and that the government had a scheme to repair any damage that was caused free of charge.

Myself with milk bucket at Bankhurst farm in 1943

Southways farm showing how haystacks were
cut into flakes to feed cattle

Then he brought my uncle down to earth pretty quickly by saying, "You must realise, Mr. Mewett, that half these chaps will not come back from the front fighting lines once they are in operation there."

As I have said before, chicken were kept and my aunty used to fatten a few cockerels, put a few eggs under a broody hen, and of course, the main produce were eggs. Well, there used to be a line of tallish trees very near the farm house and the hen house, and sometimes, just at roosting time, some of the chicken used to roost in the trees. One morning the foxes had killed two or three, laying strewn about, feathers all over the place, and no doubt carried one or two off. My uncle used to say he reckoned the fox used to mesmerize them out of the trees, but whether that was true I do not know. After that, every endeavour was made to get them down out of the trees. However, a gentleman my uncle knew: came along and said to him "If you let me have one of the dead chicken, I'll put some strychnine in the outside parts of the body and I think, if we put that down where it was left, we will get our toby (fox). Well, it happened exactly how he said it would; the fox took the bait, and never got very far before he died. I saw my uncle use some of this poison when I was working there, and the fox ate some of this particular chicken, and my goodness, he only got about twenty five yards down along the other side of the hedge and that was the finish of him!

Two or three weeks after, my uncle met the gentleman that introduced him to putting strychnine into a dead chicken that the fox had killed and left. After saying "Hello, how are you?" to each other, the gentleman in question said: "How did you get on after I treated that dead chicken with strychnine?" "It certainly did the job," my uncle replied. Well, his gentleman friend said, "It damn near killed me," to which my uncle said: "How was that?" "Well, I used the same pocket knife I used to put the poison in the chicken and I forgot to wash it, and I cut an apple with the knife before eating it. I had to have the doctor, and was quite ill for two or three days."

Strychnine is a very lethal poison, and one has to be very, very careful with the use of it.

During the war, when I was working at Bankhurst Farm, we lived only about four miles from the sea as the crow flies. The farm house and buildings were on a hill much higher than the village itself, so it could be seen very easily by low flying aircraft.

Well, in that period, the Germans sent over what was called hit and run aircraft. They used to fly sometimes just on the coast, or a few miles inland, drop their bombs, and then fire cannon shell or machine gun bullets at buildings that came into view at low level flying.

I remember one morning after breakfast, I went back to the cowshed, just got through the door, and shut it, when I heard a roar of aeroplane engines, and as I looked out of the cowshed windows, the view I had was the farm house, and my uncle walking in front of the house carrying a trug full of sliced mangels mixed with crushed oats for the ewes. In that split second, there was this gun fire that must have been tracer shells of the cannon fire, as I could see the shells hit the house, and two or three hit the ground not far from my uncle. It happened in seconds, and they flew straight on.

I thought they were coming round again, so I threw myself on the floor immediately, but, of course, they were over the coast nearby by then. As the cows were still in at that time of year, it was a blessing they were not flying another sixty yards to their right, or there would have been several cows killed.

My aunty was in the house - the dust that it caused nearly choked her - and she was not very well for some time, but survived. Her niece was going up the granary steps to get some corn to feed the chicken with, and at that precise moment a cannon shell imbedded itself in the side of the steps she had walked up - thank goodness it did not hit her.

Apparently these planes were Messerschmidts. When I looked out from the cowshed window, I could see the pilots very plainly as they were so low. There were three of them. They had dropped a bomb each at a nearby market town, doing quite a lot of damage and in the process, killing two or three people. They were very frightening - of course that was the object of the exercise.

The other situation that was worrying was when the doodlebugs started; coming over, we seemed to be under one of their flight paths.

I must have seen one of the first ones to come over. I was down the far end of the farm, on this particular day, and it was dull with fairly low cloud. I heard this engine noise, rather loud and different from any plane noise I had ever heard. I looked up, and at that moment I saw between the clouds this unfamiliar object with flames coming out of its tail. Later in the day we heard on the wireless news that these doodlebugs were coming over, their target London.

Wireless was mostly the thing to hear the news etc. on, and if one did not recharge the batteries, they were lifeless, but of course some households, as we call it now, had a radio. Some were dry battery and others were electric, but on the whole there were a lot of wirelesses with accumulators.

At the time of the doodlebugs, more anti aircraft guns were mounted along the coast.

The other defence was fighter planes which patrolled, generally about three, of Spitfires or Tempest. They seemed to be controlled by radar, because as soon as the doodlebugs, came these planes would appear on the scene. The object was to bring them down in the countryside before they got to London.

I have seen these fighter planes get behind them and fire cannon or machine gun. They would either hit them and they would come down immediately, or explode in the air.

One day, the weather was drizzle and low cloud, you could hear the doodlebugs but could not see them, but one could hear the fighters after them, and within a short period there were three of them shot down. One particular one, when shot down, with all the space around where there were gorse bushes, bracken and the village cricket pitch, this doodlebug had to drop right in the garden of a semi-detached cottage, where a young couple lived. They had not been married long, and the wife was pregnant. She was at home, and the husband had gone on his bicycle three or four miles away to visit his mother-in-law. He heard the explosion when the doodlebug hit the ground and he said to his mother in law, "Golly, that smoke seemed to come from near the cricket pitch which is near our home." With that he jumped on his bicycle and raced home. When he reached home, the sight of the damage was terrible, and his wife was very badly injured; she died in hospital.

What a terrible thing to happen, it wants a lot of understanding, as there was so much spare ground to fall on other than that garden. I suppose the village would not have been very happy if it had fallen in the middle of the cricket pitch, but the best thing about it would be no loss of life.

Going back to Fred, who was a friend to me when I worked for my uncle, he used to keep the cricket score most of the time, for home matches and away matches. Apparently he was very good at the job. I think he was in his eighties before he retired from it, and was presented with a very nice shield, which he was very proud of.

For years Fred used to do the Sunday paper round in all kinds of weather. He always wore an open neck shirt, winter and summer. It did not matter whether it was raining or snowing, all knew they were going to get their paper.

Fred could do that, as we never worked at haying or harvesting on Sundays; of course, the cows had to be milked and stock looked at, so Fred was off farm work every Sunday.

He was a marvel really, through all the weathers, getting wet and cold delivering the Sunday papers; it did not seem to affect him. He lived to the ripe old age of 95 years, yet his only son who got on very well in life, and never had as many of the harsh elements of weather to contend with, died at the age of sixty- nine. It reminds me of what my mother used to say, "We all have an allotted time on this earth, and when the good Lord calls, you have got to go!"

My old school friend, who used to come up to Southways Farm and eventually went in the Navy, he worked for the postal service after the war .

Well, I, my wife and son, just back from our holiday of ten days, which I took between winter barley harvest and winter wheat harvest, received a phone call from his only son, telling me he had been trying to phone me for the last ten days to tell me his father had died suddenly of a heart attack. I was so shocked, I suppose his son thought I was a little mad, as I was saying things like "He can't be dead, he was alright before we went on holiday." I just could not believe it. He was fifty years old, no age at all, it just took me back to what my mother used to say, "When the good Lord calls, you have got to go," bless her heart.

My sister came to stay a few days at Bankhurst Farm during the war. She was about fifteen years old at the time. At the same time, my aunty's niece's youngest brother came to stay. He was in the RAF. medical corps, and in my sister and my later years, she admitted she had quite a crush on him, at that time, thought he was the bee's knees.

Well, after coming out of the RAF. he eventually married, and he and his wife started a grocer shop with a second hand van, renting the grocer's shop with some money he partly borrowed. His wife used to deliver groceries and her husband stayed in the shop to attend to customers there.

Well, things went so well for them that by 1986 their modern store was so large, they sold out to a big food chain store for a few million pounds, and retired. I was so pleased for them - they retired to Jersey. They worked very hard, but through my life I have known other couples who worked very hard indeed in their aims to succeed in a certain project, but things did not work out as they would have liked. It just goes to show the old sayings - *It's not what you know, but who you know,* and *being there at the right time.* The couple who started their grocery business from scratch were called Jim and Jean. With regard to *It's not what you know, but who you know* and *being there at the right time,* no disrespect to either of them - I admire their dedication and determination, and things do happen in life like this. I can remember a few things happened to me which helped me get to where I aimed to get in life.

There came the time in 1946, when I had it in my mind that I wanted to join the police force, much to my uncle's dismay.

I tried the Sussex police, but at that time there were so many men from the armed forces, it was pretty difficult. I went to Brighton, sat an examination and medical, and was rejected for having a flat foot - that was the finding.

Then it came to pass my uncle became a very sick man. We knew that he had bladder trouble, and that he should have had an operation eighteen months before. But as fate would have it, the surgeon who was going to do the operation had his arm seriously injured by a bomb explosion, which was dropped by one of these German hit and run bomber planes. And knowing my uncle, no doubt he thought, "Well, that's let me off for a while," which was quite wrong.

For my uncle thought all hospitals were butcher shops. I suppose seeing what happened to his own father after a similar operation, frightened him.

Now his brother - my father - who was older, had a different view of hospitals. When he was about seventy years old, he was told by a doctor that he had a stomach ulcer. Straight away my father said, "Cut it out then!" By that the doctor said: "You hold on, we can disperse it by medicine and diet," which they did. It just shows the different thinking.

As my father saw all that was going on after his father's operation, it just did not effect him the same way.

I was nineteen years old when my uncle became quite ill - he also looked deathly grey.

As I have mentioned, I used to be in the cowshed at 5.30 am. I would start milking, and my uncle came to milk at 6.00 am. I remember when he came out of the farm house, which was near the cowshed, one could hear this terrible noise of my uncle reaching his heart out, but could not be sick. This was an every morning occurrence.

I dreaded hearing this reaching noise, so I used to bury my head deeper into the cow's side that I was milking, so that I could not hear it so well. It was terrible for him.

In the end he had to have the doctor. He sent him to have tests. Well, at this time he was going to sell the farm. They had already selected a house to retire to in a village about twenty miles away.

When he got to the hospital for these tests, he was told he should be in hospital there and then, but as the farm sale was within three or four days time, the consultant let him go back home, providing he came back to the hospital the day after the sale of live and dead stock.

The day after the sale, he went into hospital, but he was

so ill, his bladder was not emptying, and the result was the poison was going all over his body.

My aunty took me to see him. There seemed to be little tubes all over his body, and quite a different smell that I had not come across, being so young. Unfortunately he didn't have much of a chance to live, and died on Christmas Day, 1946.

Bankhurst Farm was sold by then to a captain in the army. My aunty, her niece and myself stayed on until the February of 1947. In January we had a large fall of snow. After the snow disappeared, I used to walk up to the bus stop about one mile away, five days a week take the bus to the near by town, then change over to the bus that went to Dicehurst, where my uncle and aunt had purchased a house to retire to.

About sixty yards down this by lane, where the house was situated, on the other side of the road there was a piece of ground belonging to the house which was the vegetable garden.

My job when I got to the house was to go down to the garden, which was quite a large piece of ground, cut the long grass down, so that it looked tidy, and dig the different sections for vegetables. I took my lunch with me, and about 4.00 pm. I had to catch the bus back again to Eastfield village, and walk home to Bankhurst Farm.

Then came the day when we moved to Dicehurst. I was twenty years old. We settled down in the house well, and then I had to find a job. I saw a farm job advertised and applied for it. The job was in Kent, the town area of Whitstable. I applied for this situation by phone, and as I had never used a phone in my life, and me being so shy, it was rather a nerve-racking experience. Anyhow, I got through to this particular farmer, and he arranged to meet me at the station of the cathedral city near to Whitstable.

It was the farthest train journey I had ever taken, or any other journey for that matter.

Anyhow, he met me on time, took me to look at the cowsheds and also to where one would lodge, this being a bungalow where the tractor driver and his wife lived, then back to the office, for a discussion. He outlined what I would have to do. There were forty cows to milk by hand, which were accredited, five milkers who started at 5.00 in the morning, and four milkers in the afternoon. My job would be to milk two days a week, also four weekends in five and half a day a week off, but, of course, he said "Within a year we will have Alfa Laval milking machines installed, and that would mean starting at 5.30 am. having one day a week off, and one weekend off in three." The time I was not milking, of course, the job would be general farm work, mostly with a tractor. The wage - four pounds and ten shillings a week.

Well, he took me back to the station, and expressed his wish for me to phone him the following evening.

I remember coming home, and thinking a lot about it, and decided I would decline the offer.

So, after I had my tea the next day, I walked up to the phone box in the village and phoned him, and to my surprise he was out, and it was his wife that answered. I explained that I did not think I would take the job, and her answer was that her husband would be very disappointed! "He would have liked you to have taken the job," she said, and she was so persuasive, and then said, "Why don't you try the job?" and of course I gave in, and accepted. What a soft touch I must have been by the sound of her voice! So eventually, in April 1947, I went by train to my first job in Kent.

Well, my landlord and landlady were Mr. and Mrs. Bert Walters. One thing I did not like was having to use a bucket lavatory, and newspaper to wipe one's backside with. I had certainly not been used to that!

But Mrs. Walters looked after me very well, and was a lovely cook. She was a Yorkshire lady.

Bert, who worked on the same farm as myself, owned an Austin Seven tourer soft top. He was very often doing something to the engine, but it went very well indeed.

My father let me have his bicycle to ride to work, which gave me good service for twelve years.

Home Farm used to be the base we took orders and worked from. This farm was where the cows were, and within twenty five yards of the cowsheds there was the bottling milk plant, where they distributed bottled milk by electric trucks. The firm, Barton and Bison, was painted on every truck and lorry, and they had the monopoly of Whitstable and the neighbouring town. The firm had a lorry, which collected milk from neighbouring farms to supply the bottling plant.

Well, Mr. Barton was as good as his word! Within the year that I started work, Alfa Laval milking machines were installed. Milking started at 5.30 am. instead of 5.00 am. and we had a day a week off, which I generally worked, and one weekend in three off.

As my parents lived on the Sussex coast, which was fifty five miles away, the governor, as I always called my employer, let me have the Monday off with my weekend, so that worked very well.

Going back to the cowsheds, each bucket of milk or part bucket, depending on how much the cow gave you had just milked, one tipped into a container strapped to the wall, from that the milk was regulated over the water cooler, which hung under the container; from the cooler the milk went straight into the ten gallon churn. When the milking was finished, we rolled the full churns over to the bottling plant.

When the cows were milked, they were turned out through the top end door, which led straight in to a strawed yard, enough room for forty cows, with roof covering running around the outside wall, enough room for forty cows, and in one corner adjacent to the cowshed was the bull pen. The milking machines were bucket type with pulsator on top of the lid of the bucket, with a rubber pipe leading from the top of the bucket to the vacuum line, which ran along above the cows' heads.

On Home Farm there were stables, which housed two cart horses, and a grey hunter. He was a big horse, what I would call a charger. There was a man who looked after them, and worked the two cart horses for odd jobs, harvest and mangel carting, as there was ground belonging to the Home farm that was situated about one mile and a half away, where mangel and kale were grown for the cows. This ground was named Longfields.

At Longfields there was a smithy, fire and bellows and other blacksmith equipment. The smithy was joined onto another building which housed farm implements.

So, when the horses wanted shoeing, they were led up to the smithy where a blacksmith would be waiting to shoe them.

One day, when the hunter wanted shoeing, the governor got me to ride this hunter up to Longfields. I never discovered why; I had never ridden a hunter before. It must have been seventeen hands in height, all I had ever ridden was a Shetland pony that belonged to the children on the next farm. I remember I was about five years old then.

However, I rode it up there without falling off. The governor came along just as we were ready to go back to Home Farm. He gave me a leg up, but I suppose I put too much strength into it, and found myself the other side of the horse! Both the blacksmith and the governor, well, they had to laugh, as it was a funny sight.

Eventually, off I went down the country road, and got a bit more ambitious as there was no traffic on the first part of the journey. We got to trotting; just before we got to our destination we got to a walk, as one had to be very careful, because passing right beside the farm was the main arterial road to a well known seaside town. We got safely back and I stabled the hunter and was quite pleased with myself.

But the next morning, gosh! I had back ache. I said to myself, "Well, I cannot understand it as I have not been hand hoeing mangels or kale all day. It must have been when I was on the hunter: I trotted with him, and not being used to riding, I used muscles I had never used before." But I was pleased I rode him safely.

In the winter, each one of us that was employed on the farm had to take it in turns to water the horses about seven o'clock in the evening. My night was Thursday.

Well, the first time I watered this new hunter, which was stabled with two cart horses, he had only just been purchased in place of the old hunter, just about the same size and colour as the old one. I watered the two cart horses, then went round to the hunter, stood the bucket down for him to drink. I just stood there as I always did, waiting for him to drink, wearing my heavy old second hand police overcoat, as it was jolly cold cycling down to the farm. Well, there I stood, thinking of nothing in particular, and, as I call it, my sixth sense told me his head was coming round, teeth bared, and bit me on the shoulder. As quick as a flash, I, with open hand, hit him flat on his nose with all my weight. That certainly taught him a lesson for he never did it again. What I call shock treatment. He jolly well hurt my shoulder, and made an L shape tear in my overcoat.

I think, if I had only a shirt on, the force was so much he would have had a piece out of my shoulder, so I was very lucky. But it did not affect me liking horses. Eventually the two cart horses were sold.

Then came the day when all the cows had their horns sawn off. Two vets came, injected at a particular place where the horn comes out of the head, tied a ligature with binder twine at the top of the head just underneath the horns, then another piece of string mid way along the head string, and pulled that as tight as possible so that when the horn was sawn off there was not the bleeding from the blood vessels. If there was, one would just tie another piece of string around the string that was running along the top of the head that was making the ligature, pull it as tight as possible, and that soon stopped the bleeding. The other thing that had to be done was, as there was quiet a hole left where the horn came off, sulphonamide powder was put in to help close it in time.

Well, there is generally a boss cow in the herd, and in this particular herd it was a brindle coloured cow with horns like an Aryshire, and, by golly, she did like using those horns on her other female friends!

When it came to her turn to be turned out in the yard without her horns on, as I have said the yard was connected to the cowshed, I drove her out into the yard with a few others, and as soon as she got beside another cow, she went to give her a good butt with her horns. It was so funny to see, she did not realise that her horns had gone, and she lost balance and down on her knees she went. By the expression on her face, she could not understand why her horns had not connected. That soon stopped her making scars on one or two of the other cows.

The other good thing about the yard was even in the winter the cows never laid in the cowshed. As soon as they were milked they were turned out into the yard.

Before the cows were milked, each one was washed down on the flanks and udder with a water hose and brush. There were three tractors on the farm, one Fordson major half track, one Fordson major, and a standard Fordson, all on rubber tyres - the standard Fordson was always on rubber tyres. When we got into a lot of arable work, the rubber tyred Fordson major, the rubber tyres were changed by jacking one side up, changing the wheels for a stacey wheel, and the same procedure on the other side. Stacey wheels were iron circumference, with something like nine inch spades attached on each side of the iron centre, so the weight of the tractor did not compact the soil, as it was very heavy soil on that particular farm. Getting ready for spring barley, I have known us to disc a field four or five times before it was ready for sowing. Those were the days when as the winter corn was six or seven inches tall, we walked up and down the field hand sowing sulphate of ammonia to put a little more nitrogen on to boost the growth. I must say we had some very good yields.

I remember saying to the governor at the time, "I disced a field for spring barley five times before we were able to sow," and he said, "Well, what we lose on the roundabout we gain on the swings." He was right, as we had very good yields with, of course, the help of phosphate and other fertilisers.

When kale and mangels were sown, and growing well, about the two and a half inch stage of growth, we started singling them to one plant, that is the mangel - the kale we just hand hoed, singling was done by hand.

I remember a chap coming to work on the farm by the name of Bill. He lived in Whitstable, and cycled to work every morning. I had never known him to be late for work. Bill would be about fifty at that time, and he had been in the Grenadier Guards in the 1914-18 war. He was a stocky chap, about five feet ten inches tall, very strong guy.

His previous job was on a dairy and market garden farm of four hundred acres, where he had worked a tremendous amount of piece work, singling out different crops with a hoe.

Sometimes there would be four of us at this singling mangels, but most times it was myself and Bill. It certainly was a back breaking job, but Bill was so quick and precisioned, I had a job to keep up with him, he just made it look so easy.

Bill was a great friend to me, and, of course, he knew I was pretty shy, as did the rest of the chaps. It was very rarely he talked about the Great War, but one day we were hoeing together and he told me he had lain on the battle field, wounded, for three days, and eventually was picked up and taken to the English hospital camp, and survived. It cost him a year "in dock," as he said, meaning hospital. Then he talked about the army - when he was in France, he was with two of his soldier mates, and the Germans started shelling again; mind you, there were shell holes all over the place where they were at that moment. They heard this shell; they all three jumped into a big shell crater for protection; he crouched between this two mates, and very close was a terrific explosion, and when the dust cleared away he was alive and his two mates were dead, with hardly a mark on them. So if that was not fate, I do not know. It comes to mind what my dear mother used to say "Ah, my boy, we have all got an allotted time on this earth, and when the good Lord calls, you have got to go."

But going back to Bill, and our hand hoeing, the next thing he said, when he was in France, his unit had a roll call every so often. They had to line up, pull their penises out for inspection for venereal diseases.

The sergeant major used to come up and down the lines with cane under his arm; if he noticed there was something not right with a penis, he would tap it in no uncertain terms with his cane and order the poor devil to the medical officer. Just imagine having one's penis hit with a cane!

Then they had several soldiers in the unit with a venereal disease. They could not make out why, so they put the Military Police onto it to try and trace the source, as a lot of these chaps were young and had only just come out to the front.

Myself with my good friend Bill at Barnlands farm in the 1950s

Myself driving the Fordson tractor at Barnlands farm in the 1950s

Well, what they eventually came up with was a place where there was an elderly lady, and the chaps had been lining up one after the other having sex with her for half a crown a time. Of course, they were banned from going there again as she was full of the disease!

You can just imagine, me a loner at 22 years old, never been out with a girl! Well, I was so embarrassed, blushed terribly and all I could blurt out was, "That is not true." He jolly soon told me it certainly was, and, of course, it was. I certainly started to learn things!

Then the next job, the haying, came along, mostly grass leys with clover in them. The stack, used to be made, in the same field as it was grown.

The hay was swept in by the standard Fordson, pitched in the elevator onto the stack.

One stack after it was made heated so much, one saw in the roof sunken places where it had got so hot. Gosh! how it did not catch fire, I do not know. Another one the following year, we had to turn and make another stack. That was a performance. There was an old chap, Sid Strange, who used to thatch each stack, then in the winter, cut the hay out in bales and tie it up ready to carry it away by tractor and trailer to the cows. That was mostly my job with the rubber tyred standard Forsdon tractor, as it was all road work. Sid used to be the stack builder, and what a marvellous job he made of it too. He use to live with his sister, and I always thought he was about sixty years old, but by golly, he was fit, and he had to be, cutting out all those bales of hay.

He used to be pretty serious, never seemed to laugh or chuckle. I thought, one day he will. There came a day one summer, he was building a hay stack. I was on the stack and pitching hay to him to bind the outside as he used to say, and something I said to try and make him laugh or smile, on this particular day, for the life of me I cannot remember what it was, but it tickled him so much he started to laugh

72

and chuckle. Well! none of us could believe it. I felt I had achieved so much, it certainly made my year. Sid used to thatch all the stacks, hay and corn, well, straw stacks, when the combine came into operation.

Anyhow, Sid had a ladder that reached up to the top of the roof of the stack he was thatching. He was a lover of cold tea and chewing tobacco. As he was going up the ladder he sometimes turned his head around and had a good spit! Of course the spit was a lovely colour brown from the tobacco, and some times hit the ladder, and that got a brown colour as well. But he was a wonderful old chap.

Then came the time when a farm was purchased between Manor Farm and Longfields, which joined the two farms up.

THE MAKING OF A NEW FARM

The name of the new farm was Barnlands. The farm house was renovated and one part of it was divided as a dwelling for a herdsman. New buildings were put up, the part being a yard and parlour for sixty cows. The year was about 1950. The parlour was made up of eight standings, between each two standings there was a set of teat cups, a four gallon glass jar suspended on a weighing machine; from the glass jar there was a rubber hose fitted to a special top, whereby one put the ten gallon churn, and took the churns lid off and fitted this special top on; the teat cups were connected to the glass jar. In the division between the two cows there was a hopper for concentrates, generally mixture of barley, oats, and one or two other ingredients.

There was a small trough beside each cow where she would eat her concentrates; the amount each cow had was according to her yield, which had to be recorded at each milking, so each cow's name had to be known, as there were no numbers branded on any of the cows.

It was surprising how one got to know each cow by name, just looking at her, and they certainly did not come through into the parlour in the same order, whereas in a cowshed they always knew their own stall.

Once a ten gallon churn was full, it was rolled back a couple of feet and an empty one connected, then the full churn was taken next door to where the six churn ice bank cooler stood. One lifted the full churn up about two feet to get it on top of the cooler, took the lid off the churn, and put a special top on, with a double tube leading from the top of this contraption, where it was connected to the ice bank cooler. The flow of ice water being pumped through the connecting hose, turned the double stainless-steel tube, which was inserted into the milk, stirring the milk gently at the same time ice water flowed over the churn, and that is how the milk was cooled.

When the milking was finished, we had a van to take the full churns up to the dairy bottling plant at Home Farm.

All concreting of this new set-up was done by farm staff. There was a collecting yard, a dispersal yard, which was connected to the milking parlour, where the cows came in from one side of the yard and dispersed on the other side or down the passage side between the mangers.

The cow herd was a mixed sample, and they seemed to milk pretty well. The old cowshed at Home Farm was turned into rendered sections with a small gate to each pen for the calves that were retained from the dairy herd at Barnlands Farm - the old yard was for dry cows.

The yard was cleaned out with an elevator, and a winch on two wheels. Leading from the winch was a wire rope connected to a very large four pronged fork with a T handle. When out of the dung, it stood about three feet long. What happened was, one chap operated the clutch, another the big fork with the trailer under the elevator, and it wasn't long before you had a trailer load. These loads of dung were carted along the road to Longfields, unloaded in a heap to rot down.

I remember we had a young cow, second calver, who was just starting to calve or trying to - that was five-thirty in the morning. By nine-thirty, she had not calved, so we called the vet. As soon as he saw her he said; "She has a twisted womb," and to my surprise he said, "I want a tractor and a wagon rope." Well! we led this cow out to the field, where he attached the rope around the head; it went along her neck line, around the body, behind her front legs, like a loop around her, along her back, another loop round her body, in front of her udder, then the rope continuing along the back over the tail and hitched on the tractor. Two men pulled on the rope, the tractor took the slack of the rope, and she went down as easy as pushing over a toy cow. As the rope was held tight by the tractor, which stood about six yards away, one man held her head, I held her back legs, another chap held her front legs, while the vet got his arm into the vagina to feel the calf. Now, on his instructions, he was laying flat on the ground with his arm up this cow, all of a sudden he said; "Pull her legs up so that she is on her back, now down again," and this procedure was repeated about four times, and, by gosh! he calved her a lovely calf and alive. I thought that was an achievement. We unhitched the rope, it went slack, and the mother got up straight away and was licking her calf. I certainly learnt something that day.

After acquiring the new farm, Barnlands by name, as well as more grass, the arable increased. That is when we had the first new combine, very much different to the binder and sheaves.

The combine was a German Class, six foot cut, drawn by a Fordson Major tractor. The actual driving of the combine mechanism was by an engine mounted on top. I believe it was a Ferguson 35 engine, as far as I can remember. But that combine was a lovely machine, if one got it set right it made a very good sample. We did not spray the cereals at that time, so when on some of this particular ground we grew wheat, and an odd time or two we came across a patch of thistle, a lovely crop of wheat, but so were the thistles, and where they were so vigorous it used to block the drum up and stop the portable engine. Then the procedure was to open the top of the drum, and out with an iron bar to move the cylinder or concave, by putting the iron bar through the concave bars, and heave to get it to move, and pulling out the thistles which were about three foot long, jammed quite juicy, too, in between cylinder and drum; sometimes it was quite hard removing this juicy mass. But then away we would go, no trouble.

With this type of combine, the grain itself was elevated into a kind of drum which stood on top of the combine. As far as I can remember, about four feet wide and about three and a half feet high, where there were three or four openings where corn sacks could be clamped on, and slides to push up when one wanted the grain to flow into a particular sack, and push down to stop the flow. They were West of England sacks, and when full, one tied them up, put them down the special chute, which had a stop at the end of it, so that sacks could be released near enough in line across the field. Thinking about the moisture content of the grain, some of it must have been 20%.

The sacks were picked up by two hersdmen after afternoon milking. I was on the combine, when weather was fine at harvest time, on Mondays, Wednesdays and Thursdays. The other days I was relief milking, and on relief milking times I was one of the herdsmen that picked up these full corn sacks, by using tractor and foreloader, handling them onto the foreloader, then stacking them on to the trailer, and away we went.

The covered yards for the dairy cows were not used and had been cleaned out for the summer, so we stacked the sacks of corn, two high, with a thick layer of straw on the floor; as we worked our way back with these rows of sacks of wheat, we never had a drier.

I know our knuckles got very sore handling these thick corn sacks. I remember one year a few sacks were getting a little warm after two or three weeks storing, so we brought the combine down to the covered yard and put it all through the combine again, just before the miller company took it all away. By the way, that combine also tied the straw up when coming out of the combine. The ground was heavy, and by golly, it could yield cereals well, so there was quite a lot of straw. One year, towards the end of harvest, I believe something went wrong with the trusser at the back of the

77

combine, and therefore the straw was loose in rows behind the combine. As far as I remember it must have been part of the last field of the harvest.

I know we acquired a big baler with a portable diesel engine fixed on top to drive the mechanism. It was a little later on in the year that we went baling this straw up, and I remember we just started to have white frost some mornings, quite cold it was, but as the diesel engine on the baler had to be started by swinging the handle, as there wasn't any press button battery starter, by golly that did want some swinging. The colder the temperature, the harder it was to swing, but one soon warmed up. I used to think the paraffin tractors wanted a bit of swinging especially on cold mornings, but this diesel engine was harder.

Now I am seventy years old I can hardly believe we had to swing these handles to start these engines - thank goodness for modern times! It is a wonder we did not get ruptures, or a broken wrist or arm, especially when the engine used to kick back.

On this farm, as I mentioned, we grew spring barley as well as winter wheat.

Myself and the tractor driver I lodged with, cycled home to lunch, generally a cooked lunch. It was in the month of May and jolly warm it was too! The sun was so strong by mid-day that the mudguards of the standard Fordson were so hot one kept one's arms off them.

Well, this particular day, I was rolling spring barley with the standard Forsdon that was always on rubber tyres. I had just started off rolling after my lunch or dinner, whatever one wants to call it. Driving down across the field, I came over all sleepy, and all of a sudden I opened my eyes to see the hedge looming up before me. As quick as lightning I swung the steering wheel round just in time; it was so close I could feel the hedge brushing hard against the front wheel. I was strong enough to hold the steering so that it could not pull the front wheels into the hedge. All this happened in split seconds. How I did not go through that hedge I shall never know, but it taught me a lesson, and I saw it never happened again. It was fortunate it never happened further along the field, as on the headland, in Kent called the foreacre, there was a dike instead of a hedge, and if I had gone in there it would have been more of a fatal accident. It just shows, after a hot meal and being a very warm day, sitting on a tractor, no cabs in those days so no shelter from the sun, how sleepy one can get. I do not think I was the only farm worker it did not effect at one time or the other. No doubt I was lucky, like my dear old mum would say, it was not to be!

As we had a dairy herd, I remember in an adjacent field to the dairy unit, a young Shorthorn bull ran with some heifers, and one or two cows. It was Autumn time. They were fed hay once a day by carrying it on a fork, throwing it over the hedge and one strand of barbed wire which protected the ditch. Then, when getting over the two obstacles, one took it further out in the field to spread it about. Well, that is what I did, so the animals could have a fair share of the hay. As soon as I spread it they came running across the field. As they came to the hay, I counted them and saw they were alright. I walked away with the fork in my hand. But instead of the bull feeding with the heifers, he came running after me. I stood my ground with the two pronged fork in my hand. He went snorting and bellowing around me in a circle, and I thought, well, after having a terrible experience a few years before with a bull, at least I had got a fork in my hand, and if he came at me close enough, I would have to use it on his nose, if possible. I did not want to, and he seemed to know this, as he kept away just far enough out of reach. There I was, jabbing at him and shouting, "Get away you old devil - what do you think you are doing?" and as I have a very loud voice, I expect that frightened him a bit. The only thing I could do was to back closer to the hedge, but with him jumping round me it was more difficult. But I achieved it, and as I was very fit, I was over the barbed wire and hedge like a shot out of a gun. I was on that day as relief herdsman, so it was my job to feed these particular animals. That is how I came to know what this bull was like, and getting to that hedge and over the wire and hedge felt as though it was hours instead of minutes.

The second day I told my old friend Bill, a fellow worker, much older than myself, and he said: "I had to feed them yesterday and the bull started the prank. I never messed about because he would knock one over if he could, so I jabbed him right on the nose, and it certainly stopped him." We never had any more trouble with him after that - shock treatment I suppose.

The other thing I have not mentioned is, Mr. Barton would not have any harvesting or haying operations attempted on a Sunday; I suppose it was because he took his religion seriously as did his father. Of course, cows had to be milked and stock fed whatever day it was.

Going back to harvesting and haying at Barnlands Farm, a piece of hay machinery broke down, an agricultural engineer was sent out to fix it, and the gentleman in question was a puggish lined-face individual, but, of course, knew his job. He got underneath the machine, fixed a new part on it, and by golly, it worked. He crawled out from under the machine, stood up and said, "It is not all a pretty face you know!" It seemed so funny, because to look at him he was far from a pretty face!

Now, before we had a combine, like every one else, we had to store the corn sheaves in stacks. One particular stack was built in the same corner it was grown, and it was adjacent to a small holding where they kept goats tethered near their individual sheds. Whether that made any difference I do not know, but when we came to thrash this stack, and we always put small mesh netting about three feet away from the stack so it encircled the whole stack, the netting was about two and a half feet high, purposely to stop mice and rats running away. Well, by the time we got down to the bottom of the stack, admittedly we had a fox terrier with us, but by the time we had finished threshing this stack, there were about forty rats and several mice lying dead. We reckoned the dog killed about thirty rats; she was exhausted; one could soon see why it was the right thing to do, encircling the stack with this small mesh netting. I had never seen anything like it at threshing time, there may have been a few more rats dead, but I do not want to exaggerate.

Then came a time in my life I thought differently. I went home to my parents at the weekend I had off, which was one in three, and because they lived fifty five miles away on the south coast at a place called Farlight, the governor let me have the Monday off for a long weekend. In those days one did not finish work on Saturdays until 12.00 noon. I walked down to the town of Whitstable, which was about just over a mile away from where I lodged, caught a bus to a nearby cathedral city, then caught a train from the city station to the coast town nearest to Farlight, then by bus to Farlight, then walked another half mile to my parents home, so it was quite a trip.

The only person but one from work to see where my parents lived was the governor's father as, after I had picked up a hay knife, pulled the knife towards me, it hit the side of my foot and as I was wearing Wellingtons at the time, it was so sharp the knife went right through and cut the side of my foot. The governor took me straight to hospital, and as I walked in to the hospital, every step I took, the blood just squelched through the hole in my Wellingtons. They found I had cut an artery on the side of my foot. That made me feel a bit sick, I can tell you. I had to be off work for ten days, and that is why the governor's father took me home to Farlight.

I have said I was very shy, but somehow I paid into a social club run by the milk bottling plant workers.

When this particular social came about, I invited a worker on another farm to come with me. When we arrived at the hall where the social was held, couples started dancing. Neither myself nor my friend could dance; we just stood on our own drinking orange juice. Well, all of a sudden two girls came up to us, one was blonde and her friend was dark haired, about five feet six inches tall, Irish, and lovely milk white skin. The blonde was five feet ten inches and pretty attractive. They asked us if we would like to dance. We told them we could not and their reply was, "Let us teach you." OK, we said. Straight away the tall blonde took hold of my friend, who was only about five foot eight inches tall, and the Irish girl got hold of me, and as you know I am six foot six inches tall, it all looked rather out of place. The unusual part for me was I was introduced by the tall blonde to the Saturday nighters' dance and social club that was run in the winter, and that is where I learnt to dance a little more. I remember the girls used to wear flared longish skirts, and when one got to the corners you swished them round, and, by golly, I swished them around, and one noticed how they turned their head and looked down at their skirt to see how far it flared out.

Well, I went out with this tall blonde for a time, all platonic I may add. I got quite fond of her, but I heard she was seeing an RAF. chap. When I think of it, I suppose that was not quite so platonic. Anyhow, we parted amicably but it hurt me quite a lot as I am a pretty sensitive sort of chap. Then six months afterwards she wrote to me, wanting to continue our friendship, but I refused, and I never went out with another girl for three years. Then, as I have said, I lived fifty-five miles from my parents, and it meant two bus journeys and on the trains to get home.

When I was home one weekend, I mentioned to my mother I thought of getting a second-hand car. As my mother worked for a lady employer she told her of what I was thinking of doing, and her reply was "I know just the man, a Mr. Davis, he does a lot of taxi work for me, and he would be very reliable."

So with that information, I phoned him, and he eventually got me a Standard Ten saloon. It was a smart vehicle; Mr. and Mrs. Davis said it looked like a doctor's car. It was quite old. The other thing was, he knew engines because he used to strip down his Vauxhall car he used for taxi work. Then came the day the car was ready. I travelled over to Binhill, which was only about eight miles from where my parents lived, after drawing one hundred and ninety pounds out of my post office savings account. That made a hole in the account, as I was only earning, with overtime, seven pounds per week.

I came to the home of Mr. Davis, knocked on the door, which was opened by Mrs. Davis whom I thought was an attractive lady, and had a nice manner about her. She politely asked me in when I told her who I was, paid over my one hundred and ninety pounds, and in the course of doing so, she mentioned they had one daughter, her name was Patricia, and also said, "Perhaps your mother and father would like to come to tea with us one Sunday." I said that would be very nice and thanked her.

So by my next weekend, which was three weeks from the date of being asked, I took my mother and father over to Mr. and Mrs. Davis's home. We all got on very well, and enjoyed it. That is when I met Patricia. I liked her from the first meeting, so another three weeks went by, and I went home to my parents.

As I have said, I was a pretty shy individual! I thought, as I do not go back until Monday night, I will go over to her home on Sunday and ask her out to lunch. She took sandwiches as she worked for a motor and agricultural engineers in a nearby town.

How I went over to her home, knocked on the door and asked her mother if Pat was in, I do not know. Her mother said she is just along the sitting room, so I went along to this room, saw her there, said, "Hello." She replied "Hello" to me. Well, I do not know to this day how I asked her if I may take her to lunch on the Monday! And as Pat was very shy, more to the point, she accepted, and that is how I met my future wife.

Well, things developed between us, and we got engaged the summer of nineteen fifty-five. After a while I thought my job was too far away, and I may add it was all platonic, although we were in love; too shy of sex I suppose before marriage. When I think of it these days, and the openness of sex, it all seems very far fetched. I suppose, if we were the same age and met in the nineteen nineties, perhaps we would have been more relaxed about it.

Anyhow, my mother put an advert in the Sussex Express for me, wanting a foreman's or working manager's job within a twenty mile radius of Binhill.

I approached my employer, Mr. Barton, about the situation, that I had become engaged and wanted to get nearer my fiancee, and when the time came that I was accepted for another situation, would it be alright to give him a month's notice? He said it would be alright, "But you will go for a foreman's job, won't you?" and with that, I said that is what I am doing.

Anyhow, two or three days went by, then the governor asked me to see him in the farm office on the Friday afternoon. I arrived for the appointment, and he tried his best to persuade me to stay on, and work for him still, but I told him I was adamant about the situation. Then from the advert in the Sussex Express, I was asked to go for an interview on a farm with cows and sheep only about five miles away from Binhill. I was accepted for the job, and lived in the farm house, as working manager, riding down on my bicycle, machine milking cows every morning in a cowshed about a mile away from the farm house, which was situated in the village, for ten pounds per week, that being the wage.

It was a very sad thing, as the job came available through their son being drowned in a swimming accident in the local river, what a tragedy!

When I got back to work, I gave Mr. Barton a month's notice. He again tried to persuade me to stay, but to no avail. I left just before Christmas nineteen fifty- five. I'd said goodbye to the governor, then, just as I was washing down the parlour after my last milking, Mr. Barton senior came into the milking parlour to say goodbye, and also to say if the occasion arose and I wanted a job, that I could come back and work for them again, for which I thanked him very much. I thought it was very nice of him. So that was the end of my first job in Kent.

Then early in January nineteen fifty-six, I started my new job as working manager. I was looked after very well indeed. While I was in this new job, I bought a new vacuum clipper set, to clip the cows on their flanks, as they were lying in the cowshed at that time of the year, to keep them a bit cleaner. I went home to lunch at 1.00 pm. after covering these new clippers over on top of the steam chest we had to have in those days to sterilize all milking utensils. When I arrived at the cowshed at 2.00 pm., the herdsman was back already, and of course I went to get the clippers again to proceed with clipping the cows. I lifted the covering up, and there were no clippers. I asked the herdsman whether he had shifted them, but he said he had not, and as the shed was right next to the road I thought someone has stolen them. I searched in the dairy part of the cowshed and discovered the four pulsators that fitted on top of the milk buckets were missing. Well, the next thing was to report it to the local policeman. Then I had to make the five mile journey to Binfield to buy four more pulsators before we could start the afternoon's milking.

The police brought in plain clothes men, and they searched around the cowshed that ran very near the river, but found nothing. They interviewed the herdsman - I think they knew he had done the thieving but could not prove it. They certainly brought him to tears, by accusing him of this deed, and they certainly frightened him. I doubt if he would do anything like that again. They were pretty sure that he had thrown them in the river. No doubt that was the obvious place, so it was not taken any further.

Then in October, nineteen fifty-six, we decided to get married. I asked my employer whether he had a cottage for me but he had not. I tried to rent a bungalow near-by but as it was near the sea, they wanted a rent of seven pounds per week in the winter and fourteen pounds a week in the summer, so it was not possible for me to stay there.

So the most rash thing I had ever done in my life was about to come. I gave a month's notice and had not even got a job!

In the meantime, I looked in the Farmers' Weekly and saw a situation as foreman on a five hundred acre farm in Kent.

At the same time my future mother-in-law phoned me and said she had seen the same job advertised, and if I went for an interview, my future father-in-law would take me to Ashford for this purpose. Well, I eventually went for the interview at a farm called Bothanger situated two miles from Ashwood, called Kenard. I was interviewed by a Mr. Howell, who was the manager, his father was the director, and his mother owned one of the farms.

My future wife, Pat, was with me and he showed us the cottage, semi-detached, very nice it was too - No. 8

Grovernor Road, about two hundred yards from the farm buildings.

Mr. Howell showed us the cottage first, saying if the wife does not like it, it is a no goer, then looked at us and said with quite a laugh, "I am sorry, of course you are not married yet!"

At the end of the interview he said, "I will draw a short list up and if you are on it, I will want you to come and have a good look round, to make sure you would want to come." Well, another week I was summoned for another interview. I went by train to Ashford, and Mr. Howell met me at the station and took me back to the farm, showed me the three different farms and the farming system they ran. He took me back to the farm house, and conversation went like this, "Well, Mewett " (all surnames in those days!), "you are on the short list, would you like a cup of coffee?" "Yes, please!" "Well, do you want the job?" Answer: "Yes, I would please." "Well, you need not start until November." "Thank you." With that he drove me back to the station and that concluded that, and I had a job. My dear old mother would say, "Ah, my boy, it was meant to be."

So on October the eleventh nineteen fifty-six, we were married in the parish of Binfield. The church being just the opposite side of the road to where my future wife lived. The taxi did not have far to take the bride!

I was thirty years old in the November, and Pat was to be the same age in the following August. As I did not start my new job until November, we were able to have ten days honeymoon in Bournemouth. I had never had that amount of time off in my working life, and that year October was absolutely lovely weather, like an Indian summer.

And, of course, when we came back we had plenty of time to move into our first home.

Well, I started my job early November nineteen fifty-six. I must say there was a lot to take in. I had never worked on such a mixed farm in my life, and I may add, I have not done so since.

Perhaps you will see when I explain there were two herds of cows, two flocks of breeding sheep, one of Kents, one of Southdowns, both registered, a breeding herd of Wessex saddle back pigs, with a large white bore to serve them, which produced very good weaners at six and eight weeks old. There was a four hundred brick built hen battery, one bird to a cage, twenty four hour electrical feeders moving in front of the cages, with dung scrapers on glass wire mesh to take the dung down one end; out in the adjacent field there were arks with young pullets coming along ready for replenishing the hen battery. Then there were turkeys brought up ready for Christmas. I certainly did not enjoy it when I had to help kill and pluck them, all hands to the deck at those times. The worst thing was the big cock birds, or stags as they called them. Even I at six feet six inches tall had to hold them by their legs, so that their head touched the ground, then one had a piece of wood about two inches thick and about two feet long, put one foot on one side with the stag's head underneath the piece of wood, then quickly put your other foot on the other side of the piece of wood, so that the stag's head was firmly underneath the wood, dead centre, and pull hard, which broke its neck. I must say I hated to do that, but of course it had to be done. Others, if they were not too big I could kill, like a chicken.

That is the livestock side.

Now for production from the ground: there was a small apple orchard but that was phased out; there were fourteen acres of cherries, and about the beginning of June or just before, I used to be in charge of that right through the season.

First I had to be up at four thirty each morning and in the orchard at five, scaring birds with a shot gun, also a few bangers put about the different parts of the orchard. Always at that time we had an old caravan we used to take up to the

88

orchard. It had a Calor gas stove, and Pat, my wife, used to cycle up about seven in the morning to get my breakfast ready, also my lunch. It was also my office. As well as shifting the ladders for the pickers, which, by the way, were mostly women, I also would bargain how much I would pay them for a twelve pound chip of cherries, which was generally three shillings, or three shillings and three pence a chip, depending on which part of the tree they were picking. We used to have pickers, generally men, come after work from the local railway works. I used to get them to pick the cherries from the top of the highest trees for about three pence more per chip. Well, I was rather shy in those days and certainly was not used to working with women, and the things I heard them talk about. Well, it made me blush, I can tell you! I know one lunch time, they were eating and talking, and that particular day we had a lovely young couple come to pick cherries. They seemed to be all over one another. They seemed to forget their lunch and went down in the nearby wood to play! They looked pretty refreshed when they came back. I suppose it put a little more sparkle for the job in hand! Working with those women was certainly an education for a newly married man, who was very platonic before he married. Sometimes I wonder if young couples know the meaning of platonic in these times! As I say, I used to move all the ladders for the women pickers, and as soon as I placed the ladder where I thought it was safe, I used to go right to the top of it so that it gave the ladies confidence to get up it. Well, one ladder I placed, we are talking about a forty rung ladder, I went up it pretty smartish, and as I got five rungs from the top it snapped in two, and I came down quicker than I went up. I remember it was a big tall Bedford cherry tree. I grabbed at branches on the way down, but they broke, but of course it slowed my fall down a bit. I hit the ground and was lucky to get away with it. I suppose, when I look back, it did not do my hips any good.

89

The arable crops were barley, over one hundred acres, wheat - ten acres. Potatoes - ten acres, also sugar beet - ten acres. The potatoes, we had women picking them up, so much a bag. We carted them to the home farm and stored them in an old army shed, straw bales all round the outside and on top for insulation against the frost. We also put powder to every ton of potatoes to stop them sprouting. The shed held one hundred and twenty tons of them. The variety was Majestic, which we riddled out in the winter. We had a standing order of three tons per week from a wholesaler, and Saturday mornings was the morning we took orders round to different houses nearby, and several bags were sold like that.

The wheat ground was alternated with the potato ground.

Oh, by the way, the lambing used to be carried out in spring in the cherry orchard as there was more shelter for them there.

Also, kale was grown for the cows. By golly, that was a cold job on frosty mornings; it used to make one's hands ache when they were warming up.

The sugar beet was all pulled by hand after being loosened by a plough, and the tops fed to the cows. Dockets used to come, authorising us to fill a railway truck up at the local siding yard about two miles away, so we would pull enough for to load a truck, several tons mind you, and carry them from the field to the station in a second world war American six wheeler army truck. That was certainly a gate chain gear operation. If one did not get that right, there was a hell of a clatter. I know three of us were in the cab, not a lot of room, so the chap driving used to say to the next one to him, "Come on, mate, I will work the revs and double declutching and you work the gear lever." Of course, they were used to it and it worked. When we got to the railway truck we unloaded by hand with special sugar beet forks. They had little round knobs on the end of each tine so that they could not spear the beet.

Myself machine milking at Barnlands in the 1950s

The Class Combine at Barnlands

Another job in the winter was, as soon as the kale was finished, a tractor driver and myself used every morning, to go and cut out a load of silage and bring back for the cows. Of course, Saturday morning we had to cut out two loads, ready for Sunday morning. There was a cowshed for about forty cows. Then Mr. Howell, the manager, said we were to put in abreast parlour for milking, so that went in with a few alterations to the cowshed, farm labour doing the concreting. Then, on the outside yard, there was an area enough for forty cows, and to hold them in there were makeshift wooden poles bolted to upright posts with straw bales at the bottom, the conventional type fifty pounds in weight, oblong, not round bales, to make mangers where we used to feed the kale and silage. I thought it was a bit Heath Robinson, but it worked. I remember the manager said to me one day: "You know, Mewett, you want to offer these things up before you make them permanent," and when I think about it, there was a lot of sense in what he said. One day he said to me: "This dung we scrap from these chicken in the battery house, there was no straw in it. We ought to be feeding that to the pigs." I thought he was talking out the back of his head, but now I think of all the stuff that has been put into dairy and cattle cake for cheap protein, it looks as though he was talking sense after all.

I used to do relief milk three times a year for the herdsmen's holidays, and every other weekend I would relieve the pig and poultry man.

The other thing I was not keen on was cutting little piglets to castrate them. We used liquid paraffin to put on where we had cut them. I had never done it before. They seemed to survive alright, Talk about being shoved in the deep end - like the turkeys, never done it before in my life.

The manager was quite a lad. I knew he was under the specialist for his back, and that did not help matters. I went round to the cowsheds one day, and there was the manager sitting in his Land Rover, and he and the herdsman were swearing at each other - words I had not heard before in my life. I walked away again quickly to let them cool off. The manager was prone to go off the deep end sometimes over nothing. Of course, his back did not help him. When it was time for spring barley sowing, he used to spring tining five in the morning ready for the drill, and a tractor driver used to take the job over at seven o'clock in the morning. I used to harrow up behind the drill, and that particular morning I saw the tractor driver spring tining. He stopped to have a word, and said to me: "The governor," meaning the manager, "accused me of being five minutes late and swore at me something chronic, and I bloody soon swore at him; that calmed him down." Then he looked at me, "he is a feller, isn't he?" This particular tractor driver knew him better, as he had worked for him three or four years before I came on the scene. I recall one seven o'clock in the morning he drew up in his Land Rover and opened his window. He used to smoke Goldflake cigarettes. He put one in his mouth. As soon as he said "Good morning, Mewett" he lit up and drew in a deep breath, and I thought "Oh my God, look out!," and he nearly went through the roof over nothing at all. I would not row with him; I just stood there and let him rant and rave until he cooled down, then I used to talk to him calmly about the situation. Anyway, it was very often over nothing at all. Oh, he was a good manager alright, and when he did have a row, within half an hour he would forget all about it. That is a thing I admired about him, he never harped on it.

There was a chestnut wood nearby the buildings. The woodman used to cut it down to make spiles or stakes for fencing and rails, and one morning I took a couple of chaps up to the wood to collect a load of fencing stakes. Along came the manager, got out of his Land Rover and said, "Mewett, I want to speak to you." While I left the two chaps loading the fencing stakes, I followed him down through the wood. All of a sudden he stopped and confronted me. "Mewett," he said, "You are too bloody trusting, and to get these chaps to get on with it you want to frighten the buggers, you know." I said very calmly to him "Governor, you are not going to get much work out of men without trusting someone, or frightening them either." His answer was "Oh, right" and off he walked, and that was that, never heard anymore about it.

The main farm was rented from a sanatorium for TB. patients. In its heyday it made a lot of money, then of course, as TB. was depleted it certainly was a different matter.

The sanatorium owned the six cottages nearby, one of which I had lived in for two years. Apparently they wanted to sell all six cottages. Mr. Howell went to different meetings with the powers that be, but he could not save them from being sold.

So one day he came to me and said, "Well Mewett, the sanatorium authorities are going to sell these cottages, so you better look for another job. I will give you a reference, and also I have been in touch with a well known farmer in Anford, at Home Farm. His name is Alender. They want a foreman for a four hundred acre farm they rent."

Well, my wife and I went for an interview at Home Farm, and were taken up to this four hundred acre farm. I must tell you the Alenders were pretty big dairy and arable farmers.

We arrived at this particular farm, the buildings were very well kept, all wood was well creosoted. It was mostly arable, but it was where they brought up all the calves from the big dairy herd. They also kept six cows there, all the time, for milking by hand, and feeding the milk to these calves from the dairy herd. A stockman was kept to milk the cows and look after the calves at different stages of their lives. Then Mr. Alender showed us over the house, where we would live. It was built in seventeen eighty, and by golly! what a big house. We walked into the kitchen and there was a big larder adjacent, reeking with damp. We went from there to a great dining room, very high ceilings, very big windows, very wide, the height must have been ten feet. I should think one would want enough curtain material from three or four rooms in an ordinary house to have enough for one window. There was a fireplace at one end of the room. I walked over to look at it, and just before I got to it, there was a great hole through the floor into the cellar, big enough for two men to fall through. Then we went to look at the drawing room; the same size, great windows; the fireplace was at one end, and again I walked up to it and, of course, the same thing had happened, as in the other room, a great hole down into the cellar. When I spoke to Mr. Alender about it he said, "Well, you must remember we only rent the farm!" Then from there we went up stairs; big bedrooms also a snooker room. We came downstairs. The only thing I saw that was good about the house was it had a phone. I would have liked to have worked for them, as I knew they were very good farmers. Mr. Alender tried to persuade us to go there by saying to us, "What about if I decorated three or four rooms for you?" and there we were, saying what colour paint etc. we would like. Then it came the time for him to take us to the nearby station. We rode in his Land Rover down this very long drive with woods each side until we got to the main road. While driving down this long drive he said to me. "Of course, we expect the foreman to give a hand sometimes <u>with the hand milking!</u>" By golly, I certainly pricked up my ears then, as I vowed I would never hand milk another cow. I had had enough of it, five and a half years, but I never said anything. When we eventually parted, Mr. Alender said: "Give me a ring, on the phone of course, about just after six this evening, whether you would like to take the job." My wife and I got home and discussed it, and

95

I made my mind up, and phoned him at just after six pm. The conversation went like this: "Hello, Mr. Alender. I have thought about the job you offered me. Thank you for offering it to me, but I won't be coming." The answer, "Why not?" "Well, I have always vowed that I would not hand milk another cow for the rest of my life." He said to me: "I don't think you have got much guts, Mewett." I said, "I don't care whether you think I have not got much guts or not, and another thing, whose wife wants to open a door to a drawing room and dining room and find a jolly great hole in front of the fire place in to the cellar? And another thing, it is a heck of a long and wooded driveway before one gets to the main road, so that is the reason." So that ended the conversation.

Before I go on any further, I must tell of the first five months of our married life. As I have said, we moved into eight Grovernor Road in November nineteen fifty- six. I remember about ten days before Christmas we were writing cards for Christmas, and bearing in mind the cottage had a Rayburn in the kitchen, and an open fire in the sitting room, well it was quite cold, and so knowing me, I hate being cold in a house, I piled the logs on; the fire was roaring away, and after about an hour, so was the chimney. The smoke and sparks were flying out of the chimney. I suppose it was about seven o'clock in the evening, so at that time we both had bicycles for transport, I jumped on my bicycle, went tearing down the road to the phone box, and phoned the fire brigade. They were there within minutes, our admiration for that service is beyond any bounds. They did the job without any mess at all. We did not realise when we moved in that the chimney had not been swept. We certainly had chimneys swept where ever we were after that.

We had only been married a few months when my wife's father became ill. At the same time Pat wanted a puppy, so we arranged to have this puppy brought at a certain time. It was a cross golden Labrador. The father was pedigree and the mother was Labrador, but not pedigree, but he turned out to be a fine dog.

All of a sudden Pat was called away to the hospital as her father was worse. So she was away a couple or three days, and in that time her father died, poor man. But the first evening she was away, the puppy arrived. We named him Simon. Well, the lady who brought him, provided a box and a little blanket which he was used to, and I was told to hot a brick up in the oven, then put the blanket over it, settle the pup in it, and he would be alright. Well, in the evening before I went to bed, I settled him down in the box, the blanket was nice and warm. I sat there some time then thought he was asleep, so started to creep away, and out he jumped. I reckon he was foxing! I tried again, the same thing happened, so I settled him down again, this time I took my slippers off, and waited twice as long, then crept away, and to my relief he was fast asleep, still in the box, and he was quite alright after that. It was rather a shock when Pat's father died. He was only fifty-nine years old, and we only had been married a few months. But such is life; like everyone else one has to go forward, no good looking back!

Now back to nineteen fifty-eight, the months of October and November, my first interview with Mr. Alender, the job seemed OK. but the house was not, so I did not have to think any more about it. The next interview was on a farm in Oxfordshire. We went on an express train from the local railway station. By golly, we had never been on such a fast train. Pat brought a flask of coffee. About half way on the journey, I held the cup while she poured the coffee, and as the train was going so fast it swayed a bit, and of course the coffee swayed as well, and spilt. We had to laugh, and Pat, she was a giggler, she had a job to stop. Eventually we arrived at this farm, were shown where we would live - a lovely little bungalow, all fitted out newly. I had to bend down a bit in the doorways as I am very tall. Anyhow, it was very nice. Then came the interview. These people had recently bought it, never having farmed before and no doubt looked at farming through rose coloured spectacles (meaning everything looked rosy in farming!)

We sat down, and they told me about the farm a bit, then they came to the salary. The owner said: "Well, we have been told by the local Agriculture Advisory Service that a certain amount per week would be appropriate." I cannot quite remember the amount, but as soon as they mentioned the amount they were willing to pay, I lost interest. Pat and I discussed it, but it was a non-starter. So that was two interviews gone by the way.

Then there was a third interview to go to. But before I went, I spoke to Mr. Howell as to what period of notice he wanted when I eventually got a job. He said a month would be quite alright, so we both thought that was fair enough. I reiterate about Mr. Howell, my governor at the time. He was a very good farm manager, but wanted a bit of getting used to. He had a loud voice like mine, but he had been a sergeant major in the army, and no doubt came across some terrible types of men. Hence, what he tried to get across to me ("you want to frighten the buggers, Mewett"). The third interview we went to by train from the local station to the station of Heywards View. We were met by a farming lady and taken to the farm where she lived with her husband, who was a director of a brewery. She did say "he provides the money and I farm," but that wasn't quite true - she owned half of it! Also her brother and herself owned another two or three farms, all adjoining. Anyhow, their names were Mr. and Mrs. Craven. Mrs. Craven would be my immediate boss, the first lady I had ever worked for. The job was for working Farm manager on one hundred and eighty acres, thirty single sucklers with an Angus bull running with them, and they had also started a sheep flock of fifty Clun Forest ewes, which were going to be increased to one hundred and twenty. There were three small farms to be run as one. The arable was spring barley. There was a semi-detached cottage about one and a quarter miles down the road, quite out of the way from shops. It was being renovated with flush toilet, and Rayburn for hot water. There was a shed nearby that could be used as a garage. Pat and I sat with Mr. and Mrs. Craven discussing it, and the wage was ten pounds per week, with overtime, also a Bedford van. I believe it was ten cwt. van with a window each side of the van part, for our use. We thought it was a Rolls Royce, never having had a vehicle for our own use before. So we went home and discussed it and accepted the job, and moved there on the ninth of January, nineteen fifty-nine.

I must add, when I told Mr. Howell that I had accepted the situation with Mr. and Mrs.Craven, a tractor driver and me were putting long ladders that we used for cherry picking away for the winter. I was standing in the trailer sliding a ladder through an opening in the side of the shed, so that it would rest on the beams of the shed, and Alec, the tractor driver, with a two prong fork standing inside the shed, was pushing the ladders along further on the beams. As I was standing in the trailer, Mr. Howell came along, and I said: "By the way Governor, I am leaving in a month's time." That would be just before Christmas. As soon as I said that, he blew right up in the air and he said: "Mewett, that is a bloody rotten thing to do just before Christmas," and my goodness, I certainly told him in no uncertain terms that is what we agreed on, and my loud voice, I could see it shook him a bit for I had never spoken to him before like it. Anyhow, when all this shouting was going on, I saw out of the corner of my eye the pigman, just going to come through the pig yard gate. As soon as he saw what was going on, he turned around and went back from where he came. However, the governor went off round to the cowsheds. The tractor driver looked at me and said, "He is a fellow isn't he?" I said he certainly is.

After we had stacked the ladders away, I went round to the pigman to see what he wanted. He immediately said to me, "I was coming to see if you would help me move some dry sows into the yard, but when I saw what was going on, I soon came back." Well, believe it or not, less than half an hour had elapsed, and along came the governor, as though nothing had happened, and said, "Want a hand with the sows?" and he helped us get them in. That's what I admired about Mr. Howell.

I started my job for Mrs. Craven, who lived at Yewlands Farm Hand Hill, and adjoining this farm was Butterfield Farm and Senlac Farm, which were run together. We used to lamb the ewes which, by the way, soon got to one hundred and twenty in number, in buildings at Yewlands Farm, where we had to increase the lambing pens by putting up chestnut posts; the back, sides and roof were corrugated iron. When a ewe lambed, we put her and her lambs in a pen straight away, sprayed each lamb's navel with a disinfectant spray, dark blue in colour, and the ram lambs the scrotum as well then two or three hours afterwards put rubber rings on the tails. We always held them in pens for forty-eight hours before letting them out to fresh pasture. We always kept them in a straw yard at night, all the in-lamb ewes.

On the gate to the straw yard we nailed sacking soaked in creosote, which was supposed to have deterred foxes. Whether it did or not I do not know, as we had a light all night in the yard. We carried out the procedure of injecting the ewe twice before she lambed so that the lambs could get the right antibodies through the colostrum. After the lambs were about seven to eight weeks old, we would inject the lambs against pulpy kidney, also worm drench the lambs and ewes at the same time, then the lambs got worm drenched every month. Then in August, all lambs and ewes were dipped with the appropriate dip, and at the same time the lambs were weaned and put in a field as far away as possible from their mothers. Talk about a racket for a night or two with them bleating! Those that had not been sold fat by the end of September were put on feeding rape which grew about three feet high for fattening (not oilseed rape I may add!) and it worked and did the arable ground good. I supposed it is like the old saying, wherever sheep went, it was called 'the golden hoof', like another old saying when a farmer was asked whether he would employ a boy for work, his answer was: "I will employ one boy, but when it gets to two boys, you have got only half a boy, and three boys, well, you have no boys at all."

Another thing we always did was to keep a field of grass back to flush the ewes. The ewes went in about three weeks before the rams went in, but all ewes and rams were worm drenched in the autumn before they were put on this pasture. I can honestly say this attention to detail paid off After lambing was over, from that time up until when we sold all the lambs, the most lambs we lost in that period was two lambs, and sometimes one lamb per year, and our ewe mortality was no more than one or two per cent. I remember one year when the ewes were being shorn in June, dashed if one didn't die of heart failure. It was the only one in thirteen years with sheep, during shearing, that I had ever seen.

As I mentioned, there were thirty single suckler cows running with an Angus bull. He did not seem to have enough length for my liking, but I could not alter that. The cows were crossed mostly Angus from dairy herds as far as I could see. The cows certainly gave the milk, but were calving too late, April, May and June. It took three or four years before we could get them calving in January and February. Eventually we did. The calves were taken to Reading Market in October time to be sold. Just before the time to wean them, we used to get the calves used to dry grub made up of crushed oats and decorated cake, with minerals in, and the same mix we used to feed the sheep. That was a daily job, mixing that up by hand. Any how I made a coral, sort of, so that the calves could get in to feed, but the cows and bull could not; it worked quite well.

The afternoon before sale day, we got the calves settled down in different old calving boxes, then we went down to the buildings next morning at four-thirty in the morning, to load the calves, and I used to ride in the lorry to Reading Market, and come back with Mrs. Craven in her Rover saloon. I remember this Rover was quite powerful, and it also had over-drive on it, and when she went past anyone, she would sound her horn, and by golly we were gone. She certainly did not hang about.

When the cows were calving, we had a little difficulty with one, so after she eventually calved, Mrs. Craven gave me a bottle of strong ale to give to the cow; that was the first time I had drenched a cow with a bottle of ale. She said: "That will do her good." Oh, I must say in the first three years of my employment with Mr. and Mrs. Craven, they very kindly suggested that my wife and I go up to the Smithfield Show at Earls Court in London for a day. At that time I was provided with an oldish Bedford ten cwt. van. It had it's MOT. before I was given it to use. It was like a Rolls Royce to us, especially being the first vehicle I had ever had with the job of working manager.

So off we went to London in the Bedford van, and managed to park somewhere near St. Thomas's Hospital, then a bus journey to Earls Court. When coming to go home, we got in the van, but we could not go anywhere as the clutch had gone, and we had to go home by train.

So for the next two years, until my son was born, arrangements were made for my wife and I to stay in a boarding house in Sloane Square for two nights, giving us three days to see the Smithfield Show. Also we always went to some sort of variety show. It was very nice, and we also had ten pounds spending money, and in 1960 ten pounds was a fair bit of money for three days. So, as you can see, they were very fair to us.

I remember another time we had a calf go lame, so we got it in with its mother, had a look at its back foot, and it was sore between the hoof, like scald in a sheep. The vet was sent for, and as soon as he saw it, he said, "It is a kind of scald, keep it in with the mother for a few days and bathe the soreness with cotton wool and Dettol." Of course, that did the trick, but I remember that same day, after the vet had been, I went to see Mrs. Craven. As soon as I told her what had happened, she said to me: "Well, Mewett, you must put each cow through the crush and examine each hoof." My goodness, I thought, that is going to be a game, especially when the crush was built along the side of the wall of a building, and one could only get one side of this crush, but thank goodness Mr. Craven was home and overheard his wife say this to me, and straight away said, "Don't talk such bloody nonsense!" and that was the finish of that little episode. We had two more calves which had a soreness in between the foot, but with the same treatment as the first calf, it all cleared up, and we never had any more trouble.

Mrs. Craven and her husband I got on well with; they always thought of us at Christmas.

They both went down to the yards at weekends in the winter to see the cows and calves in the yards - it was nice of them to do this.

I remember on one Monday morning my boss was waiting for me at 6.55 am. when I arrived. The usual procedure, "Good morning, Mewett," and of course I greeted her with "Good morning," then to my surprise she said, "You know, Mewett, you have white scours amongst those calves." I said: "I don't think so. I think you will find the very young calves are getting too much milk, which is a good thing as one knows the cows are milking well. It will right itself."

Well, it was exactly what it did do, of course. I never heard another word about it all the time I was there. Thank goodness I had previous experience with calves from dairy cows. I suppose the accusation was to keep me on my toes. I often wondered what comment her husband had when scours were mentioned!

Another time we had our best cow with calf. I had to get her in a calving box as the mother was shaking like a leaf, grass staggers. I sent for the vet, he was there within the hour, but just as he pulled into the farm gate, down she went and died immediately. She was a lovely animal. We put minerals in boxes that were made so that the minerals could not get wet, and we never had any more trouble of that kind. The fence of the yard was sleepers for posts, and bolted to the sleepers were some very old vat pipes from a brewery; they were like a long U shape about ten feet long and a foot wide. They served the purpose of keeping the cows and calves in. But one day, I thought, "What is the matter with this calf, he does not seem to know where he is going." I got hold of him, and straight away I thought, "he is going blind." Also there was another one going like it. So I called the vet. Soon as he saw them he said: "Lead poisoning. Have you got any lead paint about here?" And I said, "Not as I know of," and Mrs. Craven said, "Oh no!." Then the vet had a look at the vat pipes; he could see chips were coming off them, and said, "This is your trouble." Mrs. Craven did not want to believe it, but the vet said "If you do not do something about it, you will have dead calves on your hands. After the vet had said that she soon got her maintenance man to put corrugated iron over the lot, which, of course, stopped the rot, as one would say.

Then one year, I noticed the Angus bull when he went to serve a cow, he got onto her and made a heck of a noise, and his penis did not go as far as it should, and he just fell off her. So the vet as called, and said, "He could have fallen and hurt himself, but in the meantime he's got to be slaughtered." And after that episode we had ten cows not in calf, so that was a blow, but we had some Blue Grey heifers coming along, so we were lucky to hire from the next farm a lovely large Canadian Hereford bull; lovely length of body he had. The calves from him were the best calves we ever had. They had size and length.

After we had sold the calves that year at Reading Market, Mrs. Craven, when she was bringing me home in her Rover car, said, "Well done," the only time she had ever said that! They had sold very well, as they had size and length, but of course that was the lovely Canadian bull that had been the positive answer to the length and size of the calves.

Well, I was my own boss as a working manager, but there were some things I could not control like buying another bull. Mrs. Craven's sights were on a Hereford bull, but when it arrived, it had not got the size and length of the Canadian bull, so consequently the calves did not have the length and size of the previous bull. It certainly was a bit of a shock when the new bull arrived. Oh, it was a nice bull, but it did not have size. It was in the period when it was said the public wanted smaller joints. It happened with the sheep industry; then all of a sudden the trend was for bigger joints.

We used to feed the cows in yards with access silage day time, and hay at nights, no concentrates. I remember one morning when we were silage making, I got to the farm where we made this silage. In those days we started work at seven-o-clock in the morning when there was no milking to do. I arrived just before seven. I could not bear to be late, and my boss was standing in the yard. The conversation was: "Good morning Mrs. Craven." "Good morning, Mewett." Then she looked at me and said, "You are not going to have enough silage!" Off we went to have a look at the silage . I said, "We shall have just as much silage as we have other years." Her answer was, "I do not think you will."

So that was that, and of course we had just the same amount of silage as we did other years, and I never heard another word about it.

As we eventually got the calving of cows round to January and February, I used to go along an evening to see that everything was alright. One such time, as I got to the yard, I heard a cow making a terrible noise. I put the lights on and there was one of the best cows we had in the herd. She had just calved, and she was going wild, knocking her own calf about, and I was afraid she would knock it against the wall and kill it. So I got her in a calving box, chained her up, saw that the calf had a good suck, then shut the calf away and proceeded to put the calf on her four times a day. It took about a week for the cow to get used to the calf, and then she was alright to put with the other cows and calves. But in the end she had to go, because the following year at calving time, another cow had just calved and this particular cow started knocking that calf about, so it was either getting rid of her or have a dead calf about the place; something used to click in her brain, after she had just calved, or another cow had calved.

For thirteen years we had breeding ewes, and I came across something similar. As I have mentioned before, in the day time as soon as a ewe lambed, I took the ewe and her lambs into a pen for forty eight hours at least. This particular ewe was young, well grown, and had twins. I got her into this pen and she just did not want to know her lambs, and knocked them about. So I suckled them on her four times a day, and each time they had finished suckling I put them behind the straw bales in the corner of the pen. It took ten days before she would take them. I turned her out and never had any more trouble, thank goodness, after that. I know they were her lambs as I walked the lambing field five times a day, and actually saw them being born.

Then we wanted to plough a ten acre field up from grass.

In those days in the sixties, one got twelve pounds an acre for ploughing up permanent pasture, and seven pounds per acre for a three year ley. This particular field had oak trees along the bottom of it, and boughs stuck out as much as twenty feet out into the field. So I got a nice galvanised ladder and a hand saw, and started cutting these boughs right back. I was proud of the way it was shaping up. The year was nineteen sixty-three, the month August. In the morning of this particular day I worm drenched all the lambs we had to put on feeding rape for fattening. At that time we took over the running of another seventy acre farm that belonged to Mrs. Craven, ploughed it up, and sowed it with spring barley.

Anyhow, I went down in the afternoon after drenching these lambs, and started cutting the boughs off these oak trees. There was a bough about twenty feet out into the field, but it was higher up than the rest, and like a fool, I thought I would just reach that. Of course, it was too upright really. I got up the top of the ladder, started sawing away, and I had forgotten that as soon as the bough I had the ladder resting on would spring up as the weight came off it. The next thing I knew, I shook myself as I had been lying on the ground. I suppose momentarily I was knocked out, and the first thing that came to my mind was 'shall I be able to get up', because all down my right side it hurt so much and I could see my right wrist was broken. But thank goodness I got to my feet, and Reg, the chap ploughing in that field, took me up to the farm, and Mrs. Craven took me to the local hospital. They plastered my arm and put it in a sling, and sent me home.

It was the same year our son was born. I was off work for ten weeks, but I used to feed Jill, the sheep dog, and take her round the sheep every morning. One morning, it was about five weeks after I had my accident, and still had my arm plastered and in a sling, there had been a thunder storm, and a lot of rain, and where the lambs were there was a stream running along the outside of the field, and it was flowing fast and full to capacity. Jill was a very good sheep dog; I had only got to put my hand to left or right and say "Away," and she was off like a shot, and she was doing the job right. The only thing was, one lamb, instead of running out into the field, it ran straight into the stream. I ran to where the lamb was, and I saw it had caught itself in brambles over-hanging the stream. The other thing was the weight of the wet wool was dragging it down. I could not let it drown, so I put one leg in the stream to get a purchase, pulled it up to the bank, could not quite get it up on the bank, and not thinking, only to save the lamb, I used my plastered arm to get a bit more purchase. But in doing so I had to have the plaster on eight instead of six weeks, but I never told anyone about it.

That period of my life, it was rather worrying. There I was off work for two and a half months, Pat was pregnant with the son she eventually had on 18th November; my arm, which had the plaster on, when it was taken off the plaster was cut off alright, the sling taken away, but I could not move the arm, so I had to go three times a week to physiotherapy to move the arm. But they told me at the same time that arthritis would eventually set in the shoulder. Well, it did. I have never been able to lift that left arm up more than seventy degrees in the air. I have done a lot of manual work since then, and it has got a little worse as I've got older, but I have lived with it, and have been a very strong man, thank goodness. It has effected my shooting with a shot gun - anything flying at a certain height, if I don't look out, I shoot under the bird, as my left shoulder won't let my arm push up far enough.

I also started to play golf after I was fifty years old, only once every six weeks, but I just cannot go through with a full swing.

At Senlac farm buildings there was quite a big barn, and a wooden sided L shaped slate roofed cowshed, not used, of course, until we put six blue grey heifers in the bottom part of it, running out into the yard. Of all things the water ran to the water tank through plastic piping above ground. There were such hard frosts, the pipes just froze. We had to use the blow lamp on them to get the water running. It was a good job the farm house was close to the building as that particular night there must have been a spark that ignited the straw. The people who rented the farm house phoned the fire brigade and, of course, saved the heifers by turning them out into the field. So that was the finish of cattle being housed down there. The floor of the cowshed was all concrete, so lambing pens were made down there, with a three foot gangway in front of the pens, just right. The pens were made up of wood and galvanised tin. Outside the barn and cowshed, which now is a sheep shed, there was quite a big enclosed yard with a ten foot gate to the entrance of the yard. In the yard was a small water tank and it was just right to keep two hundred odd in lamb ewes at night, all adjacent to the pens. In those days we lambed the ewes from the twenty first of February, so as soon as the pens were completed all the sheep were moved to Senlacs Farm. The yard was heavily strawed and that is where we proceeded with our first lambing at Senlac Farm in nineteen sixty-four.

The blue grey replacement heifers were taken to Butterfield farm, where we had just erected a new fence with a chalked floor, and strawed an old stable up so they would lay in at nights. It worked very well.

Well, at Butterfield farm, Reg erected a machinery shed. He was very good at that sort of work. He used twelve to fourteen feet larch poles, I think they were, and corrugated iron treated for roof and sides. It worked well.

After acquiring the extra seventy acres which was Hams Farm, we were eventually growing over one hundred acres of spring corn. There was an old cowshed, a barn and a stable and in the centre of these buildings was a concrete yard. From the yard to The barn there was a rise of about two or three feet, but at the back of the barn there was a rise of four feet, straight up, before one got to the double barn doors, just right for the level of a trailer when it was backed to the double doors. Well, as we had got more corn to handle, we had a contractor come in with a bigger combine, so we had to have some way to handle the increase in acreage of corn grown. Mrs. Craven got her maintenance man to dig a very large pit in the barn, and board it on the inside; it would hold about eight to ten tons of grain. Part of the front side of the barn was removed, with a ramp going up to the level of the barn floor so that the trailers could be backed up to tip the grain into the pit. From the pit there was an auger to bring the grain up to a hopper, and from the hopper there were four openings with shutes on, for bags to be put on, so that one could shut or open any one of them which ever was necessary, rather like the sacking area of a thresher, only we used ordinary bags, which one could only get about a hundred weight of barley in, then tie the bags up, load them onto the trailer and stack them three high in the various sheds. I must say, we did have a bit of mice and rat trouble, but even if the grain was eighteen per cent moisture it seemed to keep alright for four or five months. I doubt if it would have done in very thick West of England sacks. So that solved our harvest troubles. Reg used to bale the straw as soon as we had done with the combine. We had no bale collector at first, but did eventually, so I used to stack the bales in eights as soon as there were five or six acres baled, and continue on from there until they were all stacked up, and then there was the procedure of carrying and stacking the bales. I remember it rained so hard that when it was dry enough to start picking the bales up, the top two bales were no good at all on each stack of eight, so that was more work buck-racking them into a corner. In the ground that was farmed on these farms, the lime phosphate and were kept up to the right level as possible. As soon as we put a three year lay down, eight or ten hundred weight of slag was put onto the acre; of course, the slag took care of the phosphate.

At that time I was busy with calving and just started lambing. I went to Butterfield Farm, looked to see the calves and cows were alright, walked over into another field where we had a few that were that year's lambs put to the ram. I was not keen on the idea, but as we fed the ewes five or six weeks before they started lambing, we got away with it.

Perhaps you will not believe it, bearing in mind I am six foot six tall, and weighed over fifteen stones then, the van I drove was an Austin A35 with seats in the back. I had the driver's seat welded back. It only had twenty thousand miles on the clock when I first had it. I drove it for five years, 948cc. engine, and it was a marvellous little van. With all the snow on ground in January nineteen sixty three, I went anywhere on the road between the three farms, with two half hundred weight of mineral bags in the back immediately over the back axles, and my goodness, it worked very well. I thought this was of interest to mention.

Well, I got back to my van, and as I opened the door to get in and drive off, I noticed a note on the seat, and I could see the writing was my boss's, and on it she had written:

'Mewett, I read that in the north of Scotland they have a new spring barley, and it yielded fifty six hundred weight of grain to the acre'. In the sixties that was a lot of spring barley,. The note also mentioned 'I think we should grow some.' I immediately went into Yewlands Farm, and Mrs. Craven was in. I knocked on the door and explained to her that it was all very well this high yielding barley, but we are talking in the north of Scotland, not down in the south of England, and I expect that was grown on experiment.

111

Anyway, she wanted me to grow some of this barley, so I said alright. There was a field called Mayfield, the size of six acres. I said I would sow two acres at the bottom of this field with this new barley and the rest of the field with Rika barley, which we always had, and grew our own seed as it did so well on that ground.

Bearing in mind that one did not have the sprays they have today, in this particular field all the barley was growing well, and it was at a stage, about six or eight inches in length, and when one looked at it the Rika barley was quite alright, but the two acres of this new barley at the bottom of the field, it had mildew on it. It was so bad it looked as though snow had fallen on it, and, of course, it was disaster. But I never heard another word about that new barley. Thank goodness I hadn't put half our acreage in with it, that would have knocked us for six, spelling great disaster. Through my farming life, I have always been very cautious of new varieties. I always liked to see them in the commercial world for two years before I grew them. Perhaps some would say I was an old fashioned square, but in my experience it paid off.

In that same year some bigger farmers, tried a hundred acres of this new barley. They certainly didn't try the variety again. Where one is a farm manager one is responsible, and another thing is, when things go wrong, it is your job on the line, but with a farmer himself or his son, and things go wrong, it is generally one of those unfortunate things, and they carry on as usual. It certainly is a different matter.

In that same period, we sowed eighteen acres of winter wheat. It grew well, it looked like being a two tons to the acre crop. Remembering we did not have the sprays we have today, the crop looked marvellous. The ground it was growing on had been livestock for a long time, and then turfed, and ploughed up, and as I say, the crop looked perfect. Then in June it started to look different, and by the time we combined it, it did not look the same crop, and all we got to the acre was twenty two hundred weights per acre, the reason being it had glume blotch.

The thing I must mention, at Yewlands Farm there were two badger sets, and all the time we had single sucklers, and these sets were right beside the suckler yards, no more than two hundred yards away, and the badgers ran across the ground the cows used to graze, and there was an old litter pulled out of the sets along side the fields. We had single sucklers for eight years and never had a case of tuberculosis, so sometimes I wondered why we were free of this, as I have heard of areas where badgers had sets, the milking herd had a cow that went down with TB. and badgers were blamed.

While I am talking about badgers, I remember about nineteen sixty-one when we still lambed the ewes at Yewlands Farm, and I had two lambs. They had grown well and were in excellent condition. They were the two last ewes to lamb. I had them in a separate field not far away from Yewlands farm house. That particular evening, Pat and I were invited by my late mother-in-law to go to a show in a village hall about five miles away. Well, we got dressed up; the best suit I had then was my charcoal grey wedding suit, and I put that on with the black shoes. We had to drive past Yewlands Farm on the way to this village hall, so I said to Pat, "I think I'd better look at these two young ewes as they are first lambers," so we drew into Yewlands Farm and went down to the particular field. Pat stayed at the gate entrance of the field. Of course they were right down the bottom of the field, and one was in trouble. I held her down so she could not move as I could see her womb had just started to come out. I knew I had got to keep her still so that the womb did not get dirty, and at the same time shouted to Pat to go to the farm house and phone the vet and bring a bucket of hot water, soap and Dettol, also a clean towel when the vet came. Well, there I was, holding the ewe as quietly as possible, with my wedding suit on. I suppose I was about thirty yards from the bottom of the field where there was a two to three foot drop, four foot from the hedge. I suppose I was waiting about half an hour, and everything was very quiet. It would be about the third week in April. All of a sudden I heard a noise. I looked towards the hedge, and there peeping over the top of the bank was a lovely badger. It didn't stay long, but with the two badger sets on the farm, I had never seen a badger before, and never saw one for the next ten years, but to me it was quite an experience. Eventually the vet came, and the first thing he said as he knelt down was: "Well I'm buggered! I've never seen a chap holding a ewe down wearing a smart double breasted suit." He was the senior vet, and he did not mix matters. Anyhow, the lamb was alright. He dowsed the womb with Dettol water and pushed the womb back in and sewed her vagina up with tape. He was a very clever man, especially at this type of job, because if a hole is made in the womb, the sheep is dead within thirty six hours, and it is nice to say that ewe had several more lambs after that in her life. But it was goodbye to the show we were going to see! However, it saved a ewe's life, and to me that was gratifying.

As my life was farming, the only sport I had was rough shooting on Saturday afternoons in the winter. I was very lucky to have a wife who was behind me in everything I did to get on in the farming world. As you will see, we had to move four times to get where I wanted in my career. It took a long time, but I made it. I could not have done it without Pat.

During my time with Mr. and Mrs. Craven, at Christmas time we were always given twenty-five pounds, six cans of lager, three or four bottles of very strong ale, a bottle of sherry or port and a lovely box of chocolates, and some other things for Pat.

Then came the time when Mr. and Mrs. Craven wanted to retire from farming, but still retain the farms. So Mrs. Craven approached the local A.D.A.S. to see whether they could recommend a farming family of good repute to rent the farms. On paper it would be in partnership, for tax reasons I should think. Well, a Mr. Barnham was recommended and they came to some agreement, so I eventually had a new boss. They were farming dairy cows and corn, also some contract work.

Up until then, I had been addressed as Mewett, my surname, but Mr. Barnham came to me when he took me on, and said: "We are democratic - you will call me Jack, my brother Joe, and my wife Maggie." And that is how it remained.

The year, nineteen sixty-seven. In the January of that year my dear father died. He was eighty-two. I remember my dear father saying to me - this when I was in my teens, and as one knows at that age one does not take some things said to them too seriously - "My boy, hard work will not kill you, but a damn lot of worry will," and how true that is.

He came to see us one Sunday. He was eighty at the time, walked with a stick as he got pretty stiff at times, but he said to me on that occasion: "Well, my boy, if I go tomorrow (meaning out of this world!) I have had a very good innings." What a lovely way of looking at life.

Mr. Barnham took me on at a salary of one thousand pounds per year, free milk, for which he gave me a four gallon milking machine bucket, one of which they used to milk with, the type where the pulsator used to fit on top of the lid, which I used to get from the milk tank at Tracy's Farm, where the cows were kept. I used to collect the milk every two or three days for our household use. I was offered a new seven hundred weight Bedford van with seats in the back, for farm and my own use, also two or three loads of wood for burning, for which I borrowed the farm's tractor and a three point linkage saw bench, to saw the wood up. I agreed to these terms within a week, Mr. Barnham came to me and said his father and his brother would not agree to pay me a thousand pounds a year until six months time, so I agreed to nine hundred pounds a year until the six months were up. I suppose the father and brother, who were partners in the farms, thought I might not come up to expectations. However, I got the one thousand a year after six months. I always got on with the Barnham family, or I suppose anyone else I worked for, but the Barnham brothers I *liked* and treated like brothers.

Just before the farms were taken over by the Barnham family, Mrs. Craven sold the single suckler herd but the Barnhams retained the sheep flock. At Butterfield farm, the old machinery shed was pulled down, and a cattle building erected with the roof extending to the Dutch barn where the hay was kept silage was discontinued at that time; the cattle yard had beef cattle in the winter for fattening. They were fed a barley mix and hay, the barley mix being mixed by a contractor into a four or five ton trailer and brought from the dairy farm, where also the corn was stored and dried. It worked very well; the rest of the yard where the single sucklers came from was occupied by dairy heifers from the dairy herd.

We had a very unfortunate thing happen the first winter. There was a galvanised fence parting part of the yard from the other yard. One morning, when I got to this yard, one of the dairy heifers had tried to jump it, and ended up with its back legs stuck through the fence and most of its body leaning over the other side of the fence, and of course it was stone dead. Thank goodness it never happened again.

I remember Jack Barnham, when he came to see me about working for him, looked over the farms, and said to me, "Your grassland looks good. What do you do to it?" My reply was, "We keep the lime and phosphate analysis pretty well up to where it should be." "Well," he said, "I want the grass land on our other farms to be like this." I may add the Barnham family rented all their farming land, they never owned anything at that period. They also took over a farm that Mrs. Craven owned with her brother. It was all connected up to the rest of the land. Most of it we ploughed and, therefore, with the extra land they had rented that year, and the corn building up at the dairy farm being for four hundred tons, Jack Barnham said to me, "I think we shall have to extend the corn barn for another two hundred tons." I agreed it looked right to me, so it was put up for that year's harvest. It worked very well indeed, and all corn from the farms was taken by trailer to the corn drier shed. At that time the cows were fed on the best hay we could make, and kale, also brewers grains, plus cake. They milked pretty well.

On each farm we had to make hay. The haymaking always started at the dairy farm for the milking herd in June. The first week I had a week's holiday. As soon as I was back, we started the hay making. Mostly in June the weather was pretty good, and we made some lovely hay. I know the first year the hay for the dairy farm had a lovely green tinge to it in colour. I felt it, and it seemed lovely and dry, so I got it baled and we stacked it. After we had finished haying on the other farms, we are talking about the oblong hay bales, we had baled and stacked twenty-six to thirty thousand bales a year. About the beginning of the second year, Jack Barnham said to me: "That lovely hay we made last year at the dairy farm, I used to think about it with that lovely greeny colour. I thought you had baled it too soon and it was going to catch fire, but I ought to have known different, had I not! " I said, "Yes, I would not have had that baled if it wasn't dry enough to do so." I'd had eight years before that in getting hay baled up. I had five years in farming with them, and my goodness, we had very shucky weather; two years out of five we had started combining before the last bales were stacked. Silage is the most marvellous feed for animals if made properly.

Jack Barnham took me to a farm walk one evening. It was a year when it was pretty bad weather for haying. The times we had to turn and ted the hay half way through the haying was nobody's business. That same week, as we went to the farm walk, which was only about eight miles away from our farming land, Jack Barnham was talking to another farmer, and of course the conversation was making hay. Jack was asked how the haying was going. His reply was, "We made a thousand bales and stacked them." This particular farmer said, "How did you do that?" so Jack said, "Go and talk to Ken." So he did, and I said, "It was nice and dry, I got it baled and we stacked it." He said, "Well I never, I would not have thought it with the weather we had." Well, we were just lucky I suppose. I would never bale hay unless it was really dry, because if one did, the bales get mouldy inside, or if it is younger grass, there is a danger of internal combustion. Happily I never had that problem.

Well, as I said, the sheep flock was retained. Instead of mixing grub by hand, I purchased sheep nuts instead, which was a better way of feeding. The flock was increased to two hundred and twenty ewes. The first time we started to increase them they were Kerry Hill sheep. I said I'd better go to a sale and buy some, and Jack said, "I have a farmer friend who goes to the sales every year to buy Kerry Hills for himself, and he said he could get fifty on the lorry for us." Well, these sheep came - they did not look too bad, in fact OK. They arrived in October. By the beginning of January I was bringing the flock up for putting through the foot bath, bearing in mind new ewes never went anywhere near the original flock unless they were worm drenched. While bringing the flock up on that particular day, two or three started hanging back as though they could not go any further. I called the vet, as I could not understand why these ewes were like this. After inspecting the two or three very bad ones, said, "I think they have fluke." We held half a dozen in a pen and took dung samples, and that confirmed what the vet had said, and so I had to worm drench the whole flock with fluke worm drench, and kept it up every year after that episode. Before that happened, we never knew what fluke was on the farm, thank goodness, as all replacements came from the South Downs. We used to treat the wet areas, a couple of brook fields every year with copper sulphate and sand to kill the small snails, if there were any. Well, it was a precaution that worked. It's like worm drenching the ewes and rams twice per year, and lambs every month, then, after weaning, worm drench them and put them on clean pasture, and eventually on feed rape for fattening those that were left as store lambs; attention to detail paid off.

In that period I used to go to Ashford to buy two hundred store lambs, bring them back and worm drench them before putting them on feed rape, generally on fields that had spring barley year after year. These I fenced with rolls of sheep netting strung up to stakes I hammered in the ground, as the fences were no good to keep sheep in. One could see a difference when we put it back to spring barley again. They used to call it the golden hoof where sheep had been. I remember a biggish field I treated in the same way. It lay adjacent to the senior partner's farm house. I put about three hundred store lambs through the foot bath, and worm drenched them, then put them straight on this feed rape that stood about three feet high. Once the lambs were in it, you could not see them. Well, a day or two afterwards, I heard that two woodmen on the estate saw them in this giant rape, and said to the senior partner, "By gosh, won't they blow up and die on feed like that?" I may add that by that time I had about nine years experience fattening lambs on giant rape. When I was told about this, well, I have never lost any yet through rape poisoning or being blown for the past nine years, but on that same field I did lose three lambs that year, but it was gid. It is heartbreaking to see them when affected. They were lovely lambs. It affects them in a way that they cannot walk straight, and poor things, they just fall over. The only thing to do is to have them shot out of their misery. So after that I checked which farm they came from in Kent, and each year when I went to Ashford to buy store lambs, any pen of lambs that came from that farm, or farming company, it did not matter how good or well grown the lambs were, I did not bid for any of those pens, and I never had a recurrence of gid or lost a lamb on rape, until I had lambs on rape between two woods. One morning I went to check on them, and there was a lovely lamb lying dead. One could see that it had been bitten through the throat. I knew the fox hunt hounds were up through there the afternoon before, and apparently a foxhound attacked and killed it. The huntsman told us they shot the hound straight away, of course, the only right thing to do under the circumstances, as once they do it, they will do it again.

This area of ground was at Hains Farm where we put spring barley in after the lambs had finished the rape, and by golly, it did grow well. I used to allot the same amount of fertiliser to those fields as any of the other fields as it was lightish ground. I took the view that after the ploughing, discing and harrowing etc., one might as well grow as much barley as possible per acre.

Going back to sheep and the three lambs that had to be shot because of having gid: gid is caused by tape worm from dogs. It causes some infestation of the brain with a tape worm causing an abscess. There are too many dog owners who do not worm their dogs, and the biggest problem is where there is a foot path going through where sheep are grazed. So if dog owners actually saw a sheep with gid, I hope that, if they knew the cause, it would prick their conscience and they would remember to worm their dogs.

Well, as I have said, I got on very well with the Barnham family. The two brothers, Jack and Joe, I spoke and treated them as though they were brothers, but when I wanted one of them twice a year to help me inject and worm drench the lambs, either of them was about an hour late before turning up. That did annoy me, as I was always a stickler for time, and I jolly soon told them how late they were. I began to think they would be late for their own funeral. I suppose it was always on my conscience never to be late, as I have always had to work for someone else. When I started work, in those days, if men were coming to work late, or not pulling their weight, they could be called down to the farm office on Friday or, of course, Saturday morning. The boss would hand over their cards of employment and they were told that they were not wanted any more. But those days are gone, thank goodness. Anyhow, Joe was helping me worm drench the ewes, and said, "May I have a go with the drencher?" "Of course, you can," I said, not realising the screw on the part at the end of the drench was loose. Joe got hold of the ewe and drenched her alright, but at that moment, the screw on the end of the drencher came off and, of course, choked her, and she died within seconds. I did feel sorry for Joe, as it wasn't his fault, more like mine for not checking the screw on the nozzle, but I had used the same drench gun for three or four years, with no trouble at all. It must have come loose somehow. I suppose the old saying it true that there is always a first time!

It was only a few months ago I was speaking to him, and he said then: "You remember the ewe I killed with the worm drencher?" These things always stick in one's mind. It is like the time he was helping me dip the ewes and lambs. I believe he was pushing them into the dip, and he overbalanced and fell right in the dip himself. With all the talk that the dip we used in the sixties was harmful to humans, it certainly did not do him any harm, as he is still well and fit at sixty-two years old, and I am still here pretty fit, after hip replacements at seventy years old, after dipping sheep every year for thirteen years in that period of my life.

Within two years the Barnhams rented another farm that came available, joining up with the other farm ground. It was a dairy farm originally, so it had a nice covered-in building where we kept quite a number of cattle, and, of course, we had to make hay there and stack it for feed in the winter. Also, there was enough straw under cover for bedding, and, talking of bedding straw, I bedded the cattle on both this new farm and Butterfield Farm so that they were clean. I could not bear to see any cattle with dung plastered up their flanks, which I called walking dung carts. As we sold a large amount of straw bales off the fields of the four hundred acres, we had to have quite a lot of straw for each farm, which I said we would have to have, and one year too much was sold from the amount we had to have. The consequences were six hundred bales had to be bought in, but it never happened again. I think that was the year that Jack Barnham phoned me one evening. I was in the bath at the time. My wife brought the phone to me, and I said, "Hello, Jack." He said, "I think you are using too much straw for the cattle." My reply was: "Well, Jack, when you go to bed at night, do you get into a shitted and pissed up bed?" He said, "No, I do not." "Well," I said, "don't expect those cattle to then." And that was the end of that. I never heard any more about it. I remember Jack said to me one day, "Ken, do you know what you are?" I said, "No." "You are too much of a perfectionist." To which I replied "Oh, am I?" and the wonderful thing about it was there was never any animosity on either Jack or Joe's part, and through my farming life, as I became in full control of a farming enterprise, I made sure animosity never came into it.

Now, going back to harvest time, I have said the corn drier was at the dairy farm, so all corn was carted there to be dried to about fourteen to sixteen percent moisture content. The distance from where I lived was about two and a half miles around the road. Jack used to go baling. I went corn drying after I had seen to the sheep and cattle on the farms down at my end, and before I had my breakfast, I took my son Paul, and two of the neighbouring farmer's daughters to school, and the farmer's wife used to bring them back in the afternoon. It worked very well, so after breakfast I went up to the drier, getting up there about ten o'clock. To be there all day Pat used to pack my lunch and tea, and I never got back until nine o'clock at night. Talk about dust in that drier at times! Well, I used to have to use a mask over my mouth and nose, and use five filters per day. I think, if I had not taken this precaution, most likely I would have had farmer's lung, and perhaps would have died by now, so those masks are a very sensible thing to wear in dusty conditions. Each day when I was corn drying, I used to get a few grains of corn, grind it and test it for moisture content, so we kept it to about fourteen percent moisture. As this was a continuous flow drier, as soon as it was dried, an elevator took it up to the main elevator that ran along the whole of the corn building at a height of about sixteen or eighteen feet. The elevator was boxed in, and every few feet it had a slide. All slide openings were shut except the first one, so that the corn could drop straight down to the floor. As soon as that section was full, one closed the first opening and opened the next one, and so on. We used to dry six hundred tons like that.

Well, in between testing the corn for moisture content and seeing that the elevators were working alright, I used to look out of the door from time to time, the path to Joe Barnham's house ran right past the corn barn doors. Well, Joe was about thirty-five years old and he was going to marry a nice girl of about twenty years old. This particular day I saw her go to Joe's house. It was only three days before the

123

wedding. I saw the girl go, and the next thing Joe came to me, crying like a baby, very upset. I said, "What is the matter, Joe?" He just about got it out. "She has called the wedding off." "Right," I said, "I will finish feeding the calves, while you finish the dairy off, and then we will go up to your house and I will make you a cup of tea." We got up to his house, I put the kettle on, also phoned my wife, Pat, that I would not be home before ten-thirty in the evening, and that I would tell her why later. Joe and I had our cup of tea and talked and talked. Well, he was in such a state, I thought he was going to shoot himself. In the course of the conversation I said, "I know it is easy for me to talk, but of course it's much the best thing for it to happen now than in six months time after you were married, but, of course, you won't see it now, but later on you will." It does one good to talk, especially in situations like that, and as soon as I saw that he was calmer, after about three hours, I went home, and thank God, he was alive in the morning.

His brother, Jack, used to say, "Well, Ken saved my brother Joe's life." If that was the case, it was a wonderful thing to do.

I remember we tried to contain several tons of winter oats with the proper six foot corn sections to divide it from the barley. It just about held the tonnage we wanted, but next morning we opened the sliding doors of the corn barn at the bottom end, and out came the winter oats. One of the corn sections had split open, so that was a mess to clear up. Good job no one was near it at the time.

The combining was done by one big and one small Clayson combines, and replaced with a Massey Harris fourteen foot combine which worked very well.

As the farms at Hand Hill area were surrounded by several woods, Joe Barnham set up a shoot, as his father, the senior partner, loved shooting, and of course I liked shooting as well, so I was invited too. Then the shoot got bigger, and as there was a cottage that went with the farm that was last rented, a part time keeper was employed, and by that time there were paying guns.

There was another incident that happened with young cattle at Home Farm where Jack and his wife, Maggie, lived. Jack used to look after all the calves and younger stock that were based at Home Farm, originally from the dairy herd. At that time I was using Nilverm worm drench for worming the sheep. Jack phoned me one morning rather anxious. That was out of the ordinary for Jack, as he was a very calm man to deal with. I could understand his anxiety after he explained that he had to call the vet as two or three of the young cattle out grazing had become unwell. As soon as the vet examined them he told Jack, "They are full of lung worm." The two or three that were ill he'd had to inject there and then to save them. The vet said they all had to be lung worm drenched, and Nilverm was OK., so I went straight over to Home Farm to drench them. Well, we had no crush, so you can imagine there they were in this shed about the size of a calving box, I suppose about twelve square feet. Good job I was a strong guy. Jack marked them while I drenched them. Well, I said to him afterwards, I could not quite understand how he did not notice something wrong before they got so bad. I suppose it was something similar to when I never noticed those bought-in ewes with fluke until two or three got bad enough to notice, but after that little session, we drenched them every year. It just shows how things can happen to livestock. The reason I drenched and injected the sheep flock, and as I finished whichever drenching or injecting I had done that day, I wrote it in my diary, so that I knew which date it was due again, and, of course, I proceeded to the same with the young cattle out grazing. I have always found attention to detail always paid off, especially as I was responsible for the outcome.

I must say a word about Maggie, Jack's wife. She was always very nice to me whenever I had to go to Home Farm.

125

After two years being employed with the Barnham family, I was keeping tabs on all seven farms, working out the whole farming programme in terms of tons of fertiliser, seed lime, etc. for the best production of the land and grazing. I remember going up to the senior partner's farm house one morning. I wanted to see Jack Barnham about farm business. Jack happened to be there to let out his brother's shooting dogs, springer spaniels, and he had first put them back in their runs, and that is where I met him, walking down from the kennels. I said "Good morning, Jack" in my jovial voice. I saw he looked a bit downcast, and so I said, "What is the matter with you?" He said, "Well, father has been on to me that we are using too much fertiliser; he had to write out a large cheque to pay for it." I replied: "You know it is right, just take hay. If we did not proceed as we are, we would not have anything like the hay we produce now, and about February time we would have to buy in hay when it was at its most expensive time." He said. "I know that, but you tell my father that." And I did, and he seemed to see the sense of it.

Also, I was in on discussions about some of the machinery we had to acquire. As these farms were two to three miles apart, travelling round the roads was very convenient, and Jack trusted me to go ahead and do it. But one day, when I went to see him. I told him I was happy to do all of this, but I never actually purchased anything, only grass seed. So his answer to that was: "Well, if you do more than that, what am I going to do?" He also said he would be very happy if the family could get a four or five hundred acre farm on its own, and I got to manage it.

As time went on, there was a six hundred acre farm came up on the South Downs. We went to look at it, but there was no house with it. Then a farm came up joining the land we were farming, but the house was sold off with ten acres of land, so that was the finish of that. Just like my dear old mother would say, "My boy, it wasn't to be!"

There came the time when I thought about it very seriously, and I was determined to have absolutely full control in the management of a farm. In my deliberations, I looked at the situation in this way: if I stayed with the Barnham family, whose eldest son was at a very good agriculture college, and he was pretty clever education-wise, he would be there for three or four years, but when he had finished his studies he would, no doubt, eventually take over the running of the farms, and where would that leave me?

So I could see no alternative but to try and get another position. So I applied for a job in The Farmer's Weekly. The situation was about twenty-five miles away, still in East Sussex, being the full manager of a two hundred and fifty acre dairy farm, with a pedigree herd of Friesians, also a breeding flock of sheep.

It was three weeks before I heard anything. I got home about five o'clock for tea. As soon as I got in, Pat, my wife, said a gentleman had called to see me about the job I had applied for, and would call back about six o'clock. He was there on time, a very nice chap: apparently he was in the office for the farm manager, also he visited the farm once a week. The farms were owned by a very big motor company. The owner was away in Spain on holiday, so I had to go for an interview in Croydon, another part of the motor company, very modern. There I met the owner's son. He had nothing to do with the farms really. He led me into the company board room, very modern. The beautiful board room table was the longest I have ever seen at that time, with several chairs to match. Before I left, after the interview, the son said, "Well, you go down to Moat Farm and see what you think about it, and of course I would like a reference." So that weekend my wife, son and myself arrived at Moat Farm. Well, nice herd of cows, but being milked in cowsheds I was not so keen on. Lovely house, but wanted a lot of money spent on it, like some of the wooden doors of the cowsheds:

it looked as though there had not been any money spent there for years.

Well, we went home and discussed it. I looked at it as another step up to where I wanted to go. So I phoned the owner's son up in Croydon, and said before I went into that house it would want a new sink unit, and a new Rayburn, and all rooms wanted re-decorating, and if some of the important things were not done I would not be going. The answer I got was: "I cannot understand , it should be perfectly alright. I do not know what the previous manager was thinking of." To which I replied, "It isn't much good talking about that. The situation is as I have described." So we came to an agreement. A new oil fired Rayburn, new sink unit, and three rooms decorated, the rest to be done at a later date.

So the next procedure was to tell Jack Barnham and also get a reference.

That particular day Jack Barnham happened to go up to the last farm we took over called Knotlands. So I went up there in my van, looked around, saw his Land Rover, and then saw Jack coming across a field to the buildings. So I walked out to meet him. We greeted each other with "Good morning..." using our Christian names. I said, "I want to see you about a reference as I have found another job." He looked at me, and cocking one eyebrow up, which he always used to do when surprised, he said, "What have I done?" I replied, "Nothing, I want to move on, etc." Years afterwards, when I met him, as we always kept in touch, he said, "I will never forget the spot in that particular field where you told me you were leaving us."

So in October nineteen seventy two, I moved to my new job at Moat Farm.

The first thing I had done was to have all the fields tested for line, and by golly we certainly had to have several tons on straight away as it had been neglected in that area. There were seventy cows in all, milking in an L-shaped cowshed, the L piece being built on as an after thought, which made it more laborious than ever. The milking machines were a plant with pipe lines, vacuum and milk line running along side each other and the milk going straight into the old fashioned ten gallon holding tank, that regulated the milk down over the old fashioned cooler, then into a ten gallon churn. From the start we had trouble with the pulsation, which was annoying, and I thought not a good thing for the mastitis count. So we sent milk off to be tested. I had already found out that the farms were run on requisition orders, like the owner's car industry. No wonder things were in a state. It was quite a shock to me never coming across it before. I thought, well, there has to be something done about it or we are going to have trouble with mastitis. So I found out how much it would cost to have all new pulsators. The price at that time was one hundred and two pounds. I had them put in straight away. I knew it was right to do. Well, what I should have done was to send a requisition order up to the owner in London, and not ordered them until he signed the order, so I was waiting for the phone call I knew I would eventually get, and I did! The owner was eighty years old. I remember the conversation was like this: he would go back forty years to when he had bought the farm, when he had put mains water and electricity on, and I had to listen to this conversation for what could be three to five minutes until I got him onto the present time. Then he said, "Why have all new pulsators put in?" and my answer was, "For the well being of this cow herd as they were not working properly." That stopped that conversation, as the herd at Moat Farm was the best herd of the three farms. The cows in winter were fed on hay and silage, and after maintenance etc., it was dairy cake. Well, it got to February nineteen seventy-three, and I could see we were going to run out of hay. I thought at the time "what a start to a new job." We had a rep come every month from a feed firm. Brian Day was his name, a very genuine man, and I asked him if he knew anyone who had hay for sale. He said he knew two people that might sell hay. One I went to, but they had no more for sale. Then I went to a chap called Alec Teal. He had and his two sons a farm with where they ran a cattle conveyance business with three lorries. I always remember meeting him. "Hello, Mr. Teal." His reply was, "I am Alec, what do you want?" I said, "I hear you have hay for sale." "Yes, if we get up that ladder I'll show it to you, even cut a bale open so you can see." So up the ladder we got. "There you are," he said cutting a bale open. I said, "How much per ton carried in to the farm?" He said, "Sixteen pounds per ton. How much do you want?" I said "A few tons" and we agreed a price. Alec didn't waste words. He was pretty direct, and we ended up in buying five or six lorry loads. The most extraordinary thing was within eighteen to twenty months, I met Alec again and did a lot of business every year, conveying cattle I had bought every year. Funny how things turn out in life.

The other thing I had to do was to write on paper especially printed out for the purpose, every week, what work had been going on, then permission to sell a cow or a calf at which market, but I never put down the sale of cow or calf until I had sold it, as I looked at the herd as a whole. Any cow that had been in the herd for two or three years lactation and did not give more than eight hundred gallons per year, I sold. As it was a pedigree herd and closed, I could see exactly how they performed. I knew in the May of that year as they were out to grass, and we had a few fresh calvers, there was so much milk going through the pipes to the container tank over the cooler, it sometimes could not take it, and it over flowed. I could not see the point of wasting milk like this, so I got onto the owner about it. There were some difficulties but at last we had a bulk tank installed. Also, we had to have over half a mile of farm lane

Tarmacked before the bulk tank lorry would come to collect the milk, but it was achieved! One of the best things that happened to that farm.

When I went to this farm they promised me a new Ford Cortina Estate car which I got within three or four months. Very nice. It had a trailer hitch for a small trailer, as I had to take bull calves to one of the other farms, but after I had done about twelve hundred miles with this car, there came a sound in the back axle, so I took it to a Ford specialist. He got in the car, and we had not driven up the road more than two miles, when he turned to me and said, "I know what that is. It's crown and pinion trouble." So it had to have new crown and pinion. It was OK. after that. Apparently they had had a whole batch of them and that particular model was made in Germany.

The farm house itself was a lovely place, but wanted money spent on it. Being too close to the cowsheds, we certainly got a terrific lot of flies in the summer, and the previous people could not have cleaned the window paintwork for months, as they were plastered with fly marks. Pat had quite a job getting them all cleaned off, but she achieved it.

While we are on living accommodation, there were four cottages belonging to the farm. Two were the old original farm cottages, about two hundred and fifty yards from the farm buildings, and two were newer ones about three quarters of a mile away. Well, I had not been there very long before I inspected the sink units in all four cottages. I recalled something Mr. Howell, the manager on the first farm where Pat and I started our married life had said; "Mewett, if the cottage isn't up to the wife's liking, the job is no good to the man, because they are not going to be there long." And bearing in mind that the wife spends about seventy per cent of her life in the kitchen, the very important fixture was the sink units, so I inspected all four cottages, and decided they were in need of new sink units. The next thing was to write a requisition order out, and send it to the farm office in London, knowing the owner would see it straight away. As I never heard anything, I sent memos on the subject each week. I certainly was not going to give in. About the same time, we had trouble with the cesspool of the older cottages. I got an estimate for the job, and sent a requisition order to the farm office. I did not hear anything for a few days, and as there was a new born baby in the family that lived in one of the cottages, I thought this cannot go on. So I phoned the owner who, by the way, was head of the farms and the car company. No one had any authority in his family to do with the farms but himself. His name was Mr. Markham, who, by the way, was a millionaire. I did contact him that day, and in the end, after I told him there was a few days old baby in the cottage, and that we would soon have the health authority after us, he signed the requisition order and the job was done. But there was still the question of the new sink units for four cottages, and the memos I sent up were nobody's business. Eventually I phoned Mr. Markham and reminded him he had not signed the requisition for these units. Of course, it was three to five minutes before I got him to talk about these new units back to the present day. Then he said to me: "But our farm cottages are the best in Sussex." So I replied, "I do not think so," knowing the sink units wanted replacing. And then he said, "But I have signed a requisition order for them." I said, "No you did not. That was for a cesspool." Well, after that conversation the order was signed, I got the job in operation and finished. It took me eleven months to get it done.

The main man on the farm, who was provided with a mini van by the farm, if I happened not to be there and there was a break down of machinery, he would see to it, and an odd time or two he would collect my son, Nicholas, from school. One particular morning, we were in conversation about the farm, and at the same time he said to me, "There is something I have got to tell you." I said, "Oh, what is that?" His reply was, "Well, I have been on this farm for twenty nine years, and we have had four managers at different times, but you have done more in one year than any of them did in five years! "

Well, when I had to buy all this hay when I first went to Moat Farm, I was determined it would never happen again, so I wrote a memo to Mr. Markham, stating a fertiliser programme for the whole farm, so that we would not be in that position again, and suggesting all three farms should have a fertiliser programme, and that we should buy the fertiliser in order put together for all three farms. From that I had a phone call from the farm office manager, who had to come once a week to look at the farms, as I have said before. His name was John Mark, a very nice man. He did not know a lot about farming, but he did not profess to, and was willing to learn. He said: "I have just had young Mr. Markham in the farm office, and the first thing he said to me was that Mewett from Moat Farm has put forward a fertiliser programme for Moat Farm and has said the other two farms should do the same, and buy all the fertiliser from one source." John Mark told me: "I looked at young Mr. Markham and replied, that is certainly the right thing to do."

Well, I was able to get the fertiliser I wanted for the silage, hay and grazing ground, and of course, for about twenty acres of cereal ground we had every year, which was barley and oats, which was rolled for calf, young heifers and the two Friesian bulls that were kept, although I nominated two other bulls for A1, services.

I remember when John Mark came down one week to see how things were going, he said to me, "You know the old man, Mr. Markham, is in awe of you." I said "Oh, is he! " and that was that.

The other thing I did was step up the ewe flock to one hundred and twenty, and also ordered forty rolls of square stock fencing, so that we could tie the netting to the hedges to stop the sheep from getting out, as it was not sheep proof. In that way the sheep could go round the whole of the grass land in the winter; it certainly does the pastures a considerable amount of good.

When I came from my previous job, I brought my old sheep dog, Jill, with me. She became excellent at doing what I wanted with the sheep. I remember the first time I brought the fattening lambs in to put through the foot bath, she worked beautifully, and the chap who used to lamb the sheep said, "I certainly did not think that the sheep dog you have was as good as that." So that was a feather in her cap, but alas, about a year after that she slowed up a lot. I got the vet to look at her. As soon as he saw her, he diagnosed an infection of her womb, and took her back to the surgery to operate on her straight away. He did all he could, but she never survived, and I can tell, it was a hell of a shock to me. What with that, and another thing I have not mentioned, about two months after I had started this new job, I developed mumps. That certainly hit me at the age of forty five. I had to keep away from the staff for at least a fortnight. I was wondering if anything else was going to happen before the year was out.

There was another thing that puzzled me. There was a badgers' set close to the dairy buildings, and before I could get the cowshed doors repaired, and as there was a big enough hole in the top and bottom doors of the cowshed that first October and November, while the cows were lying in, the design of the shed was that one could push the cake trolley in front of the cow mangers, so, therefore, there used to be a nub or two of cake lying along the passage way, and the badgers knew it. I have seen a badger running down the passage ways, when shining a torch down these passage ways. I do not know how long this had been going on, I expect the winter before at least. However, it stopped when

134

the doors were repaired. The puzzlement was that we never had any cases of tuberculosis in the herd.

After I had been at Moat Farm, I was summoned to the office in London to see the boss, Mr. Markham. His office was more old fashioned than the office in Croydon. I remember this big desk he sat behind, with quite a large intercom box with switches on. Bearing in mind that his company owned half the buildings up one street, he could contact each building if he wanted to.

Well, I went into his office. We said the usual pleasantries to each other, and I sat down the opposite side of the desk. After talking about the farm for a while, all of a sudden he opened a drawer in his desk and pulled out a photo of a young pedigree Friesian cow from the Moat Farm herd. She had won a silver cup or two. He held it up. I immediately went round to the other side of the desk, standing behind Mr. Markham so I could get a good look at the photo, and, of course, it was a lovely cow. Then he said, "What is special about that cow?" My answer was, "Well, she has good confirmation and the other thing is she has an udder like an Ayrshire cow." He said, "That's it, that's it! " I suppose he thought "I'll see if he knows anything about this job." It is a good job I did, or he would have been on top of me like a ton of bricks. The conversation got round to increasing the sheep flock to one hundred and twenty ewes, and purchasing forty rolls of netting, so that we could graze all the pastures on the farm, and to my amazement he said, "That is right on!," and it proved right. When I got back to Moat Farm that day I thought, "Well, it looks as if I have passed the first inquisition, thank goodness."

Then came the time when John Mark from the farm office left. He told me he could not put up with any more of the old boss's way of treating him. I thought it was an unfortunate thing to happen, as he seemed just right for the job. In actual fact, I could not see the point of anyone coming down from London once a month to see the farms. However, we were without anyone for a few weeks. Then I had a phone call from Mr. Markham, telling me a new chap was coming down from the farm office twice a week to see the farms. His name was Berry. I said, "Well, I cannot see the point of him coming down twice a week." I expect he thought, "We will sort this Mewett out, down at Moat Farm," as I learnt if he could put one man against another, he was happy. He was quite a bounder for that sort of thing apparently, and all the more so as I would not sign requisition orders for anything regarding running of the farm.

Another thing that happened, we had a lovely young cow started calving, but she could not, so I called the vet, who was the senior one of the practice. He was a marvellous vet, but, by golly, he did not mince words. Well, along he came. His name was Hopeing, but everyone called him Hopey. I took him in the calving box, tied the cow up, fastening her halter to a ring in the wall. As he was washing his hands in disinfectant hot water, I said to him: "It reminds me when I was at Whitstable in my twenties, we had a second calver and that could not calve, and as soon as the vet examined her, he said, "She has got a twisted womb." Well, Hopey put his hand up into her vagina, and he looked at me and the language was terrible. "You effing clever bugger! ! That is just what she has got, a twisted womb," and to that I said, "Have we got to get a wagon rope to pull her down and tractor to hold the rope stable, as that is what we had to do with the cow all those years ago at Whitstable." "No," he said, "I am calving her as she is standing up." He was a very strong man, but the perspiration that was coming off him with the effort it took to calve her was nobody's business, but he succeeded, and cow and calf did very well.

And, as we had increased the sheep flock, I purchased a couple of new Dorset Down Rams. I netted a sizable piece of grass that ran parallel to the short drive to the farm house.

It was just right for them to graze. When I was putting up this netting I never noticed there was a dip in the ground. After about a week, low and behold, early one morning when I went to look at them, one of them lay dead. He could not get off his back. The only little hollow in the ground and he had to find it. They are the sort of fatalities that occur with livestock. It was very upsetting, especially the rams only being on the farm for a week.

There was an incident in the cow herd: one of the best cows went very lame. I called the vet, and his diagnosis was that there was an infection in one claw, and to save the cow, that claw would have to come off. The vet also said the success rate was quite high in these cases, so I said do it, and they operated on her in the cowshed. I had been several years involved with cows, and I had never seen this operation before, and it was a great success.

Now for the time when I first met the new chap from the farm office, who was coming down twice a week to see what was going on at the farms. He came down one particular morning. He introduced himself, and we shook hands, and as I have what I call a sixth sense, as I first meet anyone I can weigh them up pretty well, and over the years, I have been ninety per cent right in my estimation. As we shook hands, and I looked into his eyes, and the way he introduced himself, like he said I used to be an under manager on a sixteen hundred acre estate, mostly dairy, and that he would be in the office eight-thirty in the morning. My goodness, we have got a right one here, and how right I was! I had occasion to phone the farm office in London, and he certainly was not there at eight-thirty in the morning. He was one of those chaps, with the experience he said he had, I do not think he knew half what he should have done, so he tried to bluff his way through. I met him one morning in the farm yard, in front of the calving boxes, and there in one of the boxes was a freshly calved cow and her calf, and the things he tried to tell me about a cow calving! He went on about this cow, and I just stood there, well, I was laughing at him inwardly, and thought at the same time, he must think I am green. Well, I let it go for a while, and then he started to get a bit too big for his boots, trying to override my decisions later on, and I must say that was a fatal thing to do to me, as you will see as I write on further.

One day, when Alec Berry was talking about the dairy herd at Moat Farm, as I have mentioned I nominated two bulls' semen for all A1, I cannot remember the name of one particular bull, I will call it Sunbeam for argument's sake, he was just about to go home and he tried to argue that Sunbeam was not the right bull. He wanted another bull, and I said that bull stands for the herd. With that, as he could not get his way, he came up with saying, "Mr. Markham wants some other bull nominated." I was standing one side of the bonnet of his car, and he was standing the other side of the bonnet. I upped with my fist and smashed it down on the car bonnet, and said, "I don't care what Mr. Markham wants in nominated bulls, Sunbeam stays." It was a wonder I didn't bend the bonnet of his car, for I was quite sure it was himself that wanted it changed, and not Mr. Markham. So that was the end of that conversation, and, of course, I never heard anymore about it. Another thing Alec Berry used to do was he always filled his car with petrol, booking the petrol to the Moat Farm account.

I also had labour trouble regarding the dairy herd, and with the head herdsman, who was single and lived with his mother. In the end we had to dispense with his services. He was a good time keeper, but at the same time he was a Jekyll and Hyde character, and one day he would be putting his arm around a cow's neck and telling her she was an old darling, and the next day I caught him swearing at a cow, also hitting her, absolutely a changed man over night. So the under herdsman became the head herdsman, and I had to find another under herdsman, which I did in about ten days.

When it came for the dismissed herdsman to vacate the cottage, two or three days before leaving, he came to me and said, "I am sorry, but when my mother and I were clearing out items we did not want, and putting them on the bonfire, the herds records accidentally got burnt." So I can tell you that caused a few problems, but I must say the head herdsman, he was only a young chap, in time he got them all up to date, thank goodness.

One evening, my previous employer phoned me and said his friend was looking for another herdsman and wanted to know about the one that was leaving me. I actually knew his friend, who was in a big way with three dairy herds. My answer was I would be reluctant to take him on as he had burnt the herds records. I just told the truth, what else could I say? I never went into any more details. Then in the following spring, the new, older herdsman, after helping clean out all the cow stands as the cows were just turned out, I do not know what the argument was about, but he downed his fork and went home on the spot. Dashed if the head herdsman didn't do the same, so I had to go on milking and also hire another chap for just milking twice a day. I tried to persuade the head herdsman to come back. It took a week before they did. Of course, they got a reprimand and also a reduction in money, but after that it all blew over, but it was a hell of an experience I never had to face again!

However, I went in the cowshed one day and the head herdsman said to me, "I cannot understand it, Mr. Berry says I must only give two pints of milk twice a day to the calves up to five weeks of age, and one or two other things he said." Well, I did not know about any of this. He had been going behind my back. I said, "Now you look here. You carry on exactly how I want you to, and if Mr. Berry says any more about it you send him straight to me. If we go on like he wants to, we will have half the calves dead." That did annoy me! Well, I let these things go for two or three months as long as nothing changed but if he kept going behind my back like this, I would eventually put my foot down, and by golly, he would know all about it!

Then one day, we knew Mr. Markham was coming down on a Wednesday. Of course, he was driven in a Rolls Royce car. It was a lovely car. It was the time we were haying, and Mr. Berry got down before him and went down to the hay field and loaded a load of hay. He had never done it before. Afterwards he came back to meet Mr. Markham. He had put a few wisps of hay on himself and made out he was brushing out hay from his hair, and said, "Afternoon sir, hot work this haying." Talk about a comedy! I believe the old man saw right through him, but at the same time I think he thought it will stir this Mewett up a bit.

Then came the time I went for the second time to see Mr. Markham in his London office. When I thought about it, it seemed to me it was like being thrown a sprat to catch a mackerel. Anyhow, I arrived at the office, always ten minutes before my appointment, and I was made to wait half an hour. I expect the boss thought, "Make him sweat a bit before I call him in." That's what it seemed to be at the time. Eventually I went in. We greeted each other. I knew the exercise was to try and get me to plough up ten acres of pasture for some silly scheme, but I explained that Moat Farm was mostly a dairy farm, and we wanted all the pasture we could get, especially as the herd was increasing in numbers. Also, I did not want to see the situation again, where we had to buy four or five loads of hay in February and March to keep the herd with enough fodder to eat. As soon as I explained about it, and as I have said before, I never told lies or tried to bluff any one, he just got off the subject and went on to the next item.

Then he looked across at me, with his face going red, at the same time pulling his white handkerchief from under his shirt cuff, slammed it down on the office desk, and said, "You do not think we know anything about farming!" to which I replied, "Mr. Markham, I have never said anything of the sort!" so he calmed down and went on to one or two other items he wanted to ask me, then said, "We will be taking you to the RAC. Club for lunch." I said, "That would be nice, thank you." Within about ten minutes his son came in, the same gentleman that interviewed me at Croydon. He was ready for his lunch at one o'clock. As soon as the son walked into the office, his father looked up to him and said, "Now, what else was it we were going to ask him?" meaning me. The son stood there and came up with one or two other items, but his father said, "No that is not it." Then there was the mention of vets. "Ah," the old boss said, "that's it!" Then he looked at me and soon told me that the vet's bills on Moat Farm were the highest they had ever been, to which I explained, "Well, we have each cow pregnancy tested, and pre-serviced, and if one does not do that you are likely to lose thirty to ninety pounds per cow, and another thing, that over twelve months, the yield per cow has risen by one hundred and twenty gallons per cow." He just did not want to know, and went on about something else. It seemed to me he never had an answer for my answer to his questions. I think he was hoping to trip me up, but he never did, thank goodness.

Well, after that little session, we went down stairs, ready to be taken to lunch. As we got to the door, there was the old boss's Rolls Royce waiting for us. I got in front with the chauffeur. As soon as I got, in the son said to me, "My goodness, they would have to make a Rolls Royce for you!" Away we went. We came to a junction where we had to stop at traffic lights. While we were waiting for the lights to change it was so quiet I thought the engine must have been turned off, but as soon as the lights changed, the chauffeur let the clutch in and away we went, and that is how quiet that engine was. Also, the ride was like riding in an arm chair, which was the most comfortable arm chair one could get. We arrived at the RAC. club, lovely old place, a lot of marble about, very nice swimming pool where the son had a swim before lunch; then, after this lunch, the Rolls was waiting for us, and I was taken back to the office, and from there made my way back to Moat Farm. How the other half live!

Then came shearing time, which was carried out about three quarters of a mile up the road right opposite the two newer cottages. All hands on deck to get the sheep to the shearers. I was helping get the sheep to the shearer, when all of a sudden, Alec Berry appeared. He said hello to us, then I thought, "Now is the time to have things put straight," so I got one of the chaps to take over from me. I walked away from the sheep pens, and said to Alec Berry, "I would like to see you now. What's all this business about going behind my back and telling the herdsman that you wanted him to give less milk to the calves and trying to alter one or two other things?" and as I have a loud voice it must have nearly broken his ear drums, as I really went to town over it. I said, "If we went on like you want things done, we would have half the calves dead by now." He looked pretty sheepish, and then he said, "I am manager as well." "Oh no, you are not, I am the manager here and that is how it is going to stay." That was the end of the conversation, but by golly he was a different man after that episode.

About eight months after I had been at Moat Farm, a lovely cow herd I may add, but to stop these labour problems I wanted Mr. Markham to put up a modern cow unit for one hundred and twenty cows, but he refused. I reviewed the situation seriously and started to put out a feeler or two for another job. The contacts were two reps I knew pretty well. Well, one came up with a job within six months of asking. The first thing I asked was how many acres was the farm.

The reply was, "One hundred and eighty acres." I said, "thank you for trying on my behalf, but it is too small for my liking." So I just got on with the job I had, and managed it to the best of my ability, and of course waited patiently.

Going back to the fertiliser programme, it paid off well, as before I left Moat Farm we had about thirty tons of silage, and fifteen tons of hay left over after the cows were turned out.

Well, in March nineteen seventy-four, all the rooms of the farm house were decorated by a local firm, and I must say they made a beautiful job of it. Coming up to Easter of that year, the rep I knew the longest phoned me and said that where he had a customer, the farm had been bought by a lady. It was five hundred acres in all, and it had been run down for the last twelve or fourteen years, as the owner had been there for fifty-nine years and had been a very good farmer. He had seven children and, of course, when the father died at the age of ninety-three, they sold the farm.

The rep's name was Brian Day, and I had known him for several years. A most practical and honest man, When I had come across as a rep. When he first told me about this vacant post, he said, "Well, it will only take a phone call to the appropriate agents!, and, by the way, it has not been advertised yet."

Well, I thought about it, and one morning after breakfast, I phoned the agents and made an appointment the following Thursday at 2.30 pm. I came from the phone into the kitchen - just remember that the whole house had been redecorated and Pat, my wife, was washing up at the sink when I told her that I had made an appointment for an interview on Thursday at 2.30 pm. Pat turned round to me and said, "What have you done?" and I can tell you I wanted a hole to come and for me to drop in it, but I said, "I have got to do something as it is not going to be any good staying here."

Now before I go any further about going for an interview, I am going back to the herd itself. There used to be a chap, whose name was John Reeve, come round from the British Friesian Society. What he was looking for was a cow with very good conformation, udder shape and also lactation. There was one such cow he liked in the Moat Farm herd. In the end he said, "I will get the selector to come and have a look at her." The purpose was to put one of their best bull's semen AI. when she came on heat, hoping for a bull calf to replenish the AI. centre.

Well, the day arrived when the selector came. His name was Joe Cade. I was introduced to him. He was a man of few words, but very experienced. The herdsman led this particular cow out. Mr. Cade had already been briefed on her lactation and butterfat. I stood with John Reeve watching Joe Cade examine this young cow. John Reeve knew the expression and time Mr. Cade was taking. John Reeve looked at me and whispered to me "I think she is in! ," and all of a sudden the old gentleman said, "She'll do!" and, of course, she was selected. Then I said, "Would you like a cup of coffee?" and they said "Yes, please." I always remember going in through the front door of Moat Farm House, and Mr. Cade took his Wellingtons off before he went into the house, and of course his cap, and Pat, my wife, was very impressed and said, "What a gentleman!" Now the selected cow was put to AI. but unfortunately she had a heifer calf.

I certainly did not think at that stage of my life I would be meeting Mr. Cade again, but you will see in the future I did.

Then came the afternoon that I went to the agents, M. & A. Turner, for the interview at 2.30 pm. and I was interviewed by Jack Ram. I told him about myself, then he produced a map, then said, "There are about five hundred acres, I think. Grow a hundred acres of wheat, and as there is fattening land for cattle, the rest farmed like that." Then he put the map round so I could see it, and said, "You think that is about right?" To which I replied, "Well, I do not know until I see the land and buildings first," and he said, "I want you to go to the farm, have a good look round, and as Easter is this weekend, I want you to phone me Tuesday morning to let me know what you think of it." Well, on Easter Monday, Pat and I went down to this farm, and it was at the time when I had recently purchased a new pair of walking shoes for Pat, and they were the shoes she wore. We walked the fields by map, and then only went half the length of the farm, as it was about two miles in length from one end to the other. Then we came back and looked at the farm buildings, then looked at the house where the manager would live, called Clinton Court. It was an older house than the main farm house, with eighteen inch thick walls, but about sixty years before it had been turned into a double dwelling, I think for a herdsman and carter in those days. As I have said, the place had been run down, and when we looked at it, one half had not been lived in for three years, and the other half had not been lived in for eight years, and half the wall plaster had fallen down, birds dung and feathers all over the place, so all in all it was a sorry sight. When we got home and were discussing it, Pat looked at me and said, "You know what I think about it." I looked at her and straight away she put her hand up and her thumb down, meaning it was not on! But I said, "But the house, Clinton Court, is going to be all modernised, and as for the farm ground, it is going to be a very big challenge. It will want tons of lime for a start, and some of these buildings have got to come down. They required too much labour and to run that farm with two men it is not on." Of course, I did not realise at that time how big the challenge would be. Anyway, I went ahead and phoned Jack Ram. The first thing I said to him was, "Well, some of these buildings want coming down, and one or two new ones put up for the running of that farm with two men," to which he replied, "Oh, my client is quite prepared to do that, and I will get back to you in a day or two." We never forgot that Easter Monday, as poor Pat, my wife, got a blister on her heel from all the walking.

The next thing was I had a phone call from Jack Ram, the agent, asking me to meet him and his client at nine o'clock on a particular morning. Well, I was at Coleman's Farm ten minutes before time. Along came Jack Ram. As previously, I told him he could get a reference regarding myself from Jack Barnham, but when he arrived, I said to him, "Did you get a reference from Jack Barnham?" and his reply was, "No, I got it from his brother Joe Barnham." Then he looked at me and said, "I think it is going to be alright." Within ten minutes a car arrived, and a tall lady got out, and I was introduced to her. Her name was Mrs. Berry. After the introduction, Jack Ram said "Let's go up to the farm buildings." As we got to the farm buildings, he turned round to me and said, "Now tell Mrs. Berry what you have told me about yourself." My goodness, am I going to remember everything, I asked myself. But I remembered it pretty well. When I mentioned I went to school at Eastfield, and was a farmer's son, and mentioned the vicar at the village church was a Canon Bright, and that Sir James and Lady Knight lived at Eastfield Place, Mrs. Berry said, "That is quite right. They bought it from my father." Well, you could have knocked me down with a feather!

Then the conversation got around to which old building should be knocked down, and new ones put up for the running of the farm. There was a granary with slate roof, a building with places to tie up cows with chains, two single cow sheds and tin and wooden calving boxes which would have to come down. Mrs. Berry said, "If it is for the good of running the farm, I agree that they come down." That only left a cowshed for fifty cows, and we put wider and higher doors onto it and used it for a fertiliser shed, as one

146

could go in one end and straight out the other. The one mistake I made was not having the partitions and mangers knocked out, but it was a very good building. It was only built in nineteen forty-two. At the end of the meeting at Colemans Farm, I said goodbye to the agent and owner, and was told by the agent, "I will let you know further in a day or two." So off I went, but I think it was the next day Jack Ram phoned me and told me the job was mine if I wanted it, and, of course, I proceeded to give in my notice.

I sent a letter to Mr. Markham, giving a month's notice, saying I would vacate the job and house by the end of May, nineteen seventy-four. Just before I was due to leave this post, I had a request to go up to Mr. Markham's office in London, and at the same time bring a map, showing the different fields for the grazing, the silage, the hay and the small amount of corn we grew, which I did. I remember my wife, Pat, came for the ride. I parked not far away from Mr. Markham's office. Pat sat in the car while I kept my appointment with Mr. Markham. I still had to wait a while, but eventually he called me in. We said hello to each other and then got down to business. I gave him the map he wanted, and then as we were shaking hands to say goodbye, he looked at me and said, "I will give you about two years on this new job of yours." I thought, right, I will tell you exactly what I think, and I did! "Well, Mr. Markham, your requisition orders may be alright for your car company, but there are certainly no good for your farming enterprise, and I will give you four years in farming - no more." With that, he walked down to where I had parked the car, and on the way said, "There is no damage to the car is there?" I said, "No." But he had to have a look as I do not think he believed me. So that was the last meeting I had with Mr. Markham.

Of course it was coincidence, but within four years all three farms of Mr. Markham's were sold. I believe also the whole business changed hands. I could not see the farming business going on for too long, as I suspect it went back to requisition orders, and that was fatal.

While we where at Moat Farm in February 1974, my mother was staying with us and in the course of conversation, my mother told us when she was pregnant with me, she walked down the lane, opposite the farm buildings; the dairy cows were grazing in a field. She went through the gate, shut the gate behind her and walked along the side of a two strand barbed-wire fence, which was the boundary of the field. Unknown to my mother who was a town lady, this particular cow had first calved and came running up to her. She was so frightened she arched her back got down on her knee's and crawled under the barb-wire fence to safety, if she had not I most likely would not have been here to tell the tale, that was in 1926.

That same year in October, my father bought a gallon of walnuts and put them in a cupboard for Christmas. When he went to get them at Christmas they were all gone, my mother had eaten the lot.

I have always thought it is right to encourage children to visit farms, and while I was at Moat Farm, on fifth April, nineteen seventy-four, I was asked by a local junior school if they could bring their junior pupils to view the farm. I accepted and they came on that arranged date. Afterwards, the pupils wrote letters of thanks: I thought the outstanding letter was from a little girl. Her letter was:

> "Thank you for letting us come to visit you on your farm. It was very interesting to see, and it was a sunny day. I did not know that you had two bulls, but it scared me very much, and at the end of the stable (meaning the bull pens) the end one which is near the milking parlour (cowshed) the fierce bull is dangerous. He kept going up and down, which is like a horse called Buckaroo.

148

The part I liked best on your farm were the sheep with their lambs on the big field. It is very funny when you tried to catch the black lamb where it was near us. I enjoyed it very much.

Bye for now, Karon Tate.

The teacher wrote underneath: "This little girl is the one with the hearing aid. She has very high hearing loss, about one fifth of normal, and she and I normally wear a person to person, a high powered transmitter/receiver, so you can imagine I am very pleased with this result."

It must have been my loud voice! They were very well behaved.

The extraordinary thing was, I was asked to buy a Southdown ram for a gentleman at Findon Fair. It was the first autumn I was at Coleman's Farm, and we were living in the first cottage at the main entrance to the farm.

I purchased a very nice ram. It had French blood in it, I believe. It was from a Southdown flock, and, believe it or not, the owner of the flock was Mr. Wade, whom I first met as a British Friesian Selector of the best cows in herds, purposely and hopefully to breed a good bull for the AI. centre. I believe I am right in saying Mr. Wade's flock was the seventh oldest Southdown flock in the country. What a coincidence!

Before I actually moved to Coleman's Farm, I was allowed to buy cattle for fattening, as the time factor was going too swiftly for fattening cattle off grass. When I started being quite a strong buyer for store cattle from the local markets, especially the nearest market, I think they wondered who the devil I was, but they soon found out. The idea was I would buy the cattle, get them transported to Coleman's Farm, and Mrs. Berry said her husband would look at them and count them. So that is what happened until we came to live at Coleman's Farm. Well, before I purchased the cattle

Mrs. Berry said to me, "I want Alec Teal to do the conveying of cattle for the farm," as she knew him very well. So, as I have mentioned before, it was the same Alec Teal I had bought the four or five loads of hay from when I was at Moat Farm. It is rather a small world when one comes to think about it.

I also attended the farm sale a Coleman's Farm, and while I was looking at different items, to my surprise, I met Mr. Wade. We said hello to each other, and he said, "I hear you are going to be the manager on this farm." I replied, "Yes, I am," to which he said, "I know Mrs. Berry very well" and then said, "If you behave yourself you will be alright." I did not know exactly what he meant by that, but I must have been a good boy, as I was there eleven and a half years.

Oh, by the way, Mr. Wade was the selector for special cows from the Pedigree British Friesian Herds Society, I met him at Moat Farm, and got to know him and his sons over the years. They lived and farmed only about three miles away from Coleman's Farm. When we did move to Coleman's Farm we would have to live in a semi-attached cottage at the entrance of Coleman's Farm, as it would take some time to renovate Clinton Court. It was pretty dirty inside the cottage, so the down stairs was emulsioned white, but upstairs was not very pretty, and my wife's school friend, Peggy, used to visit us every year for a week, about September time, but when we got to live in this cottage, Pat just would not have Peggy to stay until we got into the renovated house, as she said the bedrooms were dirty dicks! So that was that, but, of course, Peggy came every year after that.

Well, we eventually moved into the cottage on the third of June, nineteen seventy-four.

As I have said, I purchased cattle before I actually lived at Coleman's Farm. I went to the nearest local store cattle sales on second of May, nineteen seventy- four to purchase my first lot of cattle for Coleman's Farm and purchased sixty steers that day. No wonder the farmers and dealers wondered where I had come from. The next big purchase was at Haywards Heath store sale on sixth of May, nineteen seventy-four. Haywards Heath was a big store sale market, and I purchased eighty steers that day, and by twentieth of May, I finished cattle purchases as a time factor for fattening off grass and in that time I had purchased one hundred and ninety steers, mostly Black Hereford cross Friesian, not Holstein! as if they were Holstein crosses, half of them would not grade when fat. That is why, if I thought Holstein was in the cross, I never bidded for them. The other thing was I never bid for pens of cattle until the auctioneer was on the last run of bidding. I never ran anything but was a strong buyer for the right cattle for our system.

As I mentioned before, when I walked Coleman's Farm, I immediately thought that the farm wanted a lot of lime on it, and by golly, it certainly did. By third of July nineteen seventy-four, we had to have 974 tons - 17 cwts. of lime spread. Well, no wonder as I heard afterwards there had not been any lime put on for eighteen years.

Going back to buildings, there was another old main building we left besides the fifty stall cowshed. It was the Dutch barn, which was put up in nineteen twenty-six. Very modern in those days. We had it treated to last longer with a ten year guarantee. It was still going well after eleven years.

In the spring of nineteen seventy-five, as previously I had said I wanted a cattle building up with raised passage for one hundred and twenty store cattle, with silage clamp adjacent, and a corn barn drying unit for five hundred tons plus, and the erecting proceeded. One has to look at least five years ahead.

I have not mentioned that when I first went to Coleman's Farm, there were six ponds, five dykes with bay boards that the water board looked after as there was quite a lot of water about the place. It was actually the wettest farm that I had ever been on out of five different farms I had anything to do with. The dyke bay boards were put up in the summer to hold the water, and taken out in the winter to let the water flow.

On this five hundred acre, by the time one took out the ponds, hedges, dykes, two small woods and the ground which the buildings were on, I must emphasise that there had been three recently new buildings, two put up near cattle yards, the other one adjoining a big old barn called Marchant Barn, so they were scattered about a bit, so actual ground one could do for cultivation or grazing, hay or silage was about four hundred and seventy acres.

The first summer I was there, after stocking the farm with one hundred and ninety cattle, which amongst the cattle I had quite a few New Forest cases, also five or six foul of the foot cases, which I found out I had to live with over the years. I just got them in a box, kept them in for about a week, injecting them with a vaccine the first three days, and then they were alright.

There were only about forty acres of arable on the farm, and as I was on my own, I had to get contractors in to deal with all the hay I had to make. Fortunately, Marchant Barn could take some and the main amount went into a four bay Dutch barns and lean-to. But I was determined to plough up another one hundred and forty acres for winter wheat. At the same time I wondered what sort of problem I would have with wild oats, as the forty acres of arable on the farm was full of wild oats, and I mean wild oats. It got impossible to rogue them, and one four acre field we had to leave. I reckon half of the crop was wild oats, so I soon put it down to grass. The rest of the arable went to spring barley, and we sprayed for wild oats every year. The spray was called Avenge. It cost fifteen pounds per acre, but it must have been ninety nine per cent effective, as one did not see a wild oat anywhere in the crop, except one or two in the hedgerow, so I stuck to that spray, and always thirty six acres of spring barley on that infected ground. All ground that was ploughed up was always walked to rogue wild oats, but it was a very small problem. In the first year I was there I was on my own for two and a half months, then I engaged a young chap who was just getting married, and he started on the nineteenth of August nineteen seventy-four. Therefore I could get cracking on the fields I wanted to plough up for wheat.

We had to start from scratch. Nearly all new machinery had to be purchased, so I had to get it pretty right. Tractors, two new seventy odd horse power ones, one nearly new sixty-five horse power with loader and bucket on, only ninety-two hours on the clock. I found out the price of that one new before I went to the sale because I have seen some ridiculous prices paid for second hand machinery. I must say there was another chap there who wanted it badly, and I must say he made me sweat before I got it! But then it was cheaper than new.

Then I purchased a three furrow plough, drill, hydraulic harrow, fertiliser spreader disc and two five to six ton trailers, also one three ton trailer, all with silage sides and hay ladders, and a mower tedder and a precision chop forage harvester, so we got set up pretty well. I also got a silage cutter and an auger with hopper for dealing with corn in the corn barn. The corn barn was set up on the floor, drying set up Rowlands, with a forty horse power electric fan with heaters. The heaters I hardly ever used, for the best thing was the cold air I found, and I never had any trouble whatsoever, but I must admit I operated attention to detail, because the last two or three years the depth of corn was over twelve feet, 700 tons. Thank goodness the buildings I had put up and machinery I purchased proved right over the years.

The first year before the new cattle yard went up, fifty cattle were wormed, drenched with Nilzan and wintered in the modern, covered yard that was connected to old Mergins Barn, which held the hay for feed. Another thirty six steers were drenched with Nilzan, and housed in an old yard and hovel, adjacent to a three bay newish Dutch barn, and twenty two more steers were drenched and housed in a yard and hovel very close to the main farm house, all fed hay, ready to put down on the brooks about the third week in April for fattening.

I remember, going back to September nineteen seventy-four, and the local ploughing match. The first young chap I engaged won the first prize certificate and cup for three furrow one way plough, or turn over plough. A nice boost for him, and a little for me that year - at the fatstock show, we obtained second prize for outlyers. Anyhow, going back to the local ploughing match, bearing in mind that Mrs. Berry wanted to have single suckled cows on the grass land, but myself and Jack Ram, the agent, did not think it would be viable. Well, after this ploughing match, Mrs. Berry was in the orchard of Brook Farm House, planting daffodil bulbs. I went and spoke to her and asked her how she was. One must remember she had never farmed before. All of a sudden she said: "Farmers! I hate them all," I said, "What is the matter?" "Well," she said, "about half a dozen of them came to speak to me and wanted to know why I was ploughing all that lovely grass at Coleman's Farm, and that she should have single sucklers." I said to her: "Now, I'll explain why we have not gone in for single sucklers. First thing to look at is we would have to have one hundred cows on this farm," and the price of a good single suckler cow was at that time two hundred and fifty pounds, that is twenty five thousand pounds, "then one has got to have two very good bulls, with good confirmation, and that's another one thousand five hundred pounds, making a total of twenty-six and a half thousand pounds. Now, when they conceive and the calves are born, over a period of two months, that is eleven months gone. Also, I expect two per cent not to calve. Now, if one has a policy of selling the calves at nine months, that period comes to twenty months, and one has not had a single penny from them yet. Do you see what I mean?" Of course, the answer was, "Yes, I do." Now, while we have the policy of buying in the steers, I buy. One third are about twelve to fourteen months, and two thirds are anything from eighteen months to two years, the older cattle were for fattening off grass that year, and the younger ones for putting in the yard and fattened off silage, and no concentrates, in which we were successful in fattening half of them in the yard every year.

As we had no dairy herd, that was our cash flow every month. Well, in the beginning of nineteen seventy-five, we moved into Clinton Court, and what a lovely place they made of it. All oil central heated, lovely kitchen, etc., and I was so pleased for Pat, my wife. She deserved it all, and of course, that September her great friend Peggy was able to come and stay a week with us.

With the grass ground all the brooks were for fattening, and the grass that was left at the top end of the farm was perm grass, which had most of it been ploughed up in the second world war, I never reseeded any of it. I just grazed it well and got the analysis right, because I knew we had to be fairly intensive. I doubt if Mrs. Berry knew that it took me four years to get the analysis right on the arable and grass ground, but I at last achieved it, but I may add it wasn't a very easy task. In nineteen seventy-six, seven hundred and three tons of lime had to be put on. That is within twenty months of the first lot going on, but it certainly paid off. Another thing about Coleman's Farm was that there was hardly a gate or gateway any good on the place, but eventually I got them replaced. It was either that, or steers getting out from one field of steers to the next field, as I got all fattening cattle set stocked,. That means that the same batch of steers stayed in the same field until they were sold fat. The stocking rate we had meant we put on nitrogen each month in grazing season. We were eventually grazing four hundred and thirty odd cattle and growing enough silage for one hundred and thirty cattle in yards, and always twelve to fifteen hundred bales of hay to put in the Dutch barn. A few bales we sold. I always liked to have a bay and a half of hay left in the Dutch barn. I looked at it as insurance, as it was so wet two or three times in eleven years we did not turn any cattle out of yards until nearly May, and it meant we had to feed hay for ten days, and if one feeds hay as much as they can eat to one hundred and thirty cattle, because, as fat ones went out, I always bought more in to make up the number, and by golly, I can tell you it does away with a few tons of hay! I remember a manager from another farm came to see me, and he saw a bay and a half of hay left after all steers were turned out. The first thing he said "My governor would want me to sell that hay." "Well" I said, "he is a very foolish man as that is my insurance. Anyway I know if we have a very wet spring, and on this farm no one realises how wet it is, one does not dare turn out one hundred thirty cattle; when it is very wet they would stodge the grazing in no time at all, but with that hay, I know I have feed to give them in emergencies." As I have mentioned, the steers, when in the yards, were fed on as much silage as possible with access minerals. They were littered up with straw three times per week, so they kept clean. No complaints from the slaughter house ever. The days they were not littered up, there were six sections each holding twenty cattle; a bale of barley straw was put along the wall at the back of each section, so that they could pick over it if they wanted to. I kept that policy going every year, and it paid off. The policy I carried out there was, simplicity and effectiveness!

Within three or four years I had two different gentlemen wanting to see the cattle in the yards. After they had an inspection, they saw me afterwards and said, "You have certainly got something going right there." My answer was: "I know. That is why I keep to the same procedure ever year. Cattle are like humans, they have things go wrong with them like humans and other animals." I remember, after littering up, one of the chaps said, "Come and look at this steer, he isn't right somewhere." So I went to the yard. He was lying down very comfortably in the straw, but he was putting up a funny performance, chewing his cud. Although he looked well, I got the vet to look at him. As soon as he looked into his mouth he said, "He has cancer of the tongue." So he had to be put down the same day.

For three or four years I purchased about one hundred and forty odd store lambs to fatten on giant rape on two small arable fields where spring barley had been. In the year nineteen seventy-seven, on seventh of November, I put the lambs through foot baths and drenched them with Nilzan. By the 20th December I had three or four die. I had never experienced anything like it in sheep before, so I had one post-mortened and it was found that there was a parasite in the wall of the gut. It was picked up in summer and activated itself in December. The vet said the only drench that would touch it was Panacur drench, and he advised a third of an ounce or 10 mls. We drenched them immediately and never had any more trouble from them. Up until then I used to drench all steers with Nilzan, all the younger ones, which were one hundred and twenty in number. I never drenched the older cattle, which in number were three hundred and twenty odd.

The year nineteen seventy-eight, as soon as I purchased enough young cattle for grazing, by May I drenched them every two months with Panacur worm drench, and by golly, didn't it pay off! These younger cattle were meant for the yards in the winter, and I found I was selling half the number far before they went into the yards, so replaced them to make the number up. As soon as they were ready for the yard, they were all drenched with Panacur again, and as they went fat out of the yard, I replaced them; as soon as they came off the lorry, they were drenched with Panacur before being yarded. In that way we used to have five hundred steers each year go through Coleman's Farm. It certainly was not achieved over night! It took about three years to get to that number. We had a contract for three hundred fat cattle with F.M.C., which we eventually got to putting four hundred through, and with each fat steer we were paid a bonus of five pounds. We were able to do this as we had the analysis of fields up to scratch, and eventually, instead of slag for phosphate, we used phosphate 34 per cent. It lasted three years and as we had three hundred acres of grass, one hundred acres a year were dressed, and that is how we kept the phosphate at a level. I would not have achieved this amount of graded cattle with Holstein cross steers.

There was one other thing that I got going and that was having sheep in to keep from a couple of young partners in farming from Appledore. I got on with them very well, Les Rains and Ivor Pears. They used to out winter five hundred sheep on Coleman's Farm. I used to move them, so that all grass was grazed with sheep, in my opinion another asset to grass management.

By nineteen seventy-six, there was another one hundred acres acquired of rough grazing land, with quite a lot of grass tussocks in between the good grazing grass. Little did I know how wet this land really was. However, we could only sell about twelve acres of this grass for turf, the amount of grass tussocks stopped that procedure. Well, I got it contract ploughed for five pounds fifty pence per acre. It was so tough and hard they had a job to plough it. I would have said it was the hardest work those two tractors had done for some time.

One day, while I was down in these particular fields to see how it was all going, a farmer came along who had been a tenant on this land for many years. He saw what a job it was to plough and he came over to me and said, "I would give up if I was you." My reply was: "I am not going to do that. I got it ploughed and, of course, I certainly got the lime content right." As you will see, when we eventually got this land drained, the corn just rolled off it.

As regards the turning cattle out of yards in the spring, it was the earliest to date, second of April of the same year we ploughed eighty odd acres of rough grazing. That was the earliest time ever, all the time I was at Coleman's Farm. I remember that particular day I had to keep one steer back with wooden tongue, and two with eye trouble, and dashed if I didn't have another steer with wooden tongue on twenty-first September the same year. I had not seen wooden tongue in cows or cattle for some years. They both got over it with treatment, and I never had a recurrence in any steer for the rest of the time I was at Coleman's Farm. Just to reiterate, nineteen seventy-six was the driest year for two hundred years.

On the second of April that year, when we were turning the cattle out, I was opening and shutting a gate in the yard to keep the three steers I wanted kept back. As I twisted around quick, all of a sudden something went in my back. The pain was so great I did not know what to do with myself, and these particular cattle were put into fields, half a mile away. I had a job to get in and out of my Land Rover, but got them down to the fields safely. I told my wife, Pat, how my back was, and she said, "Well, sit down quietly and have a cup of tea." Well, as all cattle in the yards were fed access minerals; as soon as the cattle were out I always took two boxful of minerals down to them, so any of them could help themselves. Well, I had to get Pat to come with me and help lift the boxes in the Land Rover. Normal times I would have lifted them in myself. However, we got the job done. Well, next morning I lookered the cattle early morning. As it was Saturday, after breakfast, Pat, Nicholas and myself went to Barfield, a village about twelve miles away. I had not been there for twenty-five years. Well, my wife and son walked up to the top of the village, and I walked towards the bottom of the village. My back did not feel too bad at all. Then all of a sudden something went in my back. I could hardly walk. It was as though a couple of chaps were pulling on a ligament one each end and would not let go. I turned round, with difficulty walked up towards the top of the village where I met Pat and Nicholas coming back. I explained the situation, and Pat said, "Come and sit down and have a cup of coffee," which I did, but the pain was so great that I could not sit there, and said, while getting up, "I'll meet you down at the car park." I got down to the car park, and while waiting I just got hold of the side of the Land Rover, held it tight to put up with pain, and those three or four minutes felt like four hours. Eventually we were together, and we got in the Land Rover. I had a job to get in, and when I did, I had to lift my left leg up to put on the clutch. I could not lift it without; how I drove home I do not know. I fell in bed and Pat had to undress me. I did not know which way to turn. It did not matter what I did, I could not get rid of the pain. I had had quite a lot of pain with my back over the years, but this was so bad I would not have cared if someone had stuck a hedge stake into me, as long as they put me right out so that I did not feel any more pain. In the afternoon Pat phoned the doctor. He was out and his wife said she would get him to phone back. It happened that Pat was feeding the two dogs we took over from the last owners – they were kept in a shed next door – at the very time the phone rang, and across the landing opposite the bedroom I was in, was my office, and a phone rang. My son answered it. He was about twelve at the time. He came across to me and said, "It's the

160

doctor. Shall I get him to phone back?" I thought I had better answer it now, so I fell out of bed and crawled on all fours to the phone. I was able to sit with great difficulty, but I managed it. I explained to the doctor about it, and also told him when I wanted to pass water I had to get out on all fours, get a poe, and wee like a steer. That made him chuckle. He said, "I think you have a pinched sciatic nerve. You must lay on the hardest mattress you have, keep warm, and I will phone the pharmacist for a special pill I want you to take three times a day." Which I did. The pills were German, and by golly they were marvellous. I had to lie on my back for three and a half days. I began to think I would never walk again, but, thank goodness, I did, but I could not run as fast as I used to. I was speaking to a lady who worked in a care home, and she said the same thing happened to her after lifting a patient, and she said the pain was worse than having a baby, and she had had two children. Thank goodness I have not had a repeat of that particular problem.

As I have said, Coleman's Farm was an extremely wet farm. All arable was winter corn except thirty six acres of spring barley. I can remember going out every morning, walking this plough land and poking it with a stick to see if it would hold up a tractor with cage wheels on, as that is what mostly we had to have on the tractors. It was rather nerve racking. As soon as I thought it could hold up the tractors, we got on with the job straight away, as if one had some rain on that ground it would hold all operations up for two or three days. I know one year at the end of September, as the drill was going down at six thirty in the morning, the trailer was already in the field with the seed and fertiliser covered up, it poured with rain. It was so wet, we never were able to touch that field for ten days. It certainly proved that I was right when I wanted to get two or three fields drained per year. Three fields were all measured out on maps. There was about 20% grant then. All of a sudden the programme was dropped. I suppose I should have argued that it must be done, but I did not. I did not realise that the owners had money at that time to invest into it, and that they had put it abroad on advice by so called experts to avoid tax, but it did not work. That is the reason the whole estate had to be sold in the end.

Contrary to people's beliefs, the farm had to pay a rent to the partners, and everything was run on a business line, not, like some farmers thought, money was a source of no limit. I had to make a cash flow statement to the bank every three months forward. Each time, thank goodness, every three months there was five hundred to one thousand pounds of cash flow more than I'd stated. I was talking to a well-known farmer one day, and happened to mention cash flow. He immediately said, "Don't talk to be about cash flow. I was down fourteen thousand pounds in the year." There's the difference between the owner or tenant farmer and the manager. Whereas the owner and tenant farmer will be able to carry on, the manager responsible for managing the farm, his job would soon be on the line! It is amazing what happens on some rather big acreage farms. I remember a farm at harvest storing rather a large amount of corn on floor drying. It was not dried efficiently, and smelt like a brewery. Goodness knows what happened to the selling of it. Another one had an infestation of corn weevil. I could not believe it! Good job they were managed by farmer and son.

In nineteen seventy-seven, we eventually had two hundred and fifty odd acres of corn. All winter corn, except thirty six acres which was spring barley. It was so wet. I hired a contractor to put the first dressing of Nitram on by plane. We took trailer loads of Nitram onto a seventeen acre field that was on higher ground where the plane could fly off from. It worked very well, and I continued that operation through the years. They also sprayed the corn through the summer, when necessary. That was an excellent operation

162

as it was all done in a day, and like the Nitram dressing, no compression of the land. Just before I made this decision, we used to spray in the spring, and put Nitram on with cage wheels fixed to the wheels, and the year before, as the arable ground got bigger, one or two times the cage wheels could not keep above ground, and if anyone has seen a cage wheeled tractor sink six inches in the ground, they will know it does a hell of a lot of damage.

So my policy was, first Nitram dressing, all spraying through the summer, like aphids, and other cereal diseases, by plane. The second nitrogen dressing was put on in April by the lighter tractor and cage wheels. The tractor had a vari-spreader on it for spreading the fertiliser.

Now, as soon as we had sown the winter corn, we used to spray for black grass with our little sprayer, and spraying that time of year did not seem as though the killing percentage was high enough, so I was advised by my spray specialist, who was an excellent man, very practical, knew his job and never pressurised you into buying spray, which would not have impressed me if he had. His name was David Brown, and he used to inspect all the cereals and watch out for the different diseases, and on his recommendation I would have it sprayed by plane. His advice for killing black grass on our continuous corn ground was, about the first week in February, to spray it. So I got a contractor in with a low pressure vehicle to put the appropriate spray on. It did such a marvellous job, although I say nothing is quite 100%, but when looking at the crop in the summer, one could not see a piece of black grass anywhere. Only once, when the sprayer turned round on the headland, there was a vee shaped patch where it had been missed, and that little piece was like a hay field with black grass. So with those results I continued the policy in the years ahead.

What really got me going on black grass was when we ploughed a field up from perm pasture, and put winter wheat

163

in, and my goodness, one would not believe it. That summer it was full of black grass, like a hay field. I know wild oats lay dormant for years. I very often wonder if black grass does. Some years we had a few acres we had to put slug pellets on. We always put it on with the smaller tractor D.B.995 with vari-spreader, and cage wheels attached to tractor wheels, the same tractor that did all grassland fertilising, and the second Nitram dressing on the arable ground.

During this period I used to, in about June, take my employer and husband down to the lower and wetter fields to show them the wheat growing, and look up the drill lines, and it looked very well. So it ought to! The analysis of the ground was right, the spray and fertiliser was put on at the right time, and yet the water was killing the crop underneath. As we looked up the drill lines, I pointed out big patches where the wheat plants were at least a foot lower than the rest of the crop. They are the patch where the underground water was killing it, and those patches would not yield more than nine or ten cwt. to the acre. But, alas, I still could not get it over that the sooner it was drained, the better.

As I have said, we had thousands of bales of hay that were made by contractors in the different barns, and of course, all through the next year we were selling hay to several people, including the same farming people I had left to come to Coleman's Farm. I suppose in the owner's mind she thought this was good, keep selling hay like this, not knowing anything about farming. So she wanted me to produce more hay, and I let my heart rule my head, and I did just that. But after haying, there was grass everywhere, except where we were grazing cattle. I saw we could not go on like this. We had got to have more cattle to fatten. I phoned Jack Ram, the agent, and told him we have got to have more cattle or we would not last long like this, to which he replied, "If you think you can fatten the amount of cattle you want, do it, and if you have any difficulty doing so, let me know straight away." Well, I went ahead and increased the cattle, and I never heard another word about more hay, but that little episode took us financially eighteen months to get over. Of course, Mrs. Berry did not realise that.

As we got in to more corn, or cereals, whichever one wants to call it, I purchased a very long twenty-two foot, made up from an old lorry, four wheeler trailer, from a man who was advertising it. Then I went to a farm sale and purchased another four wheel trailer, not so long as the other trailer. Then I got a very nice chap to pick up and stack all straw bales with his two sons. I supplied tractor and loader, elevator, and the two four wheel trailers. The straw was baled with a Cooks handling system, which left when the lever was pulled, eight bales at a time. One came along with the Cooks clamp on the foreloader, clamped the eight bales, lifted them up and away to the trailer. A very good system. About ten to twelve thousand bales were stacked each year like this, and the rest of the straw burnt. The bales were picked up, evenings and weekends. This system was operated for the rest of the years that I was at Coleman's Farm. This system was started in nineteen seventy six. I believe at that time I paid three pence per bale.

In the year nineteen seventy-eight, I could see the water under these arable fields was killing the corn. It came to a point when it got so disheartening as well as a financial loss, that I got very adamant about the start of draining the arable fields. Well, Jack Ram came down, and the discussion with Mrs. Berry in her farm house proceeded about the start of draining. I said at the time we had got to start somewhere as we could not go on like this. So it was agreed that we started with one field, and I chose a nineteen acre field near the brooks, that was one of the wettest. It was named Committee Field, and I heard a rumour that in the second world war it was ploughed up, of course, by the War

Agriculture Committee, and it was so wet they did not do much with it. But when we acquired this field, it was rough grass and tussocks, which I ploughed up in that very dry year of nineteen seventy-six, and sowed it with winter wheat. But when first ploughing it up, it was alive with leather jackets. I had never seen so many in my life. So we spread these special leather jacket pellets with a vari-spreader, and by gosh, that sorted them out. From that field, seventy-seven harvest, we managed to get about thirty five cwt. to the acre, and seventy-eight harvest was not much better. Then on the eighteenth of October seventy-eight, the draining was finished by a very good draining firm. They put a herring bone drain system in, and where the main pipe came out, a deep ditch had to be dug out down to the main dyke, where bay boards were in operation, and it was nearly unbelievable the amount of water that came out of that pipe straight away. Then, seventy-nine harvest, the wheat yield jumped up to forty nine cwts. to the acre. Then in nineteen eighty year, it became so wet, as I have mentioned, we put Nitram on every month for cattle grazing, as we set stocked, and a fairly intensive system. We always had to have cage wheels on our tractor that spread the Nitram with a vari-spreader. Well, through the brooks where the older cattle were, some one hundred and twenty odd acres, it was so wet I had to get a contract plane to fly it on. The month was June. I expect farmers wondered what I was doing, flying fertiliser over the top of cattle's backs, but it never did them any harm, as the stocking rate was that grass had to keep growing, more like set stocking dairy cows. One must remember by July we used to grade out thirty and sometimes more, fat cattle per month. That was nearly three quarters of our cash flow.

Going back to cash flow, when I first started to manage Coleman's Farm, the only way to manage that farm other than cows, which at that time would have cost about one hundred thousand pounds or more to set up, was as many fat cattle, and as much cereals or corn as possible. That is the policy I went for especially as it was so wet, hoping we would drain the arable eventually, and cash flow wise, I looked at eight months fat cattle, and four months cereals or corn, as you would like to call it, which was achieved, and the last two years at least at the farm, ten months of cash flow was achieved from cattle. As you must remember, we were putting four hundred cattle per year through the abattoir of F.M.C.

I remember we sorted out one September fifty-eight fat cattle ready to go to F.M.C. I phoned the manage of the abattoir, told him we had fifty-eight fat cattle to go, and his reply was, "I don't care whether it is one hundred and fifty-eight fat cattle you are sending, as we can always sell your cattle." I tried to get them the right fat class - it looks as though it was achieved. We used to bring the cattle up to a coral that would hold about eighty or ninety, and those I thought were right to go, we put them through a cattle crush that held two at a time. I hardly ever felt these cattle, just did it by eye. One steer, a black Limosine x Friesian, had a small lump on the side of it, about the size of a pigeon's egg. I thought at the time, this lump could get bigger, so we put him in the crush, and I felt him just to see if he would just grade, and took a chance and sent him with the other fat cattle. I was lucky, dashed if he didn't grade Q quality, so that was very pleasing. Another thing happened with young cattle, it was May time, about two days after I purchased a batch of younger cattle to make up a bunch of fifty odd. I was coming through this field with the Land Rover, and I noticed a young steer on his own, standing beside a big barn door that was in that particular field. As soon as I went up to him, he was puffing and blowing in distress. Remember, the cattle were all steers, no heifers, and when I looked at him the other steers had been riding him, as though he was a heifer I suppose, over top the of his back tail end he was raw. But at last they had left him alone.

I got him up to the yards, straight away phoned the vet, told him what had happened and the condition of the steer. His reply was "I cannot do a thing for him. He is drowning in his own cud. Within a few hours he will be dead." Sorry to say the vet was right. The other fatality I had with an older steer was June twelfth nineteen seventy-eight, I was looking at a batch of eighty odd cattle at six-thirty in the morning. I noticed about thirty of them, in the second field that they could run into, were all in a lump with their heads pointing to the centre. When I got to them and investigated, there lay a Sussex x steer dead, it had died in the night suddenly. I got in touch with the vet, and of course, as it was a sudden death, he examined it for anthrax, but it was free, thank goodness. It was taken away and it was found it died of a twisted gut. I am told by the vet, a terrible painful death.

The vets, there were five of them in the practice at that time, were very good. I remember going one day to pick up vaccine for foul of the foot, and the vet I met that morning at the surgery was the one that was involved in horses quite a lot. As I was telling him about a particular steer, all of a sudden the phone rang. He picked it up, and I was so close I could hear it was a woman telling him about her horses. When the conversation had finished, he put the phone down, started talking to me again, then the phone rang again. I could hear the conversation was horses again. He was telling the lady he would not be there for another hour, and to carry out what he had told her to do. He put down the phone and said, "Bloody horse women!" So I said to him, bearing in mind I am six foot six inches tall and weighed about seventeen stones, I said to him, "You catch the horse lady, I will lay on top of her, and I guarantee she will not be able to move, then you can inject her instead of the horse!" That just amused him and he said, "That is just what one or two of them want Ken!"

There was also another piece of ground I had to look

after. It was about a mile up the road. The owners were a very nice couple, and although they were titled people they always insisted we called them by their Christian names. Their business was riding horses. I suppose one would call it an equestrian system, well, a few acres of grass for horses. I used to graze five or six steers on the grazing ground there. As horses are terrible grazers, they can soon ruin a pasture, especially if out wintered on the same. The rest, which amount to twenty six acres, I ploughed up for winter wheat. The analysis was got right on that land, but the water underlying the soil was a great detriment to the crop which averaged twenty six cwts. to the acre, except one nine acre field. As it was drier, it yielded fifty cwt. to the acre. Then one day, they wanted the drier field grassed down for horses, which I had to do, and plough some more of the wet ground up to make up the same acreage. It was a great disappointment to me, so we were stuck with a yield that was no more than twenty-six cwts per acre. Financially it wasn't on, until I persuaded them to drain this wet land. As soon as the draining was finished, we ploughed it up, put in spring barley, and believe it or not, the yield went up to fifty-two cwt. per acre. I knew the wet was killing the yield. Then Mrs. Berry said, "I can hardly believe that draining that land put up the yield to that figure." But it was a fact. Then, after draining the land, they sold the property and moved to the west country.

Going back to the combining at Coleman's Farm, when we first went there, as I have said, there were only forty odd acres of corn. Each field had a ten foot gate. Well, the contractor who did the haying, carting and stacking for me said he would do the combining for me. Well, I waited and waited. He made a few excuses, and the latest one was the big combine that was coming to us had a piece of concrete go up it. Well, in the end he brought another farmer, who had got a large combine. As it happened, Mrs. Berry and I were just coming from one of these small corn fields, after looking at the ripeness of the grain. This contractor and farmer came across to us, we were introduced, and the farmer said, "You would have to dig out a gate post and a piece of hedge before I could get in to combine these fields." So that was that. After they had gone, Mrs. Berry said, "How bloody ridiculous. Dig out the gate post and a piece of hedge!" so I heard of a farmer who had two small Massey combines which he did contract work with, and so we had to wait until October before the corn was cut. The result was, as the corn was over-ripe, a lot of it lay on the ground. We ended up with one ton per acre that we had to put polythene sheeting on a dirt floor under a lean-to of a Dutch barn, and auger it up into the lorries with a four inch auger. As you can imagine that wasn't a very good start to our first year at Coleman's Farm, so when I had the gateways replaced, I had fourteen foot gates put up through the middle of the farm down to the brooks, and any field I knew I would keep arable. But all other fields were replaced with twelve foot gates. We had to have these strong gates as we are talking about five different lots of cattle being set stocked. I must say it was a bit of a pain opening and shutting gates, from six o'clock each morning, but I do not think there was once that one lot of cattle got amongst the other lot. Most fields had old ten foot wooden gates, and two or three fields just had three poles across the gateway when we first came to the farm. Ah! I do remember the first few months we were there, a young bunch of cattle rubbed a pole out, and they got into the next field; happily there were no cattle in that particular field.

Well, as I have mentioned, we had contract combining with two small Massey combines. They seemed to be breaking down too frequently for my liking, so first I discussed this problem with Mrs. Berry, and worked it out to pay for a second hand twelve foot combine over a four year period. She was in complete agreement. I spoke to my old friend Harry, a rep for the agricultural firm I purchased all my machinery from. He came up with a farmer with an M132 Bamford Lavender twelve foot cut combine. He wanted to exchange it for a new one of the same make. This combine was only two years old, and had only combined five hundred and forty acres of corn. I actually made arrangements to go down and stand on the combine in the cab while the owner was combining barley. I saw a thick clump of couch grass sticking up through the barley and said to him, "Does it choke up when it gets to all that grass?" He said, "No, just look around this field and see where I have stopped." I looked and he was right, because the tell-tale of stopping with a combine is a pile of straw each time one stops. Eventually we came to this thick clump of grass, and the combine just sailed through it. I thought this is the combine for us. So I wrote to Jack Ram, the agent, and explained the cost of the combine new, which was then, in October nineteen seventy-eight, twenty two thousand pounds; I could get it second hand for thirteen thousand seven hundred pounds, and bearing in mind that contracting would go up in price per acre at least one pound, and I based it on a four year period, and that I was convinced we were losing a little more behind the combine than we ought to, amounting to another two pounds per acre, and looking at interest we would pay over a four year period, coupled with combining when one wanted to, it was a viable proposition. I was told to go ahead straight away, which I did. So we had our own combine for the nineteen seventy-nine harvest, and I am pleased to say that the combine in question proved to be excellent, and if I was farming now, and as it was so successful in its operation with a lovely air filtered cab, which is most essential, I would, if they made the same make of combine now-a-days, go for the same model.

Now, as I have said, the first arable field to be drained was Committee field, and in June nineteen seventy-nine, at last we had a scheme to drain four more fields, wet fields, but that would not proceed until autumn nineteen eighty, which proved to be a very wet year. So wet, that when we got into the Committee field that had been drained in nineteen seventy-eight, this was, of course, on the lower wet ground and everywhere the combine went on that field, the wheels sunk in about four to five inches. But it kept going, and the yield from that field, and I am talking about corn sold off it, amounted to sixty hundred weights to the acre. So even a non farming person could see the sense of draining arable on that farm. We proceeded to the adjoining field which was twenty acres. We got in there and the combine just bogged down, and that was the finish of that field. It was so heart-breaking to me. It was all winter wheat and standing up well, the variety was Flanders. It seemed to yield well on that soil and I stuck to it the last five years at Coleman's Farm. I had had Maris Widgeon and Boquets, but Flanders seemed to yield better for a two bites of the cherry variety as I called it, because, if the season was right, sometimes it went for milling. But this particular field never went anywhere, as it just stood there, eventually went down and rotted away. All one could say, I had never seen so many wood pigeons that winter ever in my lifetime.

The next field was twenty six acres wheat. We started in this field; the combine bogged down about half a dozen times, and managed to back out of it. How the double belting etc. put up with all this shunting out after being bogged down I shall never know. But it did. In the end we had to leave six acres to rot away, and pigeon feed.

The next field to it was twenty acres of wheat, and the combine had the same problems, and alas!-we had to leave six acres to rot away. If that is not heart- breaking, I do not know what is in corn growing!.

But that was not all of it. As soon as the straw was off, we could not plough it up that autumn, as a lot of it was laid wheat, and where it was free of laid wheat and straw, it was so wet we could not touch the ground with the plough. We tried a piece, and got bogged down and had to have a big caterpillar water board digger, which was near by in the next field, pull the tractor and plough out, so that was the end of that little episode

As for Committee Field, this very wet year of nineteen eighty, on 25th September, we went to get two loads of baled straw, and one must remember this field was the first field to be drained on Coleman's Farm, and we were able to combine it all and came up with the best yield of wheat we ever sold to date. These straw bales were already loaded. We went to pull them away with the two tractors, and could not move them. We had to unload several bales from each trailer onto two more empty trailers before we could move either of them. It seemed to be a wet autumn, coupled with the rest of the year being very wet, what with all the complications we encountered, one had to have nerves of steel!

In October of the same year, we were trying to plough and sow the winter corn on the higher ground of the farm. We were coming up against three quarters of an inch of rain on the 7th, then one and three quarters inches on 11th, and then on the 16th, the brooks that were joining Committee Field and the fields we had so much trouble combining, flooded again with two inches of rainfall, and that year we had to put on more slug pellets on winter corn than I had ever come across before. In September nineteen eighty-one, we did eventually plough it after two or three attempts. On 23rd September six acres were sown around outside of the field, then the wet stopped drilling. I was determined to sow that field and on 10th November we sowed the whole field with Armada wheat, put on by vari-spreader and harrowed on 11th November. Slug pellets, 14lbs per acre, were spread, and by harvest time we had a yield of 42 cwt. per acre. That was certainly better than being fallow. Even Committee field we were unable to plough, along with the adjoining sixty-six acres, making a total of sixty six acres with no crop at all. That certainly hit us that year financially, coupled with the twenty-six acres of corn ground a mile up the road, where we got bogged down three of four times with the combine.

The harvest of nineteen eighty-one, up on the higher ground, we had a thirty acre field and believe it or not, we had appear nine big pools of water, like little ponds. It was the biggest arable field we had on the farm. When we combined it all, we came with a yield of twenty-six hundred weight to the acre. It was a classical case of water ruining the whole crop. The field next to it had three or four twelve to fourteen foot wide strips right down through the field, where the wet had ruined the growth. The aggravating thing was the analysis was up to the standard it should be, and that same year all we produced was: W. barley, two point two tons per acre, and W. wheat, one point nine six tons to the acre, which was getting to breaking point.

I have in my diary on the twenty seventh of April of the nineteen eighty-one year: Drainage beach coming, so at last the situation looked more promising.

That was the top ground. In the spring of nineteen eighty-one, we put in a new main plastic water pipe, in a direct line through the neighbouring farmer's ground to the main water function along side the main road. The farmer concerned was excellent. He actually said at the time, "Why don't you come straight up through my land to the junction?" Which we did, and that was another problem solved, after the cost of high water charges, and getting a digger out to find the leak on the old line.

To go back to another subject which is NFU. I belonged to it, and on the tenth of November nineteen-eighty, I was persuaded by a local farmer to be his vice chairman at the local NFU. branch, and to my surprise, I was proposed and seconded. So I became vice chairman of the local branch.

I came across something I had never done before. There was a pond in front of the farm house, full of carp fish, and they started dying. The advice was from the experts, lack of oxygen, so get as much main tap water in the pond as possible. So there I was, standing there attending a main water hose pipe fully on. It saved the fish, so it made one feel better. That happened on twenty fourth of June nineteen eighty-one. Then on eighth of July the same year, I was taken by coach with many others to the Royal Agriculture Show, by the agriculture firm I dealt with in purchasing farm machinery and repairs. My old friend Harry; was the rep, and I got on well with the director, a very genuine chap; his name was Gordon. They also each year arranged for me to go to the Smithfield Show in Earls Court, London, and always took three or four of us out to dinner afterwards. I always remember when Gordon took us to the restaurant in London called Verrys, a lovely place and lovely food. It was in the basement. Well, as we came to the entrance of Earls Court, there were four of us; we had to be at the entrance by six pm. I jokingly said "Well, I suppose there will be a Rolls Royce waiting for us!" and to our surprise, there was a beautiful limousine waiting for us, the length of it was a car and a half! We had a good laugh about it. Well, that is how we arrived at the restaurant. Gordon's brother in law, Joe, met us there. We sat down. I was sitting beside Gordon, and as I was looking at the menu, Gordon said to me: "What are you going to have, Ken?" As the prices were pretty steep I hesitated, and he said: "I do not want you looking at the prices. I want to know what you actually want to eat." So I said, "What are you going to have?" He replied "Fillet steak." I said, "The same for me," and, by golly, that was the best fillet steak I had ever tasted, but I couldn't remember whether I had had one before, but I had certainly not eaten steak like it before. It cut like cutting through butter. After the sweet, we had coffee, and Joe said to me "What about a brandy with your coffee, Ken?" Well, I was fifty years of age at the time, and had never drunk a brandy in my life, which I told him. He said, "Try one," and I did, and I liked it - another experience in my life. Gordon treated me well, even when I was forced into setting up a small business of my own. Anything I purchased I always had a percentage off! Also, Harry used to arrange a taxi for myself and two other farmers, of course, himself as well, to go every year to the Smithfield Show in London, and always paid for us to go out to dinner before we came back. Also the taxi driver was always invited, paid by the firm of course.

Going back to the Royal Show, in nineteen seventy-four or five, I went with another firm's rep. We flew from Gatwick in a Dakota plane with about thirteen seats in it, and landed at Coventry, then we were taken to the Show ground by coach - my first experience of flying. I was quite alright landing, but when we came back to Gatwick, we were flying much higher, and came down quicker to land, and by gosh! my ear drums and my head were affected so much, I thought I was going to have a heart attack. I spoke to the pilot afterwards and told him, and he said he descended quicker from a much higher altitude, and to some people this could happen, and that he was very sorry it happened to me.

Just a note on Flanders wheat. I sold the nineteen eighty one harvest for one hundred and twelve pounds for January eighty-two collection. Seventy tons of barley at one hundred and six pounds per ton, that would be Sonja variety, which I grew for the rest of the years at Colelman's Farm as it yielded very well on that type of soil. Mr. and Mrs. Berry never interfered in the policy of the farm, but I remember Mr. Berry said to me, "Why don't you try some of these new varieties, Ken?" I remember he spoke at a ploughing

176

match dinner, and of course the farm was mentioned. At the time I had got the new metal gates up, all painted navy blue, and it was mentioned about trying new varieties of wheat and barley and, of course, the 'five star gateways' that I had put up, as he called them. One very well known farmer, after the dinner, said to me: "Now you have well and truly been told off! " Well, at the time he mentioned about sowing these new varieties of different corn, I said to him, "No, I will not try different seed, unless it has been in the commercial world for two years, then one knows how it performs on different soil." I was glad I was old enough to see some of these experiences of new seed on different types of soil, but I always got on with Mr. and Mrs. Berry very well.

In September of nineteen eighty, there was quite a lot of rain fall. In the end of September, the drainage firm, to my delight, started to drain twenty acre field on the lower ground, and that was the next driest one of three in that area. As soon as they set into it, believe it or not, it was tile draining on that field, and as the pipes were slotted in, they were immediately filled up with water, and even the drainage men remarked that they had not seen anything quite like it. Then overnight there was one and a half inches of rain fall, and that stopped the draining on that field, and they told me it had got to get drier. Also, the ground on the next farm, which was a mile up the road with about twenty six acres, the same there, most likely next year. So they moved up to a thirty acre field on the higher ground of the farm. They eventually got to the field, that is when we put all plastic piping instead of tiles, and Lytag, fine beach, over each runway of piping. Another problem came up which was that they had to pull the lorry loads of Lytag with their big caterpillar drainer to get it to that particular field. They managed to finish draining the field on the fifteenth of October. This particular field was the same one that, during the winter, there appeared eight or nine pools of water in different parts of the field. The consequences showed up on yield that year - twenty six cwt. to the acre - disaster financially!

It was also so wet in eighty-one we could not lift our three rows of potatoes until 9th November. Also, by this time, I had stopped buying store lambs for fattening, and put that small amount of ground in to spring barley for the remainder of the time I was at Coleman's Farm. The amount of barley after the ground was drained jumped up ten cwt. to the acre on that ground after the 30 acre field was drained. The drainers came out of there after finishing the job on the seventh of September, nineteen eighty-one.

Going back to draining on the lower ground, the drainage firm started draining the driest field on the lower ground, and finished it on 11th August, nineteen eighty -one. We ploughed on fifth September, but never sowed until 15th November, and came so wet, we had to sow it with a vari spreader and harrow it in, the variety was Armada, the other seed other than Flanders. We managed, after having to spread it by vari spreader, selling two and a half tons per acre.

By August, nineteen eighty-two, there had been two hundred and twenty acres drained of arable, the best thing that ever happened on the farm for the future, and yields after that soon showed that, as I was always convinced, it was right thing to do.

I remember the thirty acre field that I mentioned had nine pools of water in it in different parts of the field, and only yielded twenty six hundred weights to the acre. After being drained, and before being mole ploughed, it yielded forty-two hundred weight to the acre. The whole of the arable, I got a contractor to mole plough them, in September of eight-two. Eighty three harvest with Flanders wheat, this particular field it sold fifty-two cwts per acre, and in eighty-four harvest, after all the manure from the cattle yards, which amounted to about nine hundred tons, were spread. It was sown to Sonja barley, and it came up with a yield higher than I had grown anywhere, and we were able to sell seventy cwts to the acre. Then the harvest of Flanders wheat was put in, and a yield of sixty-two cwts was sold per acre. It was a crying shame that the owners could not see the great advantages that draining the arable would bring. Then there was the factor that when, the draining did start, the weather seemed to be against us during the next year to hold up operations. I suppose, when I look back at the situation, it was like bolting the stable door after the horse had gone. My dear mother would say, "Ah, it was not to be my boy!"

The thing I did like in the winter months was shooting. As I have said, my old friend Harry used to come on Saturday afternoons, on a rough shoot round the farm. Sometimes, Mr. Berry used to join us, also he used to invite me to a duck shoot. It got my mind off every day farming and I enjoyed it. I used to shoot with a twenty bore side by side shot gun, and when I was employed by Mr. Barnham, and was invited to the shoot, different shooters used to say to me on the day ,"What do you shoot with, Ken?" "It is a pop gun against your twelve bores, but I will tell you, if one holds and swings this gun how it should be aimed, it will kill anything as far off as any of your twelve bore guns." Which was quite true.

While I was at Coleman's Farm, about December time, I saw about forty teal settle down into a pond, which was in the centre of a twenty acre corn field, but the trouble was, there was no cover. So I crept across this field, crouching all the time, which was quite difficult for me as I am so tall. They all got into flight as I got about forty yards away from them, and by gosh, they are fast in flight, and to my surprise I shot one each barrel. It was an experience in my life I have never done before or since. It seemed at that moment I was as quick as my father used to be with his shooting. It was the same as in January, eighty-one. I went down to the twenty acre field with all the laid and spoiling wheat after some of these pigeons. They started coming in, and I shot seven, one after the other, and also a left and a right. After that I slowed up and started missing them.

It brings to mind a gentleman I knew. He was an excellent shot, and we were talking about slowing up in shooting. He used to go to big pheasant shoots in the north of England, and one winter when he went to this shoot, it was so cold he put on two extra pullovers. He stood at his stand; the birds started to come over and he kept missing them. He told me he might just as well have had a stick. Then he thought about it, and came to the conclusion that with these two extra pullovers on, he was slowing up on his swing, and so he quickened his swing, and down they came. He was a man like my father - when shooting, if the object was in range, they seemed hardly ever to miss. It was very entertaining to watch.

As I have said before, new buildings went up at Coleman's Farm. They were designed by Nigel Braden, and that is how I met his father, Peter Braden, who was farm manager on an estate about four miles away. Peter and Nigel came with owner's son to look at the raised passage cattle building we had put up, and which was designed by Nigel Braden. Evidently the owner's son liked what he saw, as they had the same design put up for cattle, only about twice as long, although ours was one hundred and twenty feet long, to hold one hundred and twenty cattle. Peter became my friend from that day, and that was twenty two years ago, and he has been what I call 'a real friend.' He proved he will help me any way he can over the years.

I have mentioned I was made vice chairman of the local NFU. branch. Well, after the year was up, I was made chairman, so I approached a young farmer only about three miles from where I farmed. His name was John Wade, he being the oldest son of Mr. Wade, the British Friesian Society selector, whom I met on my previous job. He was voted in, and in February or March of the following year, at our monthly meeting, the secretary came up with an item for someone to go from the branch to report on the NFU. A.G.M. in London. I was looking at the members, and thought, "I wonder who will go?," and all of a sudden a farmer got up and said, "I proposed Ken Mewett" and another one said "I second that." Well, I nearly fell off the chair in amazement, and there they were, all looking at me for my answer - yes or no? At that moment it shot through my mind what my old friend said to me one day. It was Peter Braden. He was eleven years older than me, "Ken," he said, "if you ever have a chance to go to Kensington Hall or Agriculture House, go!" I thought afterwards, what have I let myself in for! Well, when I went to the next executive meeting, the head secretary said to me: "Ken, I hear you are going to report on the A.G.M. in London. Now, when you do bring back that report we don't want about three quarters of an hour speech you know!" I said to him, "Six seconds flat, my boy." He did laugh - that amused him.

Then the time came. I went up with a farmer who was on the executive team; a local farmer, Bob Parks. I had to be up at his farm by 5.30 am. and he took me to the station. We caught the train to London, and it worked very well as the next day there was a train strike, so we went by coach. Whilst at the A.G.M. I was sitting in the Hall marking down the points I though were most important. I had never done this sort of thing before or been a chairman for that matter, but a farmer came to me and said: "Come and have a coffee in the foyer." Which I did. While I was there a well known farmer from Kent, who had been in the NFU. for twenty five years, said: "Stay and have a talk." I said, "No jolly fear. I came here to do a job and that is to report on this A.G.M." So back I went and got on with the job. The extraordinary part was, as I was chairman of the local NFU.

branch, Mr. Jack Barnham, whom I had worked for five years in my farming career, he was the County Chairman, and on the last day, Bob Parks and I were just going, and along came Jack Barnham. I can see him now - he looked quite worried. He cocked one eye brow up, which he generally did in these situations, and said to Bob Parks "You will help Ken won't you, Bob?" to which Bob replied, "I don't think Ken is going to want any help. He will be alright."

Well, when I perused what I had noted next evening, I got it down, the speech I was going to make, and my son Nicholas, had a radio cassette, with a little speaker on it so that one could record one's voice. He said I could borrow it. Well, I spoke into it, and emphasised very strongly different parts of the speech, and when I played it back, I said, "Well, that's not me talking," it sounded so different, but my wife and Nicholas said "It jolly well is," and of course it was. Then came the day I had to present it to the executive. I was listening to all the different items that are a matter of form, then Jack Barnham, the chairman, said: "Now, Ken Mewett is going to report on the A.G.M. that took place in London." Well, now you first think about it, I had never done anything like this before, and the place was filled with chairmen and vice chairmen from East Sussex and Kent, also a well known MP. was always present at the monthly meetings, which I had forgotten all about. I must say I was just a little apprehensive, as I remembered I had got this speech down to eight and a half minutes, and emphasised it just how I had put it on tape. As I have said, I wrote the most, I thought, important points of that meeting, and delivered it. Well, I can hardly believe it now, the ovation I got. I wondered for a few seconds what was going on, so I must have done something right. Even as I went out to the car park to be driven home with the vice chairman of our branch, John Wade and his brother David, all of a sudden a chap was making a hell of a noise with his motor horn. I looked round, and there was a well known farmer honking his horn, and putting his thumbs up. I had a job to believe this, but I must say it was gratifying, especially as I had never made a report on the A.G.M. of the NFU. in London before, or any other organisation for that matter. About a week or two after I had presented my report on the London A.G.M., all NFU. chairmen and vice chairmen had to meet at a village hall, about fifteen or sixteen miles away from where I lived. We were gathering in the hall, and having coffee, when in walked the local MP. I went up to him and said, "Hello, Geoffrey." He shook hands and then said "Congratulations on your report of the A.G.M. in London. You delivered it well, and in the right amount of time!" Well, I can tell you now, I felt twenty foot high instead of six foot six. I had forgotten that he would be there every time the executive met.

Within a months time, my local NFU. branch had a request from a church organisation in Brighton for someone to speak on farming, so as I was the chairman of the branch, I said I would go. Then there were two other farmers said they would be on the panel with me. So the evening came for us to be there. I arrived and was introduced to the chairwoman. Of course, as I always am, I was fifteen minutes earlier than the appointment. Well, I suppose we waited for over half an hour, and these two farmers that should have been on the panel with me, never arrived. So the chairwoman said to me, "Shall we have to cancel the meeting?" and I looked at the large amount of people that were there, and said, "No. I came to do a job and I will proceed as planned." With which she said, "Thank you," then asked me if I knew about elm disease, to which I replied "Not a lot," so she said "Would you mind a gentleman who knows a lot about elms disease sitting on the panel with you?" To which I replied, "It would be a pleasure." So that was how we started the evening. Well, as we proceeded, very few questions were put to the

183

elms disease gentleman. They seemed to be directed to me. The questions that were put to me were as follows, but I cannot remember in which order: one was, why do farmers spray the cereals as they do? I thought, by golly, how am I going to answer this, but I looked at the audience and said: "Hands up all the people who have roses in their back or front gardens and the roses do not have black spot, mildew or green fly," and I can tell you now, there was not one hand went up, and the place went so quiet one could have heard a pin drop. Then I said, farmers only spray if there is a disease on the cereals, because if they did not, the yield could drop fifteen or twenty cwts per acre, and the cost of growing one acre of cereal today, it would be pretty disastrous and in the end they would go bust.

Another question was asked about cutting hedges: why are they cut every year? I said, if they were allowed to grow each year, they would end up in growing twenty feet high and ten or twelve feet wide, the height would be cutting out a certain amount of light and air from the crops that were being grown. I can tell you, when combining, the first fourteen or fifteen feet would be so wet, one could not cut it until midday, also, as it lays much wetter, the grain itself deteriorates. As for the width of the hedges, so much ground is lost, as well as harbouring rabbits, and haying is worse than combining round these areas. As for the road hedges, if one did not keep those trimmed properly, the County Council would be after the farmer to get them cut, and if they are not cut, they will get them cut and charge you for the privilege, and a very important issue, the country side would not look like it does today, not nearly as tidy. The general public would soon cry out if it was not kept so.

I can remember before the second world war, seeing hedges very tall and wide, like I have explained, and my goodness, it certainly looked rough. The reason for most of it was, after the first world war, there were no guaranteed prices, as there were after the second world war, and prices dropped dramatically as the government of the day only thought about imports, and therefore things just deteriorated. Even some fields that werc arable in the fourteen eighteen war, through compulsion, just fell down to rubbish and wild grass as there wasn't the money available to afford to sow them down to grass, and several farmers went broke before the second world war started. Those that could hang on long enough into the second world war were made, and the recovery continued after this war, as Tom Williams from the Labour government brought out a scheme of guaranteed prices for farmers, including grants for new buildings to be put up where necessary, as between the wars a large numbers of farm buildings were falling down or in great disrepair. That is why the country side looks so tidy and shipshape today.

It was a great false economy letting farming get into a disastrous state, as when the second world war came, there had to be a subsidy for liming the ground, as the land took thousands upon thousands of tons of lime to bring the land up to the right P.H., as well as about the same amount of phosphate, in the form of slag in those days, for the purpose of getting the full potential for growing arable crops and grass production. I think there are very few people that realise how close to starvation we became, as, being an island, it became easier to make things very difficult for us all.

Another question was, why are we in the Common Market. Cannot we be on our own as we were before? My answer was, after the person had asked why not sell our products to the eastern countries like Egypt, etc.: "How long would it last? Three or five years? Then what? This is just one product. A very large amount of milk is exported to that country, but even now the amount is declining, as they are importing large herds of dairy cows and dairy

185

managers as well, so they produce their own milk. This can no doubt happen to other commodities. Then, what would happen to the sale of products, and not only in farming in this country?"

Another question I was sure would come up was straw burning at the time, and it did. My answer was, if all farmers carried out the NFU. code for straw burning, there would be nothing like the trouble there is today. When looking at the situation as a whole, the trouble is there are rebels in all walks of life. As it was mostly a church community I was speaking to, there was a vicar sitting in front listening. As soon as I mentioned about the rebels in all walks of life, he looked at me and said, "Yes, and I have got some of them!" That certainly brought a large amount of laughter, but it certainly finished the question again.

That was some of the questions I was asked, but of course there were many more, and I found I could answer them, and I was enjoying myself so much, I could have stayed there until twelve o'clock at night!

Then, came the time, to end being NFU. chairman of the local branch. Just before that happened, there was a dinner held at an hotel, where we held our monthly meetings. As I was ending my chairmanship, my wife thought she had better come with me on this occasion. Well, after dinner, of course, I had to make a speech. Well, as usual we all raised glasses to the Queen etc., then I got up and said, "Well, gentlemen, we must not forget the ladies who are behind us in our work. They have to put up with quite a lot from us, you know." The men all started looking at me, as much as to say, My God, what is he going to say now!

Going back to myself, I remember in the spring and summer when all the steers were grazing, one batch of about thirty of these steers down in the brooks, swam through the dyke, which was pretty deep, into a lot of dairy heifers, which were the next door farmer's. We went down there and had to walk the opposite side of the dyke, about one hundred and fifty yards to the field they were in. The only thing we could do was drive them through the dyke again, back to where they came from. It took a bit of a time to get them back, but we succeeded. It was pretty exhausting work. We walked back to get to our side through a small gate. I looked back, and I'm dashed if there wasn't a steer had got back over into the heifers again. I reckon he was the trouble in the first place. So we walked all the way back again, eventually got him through the dyke, and I said: "Right, we will take him back half way up the farm," which was about three quarters of a mile away, and we managed to do that. We managed to get home about, well, just after twelve o'clock, which was our lunch time. Well, I sat down to my lunch and Pat, my wife, said something, I forget what, and I just blew up over nothing at all. It was very rare for me to do that, thank goodness, but I had done it, and I was very sorry afterwards. I looked at all the gentlemen there, and said: "Of course, you do not do anything like that I suppose!" and they all started grinning, with a chuckle or two, then my next comment was: "Gentlemen, raise your glasses to the ladies for all they have done." Afterwards the secretary called me over, and said: "That was the best after dinner speech I have heard." So I was glad it went down well.

When my wife and I got home and we were undressing for bed, she turned to me and said, "I do not know how you do it." I said, "Do what?" and she said, "To speak like that." I said, "It seemed to come in my mind what happened the year before, and I was pretty sure that some of those chaps had done the same thing, and it was right to raise their glasses to you ladies."

Then came the time, the year after I had finished my period with the NFU. chairmanship. I was asked to speak on farming to eleven and twelve year old boys and girls at a nearby market town school, which I accepted. I had never done

187

this sort of thing before. When I look back on my life, and as I was rather shy of anything of this nature until the last few years of my farming life, I can hardy believe the things I got involved in, and especially as I was much slower at school than my dear sister. But as I have mentioned before, it was determination and dedication - the very important two words in life.

Well, I arrived at the school on this particular day, and was greeted very nicely by the form teacher, There were three of us there to speak on our different subjects. The first one was a chief librarian. I was the second in line, then there was a social worker. As far as I can remember we had about twenty minutes to speak. The chief librarian spoke very well, then came my time to speak, and when I thought of the time of twenty minutes, I though by gosh, that's a long time. Anyhow, I said to the form teacher "How do you want me to project this farming scene?" and she said, "Well, go from January to December," which I did, and to my surprise I went over the time I was allotted. Then we went for coffee. Also at that time I went and apologised to the social worker for going over my time, but he said "Not at all, it was most interesting." I must say, regarding his talk, being a social worker, my goodness that certainly opened one's eyes to the problems they have.

After coffee we went back to the classroom, ready to be bombarded with questions, and I must say, they were intelligent questions from eleven and twelve year old's, and I seemed to have more questions put to me than either of the other two. I cannot remember all the questions put to me, maybe a few odd ones. One was, do you think it is right to hunt foxes?, to which I replied: "You are thinking about the recent ban of fox hunting on all the council owned land. The first thing I think is, if it were banned completely there would be a large amount of unemployment, as well as a large number of horses and hounds would have to be put down. Also, what about the sheep farmers and chicken farmers? I am old enough with experience of both kinds of farming. Foxes do like newly born, or three day old lambs, and if they get into a flock of chickens, they just don't kill one or two, they kill and maim a heck of a lot of other poor chickens. Now, there is no doubt in my mind they have got to be kept down to a reasonable proportion. Fox hunting kills a very small percentage, but there are no doubt several caught by wires, and some poisoned, and a few shot. If fox hunting was to be banned, there would be organised shoots immediately on a big scale where these foxes were getting out of hand, and believe me, on these shoots, there will be people shooting at too long range. The fox is injured, goes away and takes three or four days to die. If that isn't cruel, I do not know what is."

I received lovely letters of thanks from these eleven and twelve year old's. I was delighted they took such an interest in the farming scene.

I was also asked could I tell them a funny experience I had in my farming life. One came to mind, but I thought it was not suitable for this age of pupils, so I looked at the school mistress and hesitated, and said, "I will come back to that if I may." I did come back to that and told them another funny experience. The one I was going to tell them was the time Reg, the tractor driver, came through the field where we had not long put the rams into the flock of ewes. He actually saw a ram go to mount a ewe. As soon as the ram got up to the ewe she moved forward and, of course, the end result was the ram slipped off her without penetrating. This happened three or four times. Reg just had to stay to see what happened. Well, eventually the ram got so fed up with this, he backed away from the ewe, put his head down and bunted her up the backside, and lifted the poor ewe's back legs off the ground. He just could not help laughing as it looked so funny.

I suppose when I think of it now, in this day and age, that age of pupil, if I had told them that, I suppose it would be like water running off a duck's back.

It was about February or March of nineteen eighty-three that a group of farmers, mostly those that had given up dairy farming, came to look at our silage, and the steers in the yard. Afterwards, they took me up to the local pub to lunch. These farmers belonged to the Grassland society, as did myself. While we were having lunch, the secretary of this group turned to me and said, "Ken, we are setting up a beef and sheep group, and we want you to be the chairman." Well, I nearly choked on my food, it was such a surprise. I dithered a bit, but then I agreed to do the job for one year, but in the end I took it on for two years.

It was extraordinary how farmers refused for us to see their farms. My right hand man, who was an I.C.I. rep, and a very nice chap, helped me enormously. We went to a farm once a month through the winter months. When a farmer was approached, the excuse was, we are not good enough, but of course, we persuaded some in the end. We always took the host or hostess out to lunch afterwards, booking ahead of course. We had several farmers attend our meetings, mostly smaller farmers. I was lucky I knew the sheep and beef as well as the dairy enterprises very well. So, happily, I knew hopefully what I was talking about, but in the course of these farm walks and discussions, I made different jokes along the way, as to look at some of these farmers, they certainly looked as though they wanted some cheering up. I remember going to a large scale farming enterprise. It was very well farmed. We took the host to lunch afterwards. This particular time there were quite a few of us for lunch, including ladies. Well, we were all seated for this lunch, and waiting in turn. As soon as I was presented with mine, I straight away put quite a lot of salt on my lunch. As soon as they saw what I was doing they shouted out: "Hey, Ken, you must not put on salt like that, it is very bad for you." Immediately my answer was: "Ah, ladies and gentlemen. These things taken in moderation are quite alright, even love!" That certainly brought on a few chuckles and laughs, especially from the ladies. Thank goodness it always seemed to go off pretty well, and I always enjoyed it. I know the first meeting I took on, I thought, my goodness, as soon as all our group members have arrived, I have got to introduce the host and hostess, and explain a bit about how their farm was being run. I was rather apprehensive at the time, but I seemed to cope pretty well, and after that first endeavour, it all came easier from then on.

Now back to Coleman's Farm, I remember I was walking down through a small field with Mrs. Berry and her dogs. This field was adjacent to the farm house, and while walking down to the end of the fields, in the course of conversation, bearing in mind her eldest daughter married a major in the army, and was posted in Ireland – I do not know the details, but they eventually got him out of the army and, of course, he had to find a job – Mrs. Berry turned to me and said, "You know, Ken, my son-in-law has got to find a job, and being a major in the army nowadays does not mean anything." I replied, "I know it does not." "Do you know, Ken, these majors have everything done for them, and I think when they get a civilian jobs they will find a great difference." And with that she said, "He has not got much up top, Ken." I could not believe what she was saying, then she went on to say, "That Captain Mark Phillips, he has not got much up top you know, but, by gosh, he can bloody well ride a horse.!"

Then in February, nineteen eighty-one, I had a phone call from Jack Ram, telling me that the titled gentleman had been in the office representing his wife and mother-in-law, who were partners in Coleman's Farm, and he wanted Jack Ram to go into the whole business of Coleman's Farm, as he was

191

told by his young friend who worked for the same agents that he thought that a better financial return should be coming from a farm of six hundred acres. Jack Ram said, "As I have been instructed to look at the whole business of Coleman's Farm, I shall have to do it.." I said, "Of course, you must, but I will tell you in respect of the gentleman who put the instructions forward, Jack, put your index finger round to your thumb, making an O. That is about as much as he knows about farming." And, of course, the net farmable acreage was five hundred and seventy two acres.

Well, gross margins, variable costs, etc., were all gone into. The fat cattle side came up with:

Average number of throughput of cattle during the year - 407.

Gross margin per acre - £125.

Gross margin/head, before farage costs - £115.

These figures are very exceptional considering that the accepted national average was approximately £50 per acre.

The success of the enterprise can be put down to the following factors:

1. excellent animal and grassland husbandry
2. first class fattening land ideally suited to big cattle
3. good marketing.

The local Senior Agriculture Advisor's opinion.

Mr. Mewett is one of the finest managers of beef cattle he knows, and as I have always said, there is no liquidity of capital invested in machinery, and I always reckoned to have £50,000 worth of cattle in the yards by the end of the financial year, which was, of course, liquidity.

The sheep that we had into keep gave us a gross margin of £3.75 per acre.

Recommendations:

1. the proposed drainage programme is carried out as soon as possible, this increasing the arable acreage to some 300 acres

2. An additional 100 acres is not added to the arable enterprise

3. The beef enterprise is continued under the present management policy

4. The wetter grassland around the farmstead could be improved by drainage in future if surplus capital was available.

A very good point was made on the corn side - that the price of corn is 50% more in Europe than on the World Market and it cannot be expected that European prices will be subsidised to the same extent in the future if industrial business conditions worsen in the EEC.

With the future price of corn uncertain, and an annual increase of costs up to 15% more, pressure is being put on arable farmers to increase their yields in order to maintain their profit margins.

To justify the addition of 100 acres to the arable enterprise, guaranteed yields of over 2.75 tons/acre would be required to meet the additional costs. Moreover, the capital required for the essential additional machinery would be invested in depreciating assets, whereas investment in fat cattle is appreciating and also liquid.

The partnership even went as far as, in February, nineteen eighty-one, instructing Jack Ram to stop me buying store cattle to replenish the fattening yard. I remember I went with my son to one of the biggest store cattle sales in the area. My son was on vacation, and into photography at that time, so he brought his camera. I remember him taking a photo of a Hereford bull in a pen. As we walked away down between the pens, there was Jack Ram coming up to meet us. We exchanged greetings, and Jack said, "I phoned you this morning, but you had already gone, to tell you the partnership doesn't want you to buy any more cattle at the moment." It was very upsetting at the time, and it shot through my mind - where does the partnership think the cash flow is coming from, as we did not have a dairy herd? Of course, when the summary of the whole farm business was sent to the partners, the policy was carried on as usual.

Going back to cattle, I suppose some farmers would think the minerals I used for cattle, which cost £1,000 per year, was a bit over the top. One must remember there were one hundred and thirty cattle all the time in the yards, as I replaced the fat cattle we sold each month with store cattle, and we are talking about a five month period in yards. As I said before, they had as much silage as possible, no concentrates what so ever, and the system worked so well that we were able to fatten half the cattle before they went out on grass.

Some of these cattle were pretty good in condition when turned out, and the great thing I noticed was, as they were just fed on silage and minerals, when turned out, they did not lose weight, unlike cattle fed on a lot of concentrates whilst in the yards; they seemed to melt away.

To prove my point within five or six weeks of being turned out, we used to pick out a lorry load of sixteen fat cattle.

While I am on cattle, on the fifth of April nineteen eighty-four, I went to look at eighteen and twenty month old steers at Knotlands Farm, farmed by Mr. Barnham, the gentleman I previously worked for, for five years.

I was met there by Jack Drummond, a very experienced stockman, who had the authority to sell these cattle. They were Simmital, Limosin, Sussex and Hereford cross Friesian breed not Holsteen. I purchased fifty four of these steers, which were fed on just silage for £370 per head. I thought it was a fair price to pay, and of course I knew they were not fed concentrates. It was quite an experience going to that farm, after fourteen years away. It brought back many memories. One important memory was of a certain field on that same farm, where I met Jack Barnham and asked him for a reference and told him I was leaving their employment.

194

As for marketing the fat cattle, they all went to F.M.C. abattoirs. I had a contract for three hundred, but managed to grade four hundred through F.M.C., for which I was paid five pounds per head bonus for the whole four hundred steers.

Well, I remember the local market rep phoned me one day to see if he could come to look at the steers in the yard. I made arrangements for him to come, and whilst looking at the steers, some were nearing to be graded, he turned to me and said, "Well, Ken, these would sell very well." To which I replied: "I expect they would, some of them, but we are talking about at least twenty-four to thirty-odd a month, all on a particular day, and I have been to these fat stock markets and have seen what goes on, and I have heard one butcher saying to another, 'If you don't bid for the four or five cattle I want, I won't bid for the ones you want', and besides, are you going to give me a five pound bonus for each fat steer I put through?" And the answer I got was: "Well, Ken, there are hidden costs behind all that, you know."

So I soon knew where I stood, and said to the rep, "I will stick to F.M.C. for I do know what cattle grades are at A.A.A. and Q.s and get paid accordingly," and I may add we certainly graded out quite a lot of quality fat cattle.

Of course, as I have mentioned before, we had a casualty or two. I remember on sixteenth of June, nineteen eighty-four, I was looking at the older cattle down in the brooks, early one morning, and there lay one dead. I called the vet. He examined this steer, and remarked: "Look at the blue colour around the nose, mouth and tongue," and he diagnosed poisoned by a snake bite; the first animal I had ever known in my career dying from a snake bite.

We were lucky, for the five hundred steers we grazed and yarded through the year, our mortality rate was around two steers per year.

On twentieth July, nineteen eighty-four, my wife, self and son started our ten day holiday in the Devon area. At the same time, on Saturday, twenty first, we went to Peggy and Neville Parkinson's wedding, Peggy being my wife Pat's school friend, also our maid of honour at our wedding. All went off very well, and we had a nice time the rest of the holiday, and came back on Saturday, twenty -eighth. I must mention about golf. I could not play this game very often, work came first, but on thirtieth July, nineteen eighty-four, my son and I played golf at Seaford Head golf course. It was on that day I, at last, broke the score of one hundred, and had a round of ninety-six, so one can imagine I was very pleased with myself.

On twentieth of August, nineteen eighty-four, our Laverda combine broke down, bottom feed roller broke, but was lucky enough to get a replacement from our local agriculture engineers. It was while we were fitting this part to the combine that Mr. Berry came along to us, and said to me, "Jane wants to see you," meaning my employer, Mrs. Berry, so I replied, "Nine-thirty tomorrow morning."

So the following morning, the twenty-first, I was in the farmhouse at 9.30 am. sharp. Our, greetings were: "Good morning, Mrs. Berry," "Good morning, Ken," then Mrs. Berry said, "Sit down, Ken." I instantly thought 'this is unusual' so I sat down, and Mrs. Berry hovered about, and seemed to have a job to say what she had got to tell me. It was a good job I was sitting down, or else I would have nearly fallen down, for the news she broke to me was - I was 57 years old at the time - "well," she said, "I have got to sell the farm, nothing to do with the farming business. I was advised by two solicitors to put a certain amount of money abroad to save income tax, as I was left a very large property in London by my father, and it made more money when sold than we realised. That is how I purchased Colelman's Farm, and the tax man caught up with me, and the amount of money I have got to pay them is so large I am

196

forced to sell the whole estate. I'll tell you, Ken, I could murder those bloody solicitors. The farm will be sold by the end of next year, and I want you to keep it confidential, we don't want to leave here, but we are forced to do so."

Well, this was the biggest shock of my farming career! It was so upsetting, I had to get out of that farmhouse as quickly as possible, as I was on the verge of breaking down. Where would a farm manager of 57 years old be employed as a farm manager on another farm? I was too old, so I said I would stay on, and keep the farm in the same condition it is now to sell it. I was sworn to confidentiality, which became difficult until about May nineteen eighty-five, when at last it was made official.

I remember in nineteen eight five, spring, a helicopter flew very low around the farm buildings, photographing, and of course the farm staff wanted to know what was going on, so I said I would find out. I went to Mrs. Berry, and told her the situation, and she said: "Tell them that some paper has permission to photograph the whole farm" and, of course, I had to tell them that, which was a lie. I hated it!

Then, when the spring came of nineteen eighty-five, I did not purchase any cattle for the one hundred and twenty acres of brooks. It was let out for twenty five pounds per acre for a farmer's big cattle, and I had to look at them every morning, and one of those died, so that is the kind of thing one does come across with livestock.

Mrs. Berry said: "Put an advert in the Farmers' Weekly, and I will pay for it." I did just that, and never got a reply. She did warn me, "Do not put your age." I still did not get reimbursed for this advert.

Then one day she said to me, "Of course, Ken, I will give you five thousand pounds when the farm is sold, and if it makes one million pounds, I shall give you more." I thought at the time, I don't think it will make as much as that, but it got to near it - nine hundred thousand odd pounds.

I thought at the time, five thousand pounds wasn't much for lifting the farm up to its present state in eleven years of management. I controlled the actual farm business. I had no interference at all. I knew nothing about money being put abroad.

I wish I had known that money was available, I would have pushed a lot harder to get the arable fields drained. I see by my records that on twenty-fourth of September nineteen eighty-four, I sold to John Stokoe winter wheat:

120 tonnes of Armada for November 108
150 tonnes of Flanders for December   114
150 tonnes of Flanders for January 1985   116
80 tonnes of Flanders for February 1985   118
the Flanders 12.5 protein, Armada 11.5 protein.

It was in October nineteen eighty-four I had a fifty acre field down in the brooks para plough it was a field that did not flood. Also, two small arable fields that had not been drained. I think it did quite a bit of good.

Going back to the sales of corn of eighty-four harvest, after all the arable fields had been drained except the drier two, five and seven acre fields.

The amount of corn sold was seven hundred and fifty six tonnes, something different to the yield we got overall, before the drainage was done.

I remember going to the local bank to collect money for wages, and it was the time I heard there was a new bank manager. About eighteen months had gone by and I had never met him. Well, that particular day I was drawing the wage money. There was a biggish office behind the cashier counter, and a very well dressed gentleman walked in the office to have a word with an employee. I looked at him and said, "Good morning," and he acknowledged me, and then I said, "Are you the new manager?" To which he replied. "Yes, I am," and with that, he went through his office and came out to where I was standing, and introduced himself, Geoff

198

Badle, and said he had been here for eighteen months. He then said he understood from another farmer that we had done a lot of draining at Coleman's Farm, and that he was interested to see it. I said he was quite welcome to come and with that I said "Come to coffee one morning." "I'd like that," he said, and I said, "Then after coffee I will take you to look at the wettest ground we have drained," and he replied, "Then I will take you out to lunch."

After coffee, I took him to this very wet land we had drained, the same land where we had to leave corn as it was impossible to combine. It was at the time when the plants were about four to five inches high, and looking very well. I showed him where we had to double drain in the very wet patches, which meant the drains being eleven yards apart instead of twenty two yards apart. It made such a difference that the corn was lovely and even all over the field. It was very remarkable the difference this made. Geoff was very impressed. Then we went to lunch, and that is how I first met Geoff Badle.

Now, my next door neighbours on either side of Coleman's Farm, on the east side was Tony Ruskin, and on the west side was Fred Ruskin and his son, Richard. Tony and Richard were cousins and I got on with them very well

Now, when I first went to Coleman's Farm, after a few months, I came out of our farm entrance, went along a by-road towards the main road, and I came across Fred Ruskin and his son moving five or six of their single sucklers and calves across to some ground they had on the other side of this particular road. So I stopped until they had got them safely shut into the field, then drew up towards them and said to Fred Ruskin: "Good morning, Mr. Ruskin." I had my Land Rover window slid along so that I could speak to them clearly. With that, Fred came over to me and stuck his head half through my open Land Rover window and said, "I am Fred. Mr. Ruskin is along the road," and he was referring to his brother Charles, who was Tony's father and he was getting on towards ninety years of age. Fred, himself, was getting on for eighty, so from then on, I always addressed him as Fred.

When our draining was done on our arable fields, and the plant count was very good and at harvest, corn yield was coming off the fields as I expected it would do, well, it was in fact a lovely sight to see, the evenness of the whole crop across the fields where the very patches that were being killed by water, the growth was so good, one had a job to visualise the state of it before it was drained. It made me feel that getting the analysis up to scratch on the farm was not in vain. I continued to have the fields lime tested every year right from the start. As I had to move to a different farm four times to achieve my ambition, the first thing getting the lime right, then the phosphate up to the level for that particular land, and it paid off.

One day I was passing the lane that led down to Fred and Richard Ruskin's farm, and at the top there was a large board advertising the same land drainage firm that we had employed to do our drainage at Coleman's Farm. So when I saw Richard Ruskin, I said to him "Hey Richard, what is all this then!" He looked at me and said "What is what?" "Well, I see you have the drainage boys in, how come?" His reply was: "Well, I have been looking over the hedge into your fields, and the transformation to the crops is nearly unbelievable, and I thought, well, we have got to have some of this, as it is the same type of ground, that is the reason the drainers are in." So I said to him, "Richard, this drainage you are having done will be the best thing achieved in your young farming life on this particular farm."

Richard Ruskin's father died a few years ago. He was nearly ninety years of age. Richard has a young son and daughter, and the son will no doubt take over from his father one day and, of course, this drainage will be a great advantage to him in the years to come, especially if he mole drains these fields every two or three years.

Then in nineteen eighty-five, the fateful day of leaving Coleman's Farm before I was sixty five came ever closer. When I mention sixty-five, it was the first employment where there was a pension paid in for me, but, of course, the money paid into the pension was always mentioned when the annual wage increase came into operation, and if I could have stayed to retirement age it would have been a fair pension, something different from what I ended up with after being made redundant. No one wanted to know about making my pension a better deal for me, and so I ended up with a pension twenty three pounds per week when I became sixty-five, and of course that was very little.

Then there was the situation where I had to keep the selling of the farm confidential and, therefore, could not approach the local council. I suppose I was too trusting for my own good.

The local senior Agriculture Advisor suggested to me: "Why not get into buying and selling livestock, you have experience of sheep, dairy cows and beef cattle?" He said, "Get a lorry and convey livestock as well." It all sounded OK, but I had not got the money to buy a lorry and, of course, one had to have a place to live, also five to ten acres of pasture attached to it ideally. The reason for having five to ten acres of pasture near by was one could buy a few sheep or cattle and hold them, if necessary, to sell at a later date.

I just did not have the money to do this.

One day, Mrs. Berry said to me, "Ken, I am so worried about you," when she knew that I was going to rent a cottage and start a business buying fat cattle for an abattoir, and also buying sheep and other livestock for private customers. She said, "Why don't you get a part time job, as who is going to give you two or three pounds a head for buying dairy and beef cattle?" Mrs. Berry certainly did not say, "I am so worried about you, I will help you financially to start your business," as it was no fault of mine the whole estate had to be sold.

At that time there was help for the first year for a small business from the government of forty pounds per week. Well, Mrs. Berry signed that for me. As far as I can remember I had to go on the dole for six weeks. That is a thing I had never done in my life. In nineteen eighty five, my last year at Coleman's Farm, I still managed the farm to the best of my ability.

We made the same amount of silage we had always made. There was the same amount of autumn corn sown in eighty-four, and the same amount of spring barley sown in eighty-five, with the same inputs for the maximum yield.

Then came the time the staff were told exactly what was happening, about six months before the estate was sold.

Well, I knew I had to find a cottage, so I approached a gentleman who tested the fields on the farm for lime, in fact the same one that used to do the straw cart and stacking on contract with his two sons. I asked him to look out for a cottage to rent, as I was going to start a business up livestock buying and selling. Well, after the harvest was over, I asked Mrs. Berry if it would be alright to start a little of my business before I left in the November, as two farmers had approached me about buying for them. She said "Quite alright, Ken."

One of the farmers was Richard Ruskin's next door neighbour, to buy fifty shearling ewes for replacement to his flock, and the other farmer were John Wade and his brother David, to buy a Sussex bull to put on to their dairy herd of Friesians.

It was September. I went to Findon Sheep Fair and purchased fifty very nice shearling ewes, and as it was my first customer, I did not charge him the full rate for buying them.

Myself talking to old friend Bill Skye
at Frindon Sheep Fair in 1974

203

As I was looking for a good Sussex bull, I contacted a very experienced man in the Sussex cattle world. He recommended a very good breeder in Wiltshire, so I contacted him, and he said he had three, about eighteen months old, the age I was looking for, so we arranged a day to go to see these bulls. The breeder suggested my wife and I go to lunch with him and his wife. When we arrived, the house was quite large, a bit before Victorian times, as we could see when we drove up in the Land Rover we had at that time. The drive was small beach, and there was enough space to drive up to the front door and turn round to go out again. The front door had steps going up to the entrance. I suppose really it was Georgian style, and looked as though the family had seen better days. However, we were welcomed, and given a very good lunch.

After lunch my wife stayed with the hostess, while I went with the host to look at the bulls. The farm buildings were about one hundred and fifty yards away from the house, and in an adjacent field there were three very nice bulls. I was told about each one in turn, but I still had my eye on a particular one, and I walked around him at close range three or four times. He had length, a straight back, strong legs, and good confirmation, which is essential in a breeding bull. I asked the price of this particular bull, and was told twelve hundred pounds. This was my price range, and although he was the bull I wanted, I said, "Well, it is going to cost me quite a bit to get him down to Sussex." With that my host said, "Well, I will get him down there free of charge." It generally pays never to be too eager to strike the deal, and, of course, I purchased the bull at the price mentioned, and I charged ninety pounds for my time and travelling.

So that was the first bull I had ever purchased in my small business, and Mr. Ruskin's shearling ewes were the first in the sheep line.

As I have said, I went to Findon Sheep Fair in the September. When I arrived back from the Fair that day, I got indoors of the lovely farm house we lived in, and Pat, my wife, seemed quite excited. Then she told me that Les Light had come and told her he had heard of a cottage to rent out at Baylington. I knew the farmers who owned it.

So I said, "Where is Les now?" and apparently he had gone down to get a load of straw bales up to the Dutch barn that was near the cattle yard, as Les was the gentleman who carted and stacked the straw bales every year. Well, I jumped in the Land Rover, I suppose I was a little excited, and went down the lane where I knew the load of straw bales would be travelling up to the barn, and I met Les on the way up. He stopped and I said to him, "I hear you know where there is a cottage to rent." "Yes," he said, "out at Baylington. It has been empty about a month. You know who owns it; it is Elingtons, the farmers. Ring up Barry, the younger son, I get on well with him, as I have the most dealings with him."

So that same evening I phoned Barry Elington. I told him who I was, and straight away he said, "How do you know about this?" I said, "Les Light told me." So the reply was "Oh, that is alright then." Also, he said, "Well, we had a lady look at the cottage and, of course, she will have first refusal." I said, "Well, yes, of course." After he had explained it was a four bedroom cottage on its own, I thought, just what we would want if the rent is not too high. I wish the lady no harm, but I hope she does not have it. So I had to leave it at that. Well, on the following Friday, I received a phone call from Barry Elington saying the lady who was coming to look at the cottage that was for rent had not come back to them at all, so Barry said: "Flip her! Can you come at 10.00 am. and meet my father at the farm house, and he will take you to view the house." This was the next day, on the Saturday.

So my wife and I duly arrived at 10.00 am. for Mr. Elington to show us the cottage. He took us eighty yards down from the farm house. On the opposite side of the road there was a little gate with twenty two steps leading to the cottage in question.

As we started up the steps, I looked up at the cottage: to my surprise it had lattice lead windows. It was extraordinary as Pat, my wife, had always wanted to live in a house with lattice lead windows. One must remember that we were coming from a lovely farm house with a big inglenook, where we had brasses along the beam over the fire place, also copper pieces that had come down through my wife's family, and I had a hunting horn that was three parts copper which my grandfather used when he was in charge of a pack of Beagles. So one can imagine, we thought, where are they going? But to our amazement, when we were shown the sitting room-cum-dining room, which was L shaped, there was a three quarter size inglenook with a lovely beam over the fire place, the fire place being set back a bit, making the inglenook, so there was the place for the brasses and copper. The cottage had a fair size main bedroom, and three small ones. The smaller one would be just right for my office, and as Pat said, there were a lovely lot of cupboards. The cottage had three flint walls around it, the other side of the south wall was the milking parlour with a hundred cows.

The heating in the cottage was all solid fuel, and the drainage was cesspool; a nice size lawn, rose beds, and a little bit of vegetable garden. It was ideal!.

Mr. Elington took us back to the farm house where we parked the Land Rover, which was a long wheel base safari Land Rover which I had had for eight years and which went with the job, I also took it on holiday each year for ten days in Shropshire.

I remember we stood outside the farm house, and along came Barry Elington and joined us as we were discussing the rent for the cottage. I said, "You mentioned fifty pounds per week," and Barry and his father said, "No, it is fifty five pounds per week." Then there were the rates on top of that, more than I wanted to pay, just starting this business, as I knew it was going to be a hard job to get going, as there were too many men doing the same business, and they had been in it years.

Well, we agreed we would take it on, and had permission to put a new iron gate at the top of the twenty two steps, also a close chestnut fencing, wire which held the four foot high and inch and a half split chestnut around the rest of the garden on the road side, to stop our dog, Max, from getting out. Also we asked to come at different times to decorate the whole cottage until we moved in.

Pat was very taken with it, for it had lovely views, it had space for the dog to run about, also a nice garden, as Pat loved gardening, but the biggest attraction was the lovely inglenook and plenty of cupboards.

It was just rather worrying how we were going to keep paying the rent, and pay the rates each year for a start. But my son, Nicholas, came home for the weekend from where he had just started a job in the August in Portsmouth for Ferranti, the defence people. As he was able to get a degree in combined science, he was lucky enough to get a better salary.

However, we went down to the cottage and he liked it immediately. I was telling him about the rent and we had to pay rates as well of eight hundred pounds a year.

Nicholas was only twenty-three years of age at the time, and also had a rent to pay at Portsmouth of forty pounds per week for one room in a lovely private house, where he was happy for seven years. But he had only been there two months, and said to us, "I will be home at weekends quite a bit, so I will pay the rates." And that is what happened for eighteen months, so that helped the situation enormously.

Anyway, in between running Coleman's Farm, my wife and I, about 4.00 pm., used to go down to Dove Cottage to decorate, with permission of Mrs. Berry, and that is how we decorated the whole cottage.

Now, back to farming. We are talking about around the 26th September: we had managed to get all the ploughing done, and had started sowing the corn, and what a difference the condition of the soil after the draining had been completed. In fact, it seemed a different farm. Our sowing procedure was one tractor power harrowing, another drilling, and myself driving a sixty-five horse power tractor, with an eighteen foot hydraulic harrow, coming up behind the drill. I generally started mid afternoon, and we kept going until that particular field was sown. It meant working with tractor lights on, all David Brown tractors. I remember, when I was going up and down the field harrowing, a great sorrow came over me that I would not be doing harrowing on this farm again, and thinking of the trying times I had in management to get this farm to the standard it was at that present time, but I achieved what I set out to do in the end.

If I had had a farm of my own, Nicholas would have gone into farming as he was practical as well as academic. A very lucky fellow in that respect. But I kept him out of farming for someone else, as I knew the pitfalls, and thank goodness I did. His financial position today is twice as much as it would be in farming for someone else, and, of course, if one gets made redundant there is generally a pretty good handshake at the time, and pension to go with it.

As I have said, Nicholas, our son, started work in the August. As he had to have a car, he purchased one about two or three weeks before starting work, a brown Alegro Estate car, 1500, and that car proved to be excellent. The name we gave it was Caddy; just right for a young chap being his first car. I remember all three of us going to

Portsmouth one Saturday, looking at three or four different places for Nicholas to stay while he was at Ferrantis.

One was a room with a gas oven, and at one had park the car outside in the street. We did not think much of that. We also looked at another place three floors up, and the man who owned it was pretty stand-offish, and I said to Nicholas, "I don't care if it is reasonable, you are not staying there." So they were not suitable, so home we went.

Pat, my wife, found another advert in Bedhampton in Portsmouth, so the following Saturday we went down to see the place advertised. Nicholas's cousin was staying with us at the time. He had a degree.

Anyhow, we got to Bedhampton and found this private house called The Barn. It was about a quarter of a mile from the main street in the country part, a nice enclosed yard where three or four cars could park. There was a wall dividing the house from the yard, and in about the centre of the wall there was a door. I went through the door first, Nicholas's cousin, Michael, was behind me, then Nicholas, then his mother. As soon as I got through the door, there in front of my eyes was a very attractive and petite lady, painting garden chairs white. I shall never forget it. Young Michael gave me a nudge in the back and said "Go on, Uncle Ken, sign the cheque now!"

Well, the house was quite old but had been renovated in the modern manner, all in its own grounds. We were shown a room upstairs. It was one of four being let out, the other three were occupied. It was a very nice room, all central heating, and each morning Nicholas would be given cereals and milk for breakfast for forty pounds per week, and an evening meal extra if he wanted it. So we accepted the room, and the other nice thing about it was Nicholas did not have to have his car in the street.

But as he played so much golf in the summer evenings and weekends, and did not know when he would be in, he thought it was not fair on Sandy Spence, the landlady, and declined the offer of supper. I used to go down one afternoon a year to play golf on the Portsmouth course. That was when I was running my own small business.

As he was on flexitime, he used to finish quarter past four in the afternoon, just right for his summer evening golf.

However, Nicholas was very happy there, as Sandy and her husband, Michael, were very nice people. Two or three years after he had been there, first one room was vacated, then the two other rooms were treated the same, and brought into private use. Well, one can imagine how Nicholas felt. He thought: "When am I going to get my marching orders?" Well, one morning he was coming down the stairs and he saw Sandy waiting for him. He though, "Oh my goodness, I've got to vacate my room," but when he got to the bottom of the stairs, Sandy, the landlady, bearing in mind Nicholas is six foot four inches tall, and Sandy five feet nothing, she looked up at him and said, "Nicholas, you can stay here with us as long as you like, and at the same rent, as we can trust you." So that was a great relief to him and, of course, we were very proud of him. Well, he was there for seven years, until he changed his job, as he could see what was happening to Ferrantis.

He was lucky he got another situation in Epsom, Surrey, for pension fund people, who employed a computer firm to do all their computer work. He went in to that firm as his job was computers. He was lucky, as about nine mounts after he left Ferrantis, they went into receivership. The thing that worried me was he started travelling from Portsmouth to Epsom every day. I had a talk with him about it. The sooner he got somewhere to live in Epsom, the happier I should be. Eventually he got a nice third floor flat, private grounds to put his car, eight minutes walk to the shops, seven minutes to the leisure centre, and only four minutes walk to work. He is still there at my time of writing.

But when the time came to tell Sandy he had rented a flat in Epsom and would have to leave, she looked up at him and said, "Oh, Nicholas, this is the worst news I have had all the week." So no doubt it made him feel good. The other nice thing for him is that with two or three others from his firm, he has joined a very nice golf club at Slinfold, West Sussex, about thirty-five or forty minutes journey from where he lives, and he has got on very well. But recently, the computer firm was taken over and forty of them had to go. This was November 1997. I asked him what saved his job, and he said a lot of the customers wanted a certain kind of computerisation projected forward, and he was a project manager. Well, I would not have known he was a project manager if it had not have been for this takeover situation. Nicholas will not tell you anything about his work. He was just the right chap at Ferrantis, as they had to sign a secret act paper, as it was all to do with defence work.

Now, back to the farm. Jack Ram came down to talk about the pension the farm had for me, and in the discussion he advised me to take cash of one thousand and three hundred pounds, still leaving twenty three pounds per week, which I accepted.

Well, just before the farm sale, I was sent the usual redundancy money, also a five thousand pound cheque that Mrs. Berry promised me, but I never did get the one thousand three hundred pounds, which was insurance money.

I thought about making a fuss about it. Although my wife, Pat, never said a word about how upset she was, I knew what she was going through; less fuss the better for her, I suppose.

In February of that year I had an accident with the Land Rover, while fetching crushed oats for Mrs. Berry's horse. There was a lot of snow on the ground then, and the road had not been salted and gritted. My wife was with me, and I was coming to a bridge with quite a stream running under it. I saw this car stop the other side of the bridge, so I kept going. All of a sudden, this car started over the bridge, and in split seconds, I had to decide what to do. If I slammed on the breaks I could visualise going sideways into the ditch. As I had my wife with me I decided to keep going over the bridge. All would have been well, but just as I got to the passing car, the lady panicked, put her foot on the accelerator and, of course, the back of the car slewed round into the side of the Land Rover and, believe it or not, it did a thousand pounds worth of damage.

The lady in question swore she never drove onto the bridge, but I am sorry to say she told a bare faced lie. She happened to be a solicitor's wife. She phoned me one day and swore blind she had stayed the other side of the bridge, but I told her she knew very well she had not, to which she replied "I have been told you are an awkward chap to deal with," to which I replied, "When a situation is true, I will say so." So that ended the conversation. Of course, she was claiming compensation as she said she was hurt when it had happened. She soon got out and exchanged addresses; then, after that her husband phoned me and said, "My wife said she had stayed the other side of the bridge," I said "She certainly did not." I never heard any more about it until there was a claim for some injury which passed on to the office, and I never heard any more about that. Perhaps that was in lieu of the thirteen hundred pounds I did not get, but I cannot understand why I did not hear any more about it.

I remember when I told Mrs. Berry about the accident and showed her the damage, she looked at me and said: "I expect you were going too fast." I said: "I never was, but have it your way," and that was that.

Now, in the course of events, I met the agent of the new owners that were coming into Coleman's Farm. I explained all arable fields were drained except two small ones, and he said they would plough a lot more ground up as they had no livestock, to which I replied: "It is no good ploughing any more ground up unless you drain it." His answer was: "We shall do that as the owners have the money for such an occasion." I said: "Well, that is a different matter."

But going back to land agents, I always thought of one of the most prominent and oldest agents for the wealthy, when I saw their names in the *Farmer's Weekly*. Well, it shook me when I met up with one or two, how they talked rather ridiculously about the farming. I wondered how they were employed by these estates.

Anyhow, I was in Coleman's Farm house with Mrs. Berry, and when she said, "They are going to plough more ground up, Ken," I said, "Well I told them it was no good unless they drained the ground first, and I was told they had the money for that operation." With that Mrs. Berry said: "Why is it we did not drain more?" I could not believe what I was hearing, especially when I wanted to drain two or three arable fields per year in 1975, and then they dropped the lot. I just said "God knows! as I do not." People have a very short memory.

Then, about two or three weeks before the sale at Coleman's Farm, I purchased an X registration Ford Granada estate car for my business, with fifty- eight thousand miles on the clock. . The estate car was named Snowy, as it was white. Lovely, quiet six cylinder engine, it used no oil at all. I purchased it for four thousand nine hundred pounds, so I had just a hundred pounds left from my five thousand.

To get enough money to start this business, I was forced to sell two hundred and fifty shares that I had in I.C.I. That was a bit of a blow, having to sell those. The fortunate thing was Geoff Badle, my bank manager, stood behind me in starting this business, and I was determined to succeed in getting it going.

Then we moved on the 26th November, giving us time to clear up, and burn things we did not want. Surprising how much one collects over the years. We had to give some of the furniture to my sister and two nieces, and we eventually drove out of Coleman's Farm yard at 6.00 pm. on 29th November, 1985, and I have never returned, although we are only eleven miles away.

I was invited to go to a cereal demonstration there, but I refused. It brought back too many memories. I may add, we put as much furniture in Dove Cottage as possible, and made the smaller bedroom my office.

Well, the next step was I was forced to go on the dole for six weeks, before I was entitled to the forty pounds per week on the government scheme to start up a business.

The other fortunate thing was the two farming partners from Kent who grazed five hundred sheep per year on Coleman's Farm, got me into the sheep keep business. The Kent sheep customers would ask me whether I had got farms where they could graze their sheep through the winter until March. At one time over 2,500 were grazed. I would find the keep on different farms, negotiate a price per head, and make sure these sheep would be looked at each day, as there were two or three places where I was sure they would not, so I never went any further discussing sheep keep with them.

When different farmers allowed grazing on their farms, I told them I would pay them by a fortnight after the sheep had been taken away, and I just managed to do that. Only just! After the sheep had been taken back to their own farms, I used to send a bill to the owners, then wait until I received their cheque before we could pay the grazers. I may add, once or twice we were on tender-hooks waiting for the cheque to come before we paid the farmer who grazed the sheep. That way I avoided borrowed money.

Two or three weeks before we moved to Dove Cottage, at the farm, we had seven farm cats that my wife used to feed outside Clinton Court Farm house where we lived, and one morning I looked out of the kitchen window and saw a little black kitten feeding amongst the other cats. I said to my wife, "I cannot believe it," and she came and looked and neither could she believe it, as all the cats had been doctored. All we could think of was someone had pushed it out, as they did not want it, and it mingled with the farm cats.

The amazing thing was, that as soon as he had eaten, he sat on the top of the backdoor steps away from the other cats, so we let him indoors, and provided a dirt tray for him, and he seemed quite at home. He did not look as though he was more than a month or five weeks old. However, we called him Tiddies, and took him to Dove Cottage with us where, as it happened, it had two cat door flaps where he was able to come and go as he liked.

We called him our lucky cat, as Dove Cottage seemed to us to be a God-send. It was just right for what we wanted. Tiddies, within the year, caught two large rats, and one the following year, so he was a real hunter. All the eleven years I was there, I never saw one live rat, so it seemed as if Tiddies was a deterrent to these terrible creatures.

As the years went by, at one period I wondered if he was as lucky as we thought. I had always wanted a cat in the house, as when I was a boy my mother and father had five cats that came in the house, and so I was rather used to them at that time. However, Tiddies has done very well. At this present time he is twelve and a half years old, and can tear across the lawn like a two year old, and woe betide a mouse that gets in his way, or a rat for that matter.

In December of 1985 I started looking at fat cattle for F.M.C. on different farms, to see if they were the right fat class to be sent to the abattoirs. At that time, I also purchased fat cattle from the farms my old friend, Peter, managed, mostly bull beef, which I eventually put through Borthwicks, another abattoir. Also I was doing business with John and

David Wade, sending fat cattle and bull beef to Borthwicks as it was very close to them to transport their cattle.

After I had been at Colemans for about four months, Jack Ram asked me to buy a Southdown Ram at Findon Fair for a gentleman who was running a farm for his relations. So I went to Findon Fair, purchased the ram, and amazingly it came from John and David Wade's farm, selected from their Southdown flock. I believe it had French blood in it. I think their Southdown flock is the seventh oldest in the country.

On 17th December I had to go to Worthing to an Enterprise Allowance Scheme Information Session, which was held at the Worthing Job Centre.

In November 1985, Richard Ruskin asked me to look at his fat cattle, all from single sucklers, and I sent ten to F.M.C. After that I purchased all his fat cattle for F.M.C. until the first B.S.E. scare really took hold, and I finished my business, as I was really hit by this scare, and I was no longer viable about the year of nineteen ninety-two.

On the 3rd December 1985, I was travelling to a nearby market town with my wife in the new second-hand Granada Estate car, when coming to a round about, a lorry load of big stones was coming in the opposite direction, and swayed, and dash me, a stone came off the top of this lorry, about twice as big as a cricket ball. It was bounding at great speed straight at us, but luckily it hit the radiator and did not come through the windscreen, as if it had hit either of us, we would have been killed. It was just like a cannon ball, and it damaged the radiator so much I had to have a new one put in immediately, costing one hundred and sixty pounds. I had no time to look at the number plate of the lorry. I thought at the time, what else can happen.

I see that on Monday 21st October, 1985, I judged store cattle at Haywards Heath Store Sale. I suppose they thought it would help me in my new business to get me known in a wider area. I remember I selected a pen of Friesian cross heifers. Of course, one does not know at that stage whose cattle they are, until after judging, and the extraordinary thing was, they belonged to Messrs. Barnham and Sons, the family I worked for fourteen years previously! There was a very nice gentleman there at Haywards Heath Market I had known a few years, and he knew I had purchased around three hundred cattle per year at that market for the last ten years. His advice to me when I told him I was going into the business of buying and selling cattle and sheep was: "Ken, you must really go for it. Hand out printed cards, advertise, and get round as many farms as possible." He was right, as there were too many in the same business and had been in for a few years, so I could see I had quite a task on my hands. My goodness, I did have to travel quite a few miles that first year, but I expect it paid off in the long run, although I did wonder about it at the time.

When I officially started my business in 1986, Geoff Badle recommended a very nice gentleman, John Cravet, to be my accountant. He used to do this work part time. When we first met, we got on very well, and his charge was very reasonable indeed. So you see, Geoff Badle helped me all he could. We kept in touch over the years. He used to come to tea with his wife two or three times a year when we were at Coleman's Farm, and, of course, looked round the farm in the summer months. In this same year I went to the local market and I met a very well known farmer, and I persuaded him to let me look at his fat cattle, and select them for F.M.C. His name was Richard, and his brother was Ray Bancroft. Well, both brothers had Guernsey dairy herds. Their beef was Charolia Bulls on the adult cows and Sussex Bulls on the Guernsey heifers.

The Charolias on the cows made some lovely fat cattle. The Sussex on the heifers, of course, were a bit smaller. The steers were good, but the heifers had to be sold at a lighter weight as they would get too fat.

I used to pick a few out that were ready before they went into the yards for the winter.

I remember, when I started drawing cattle from Ray Bancroft's yards, I was pleasantly surprised to see the Charolias cross Guernseys, the lovely cattle they made. They certainly had the right bulls of that breed. They had no silage, just hay and concentrates to fatten on, with that they killed out very well.

Going back to markets, Haywards Heath market, the last time I purchased cattle there was about nineteen ninety. Who would think since then that it has closed, and a super market has been built on the site. How things change.

At the beginning of 1986, one day my wife, Pat, said to me, "You know you are morose," I suppose I was , being very unusual for me, but as I have said, being made redundant at the age of fifty-eight years old was such a shock in my farming life, although I am rather a strong character, it had affected me in a way I would never have thought.

Then came the Grasslands A.G.M. at the local agriculture college which I attended. I knew that a cup was presented to a person who had done the most for the Grassland Society in the last two years. In those days there were a lot of people came to that A.G.M., the room was packed.

I sat about four or five rows from the front, and listening to, in actual fact, a very nice young gentleman from I.C.I., who was my right hand man when I was Chairman of the Beef and Sheep Group. His name, David Power.

Well, he was talking about a man, tall in stature and a few other things, and all of a sudden he said: "I am very proud to be able to present this cup for the most done in the Grassland Society in the last two years to Ken Mewett." Well, I nearly fell off the chair. I could hardly believe what I was hearing. But I recovered, and went up to receive this precious cup. I shook hands with David Power, and thanked him, then turned round to the audience and said "I am nearly lost for words, but thank you ladies and gentlemen." Then I heard one or two shout out "That will be the first time, Ken," meaning that I had been lost for words!

But from that night I came out of being morose, and seemed to go forward like a rocket. It was certainly a great boost for me.

In January of 1986, I met up with Dick Longden, who was a very successful man in buying and selling livestock over a period of years. I got on very well with him, as he gave a boost to my small business.

In my looking at fat cattle in yards, I came across a yard of cattle on a particular farm which disturbed me, as in my farming life I always kept cattle and cows well bedded down with straw so that they kept clean and comfortable. I doubt in this yard if it had seen straw for some time. Well, thank goodness it was the only yard I ever saw like it.

But at that time I thought, if the general public saw this particular yard with cattle in it, they would have every right to complain. The disturbing thing about it is, it gives a bad impression on farming as a whole. Therefore the old saying , there are rebels in all walks of life.

I remember 4th June, 1986, I took Dick Longden to a farm to purchase several bulls, which he did. Well, these bulls went to a very big estate in West Sussex that Dick Langden did a lot of business with. After they were delivered, I went in my car and Dick in his to the particular farm on the estate. When we got into the yard, I stayed seated in my car, and Dick greeted the manager. Dick was on the offside of my car, and the estate manager was on my near side, both about halfway along my estate car, but on opposite sides, and they started arguing about the crossbreed of these bulls. The argument got rather heated, and the manager banged his fist down on my car roof with such force I thought he had dented it. The argument came to a halt, but I thought at the time, by gosh, this is a dangerous job to be in.

On 6th June, Dick Longden and I took Dick Dowles, he was the dairy herd manager for a large estate, to look at in calf dairy heifers from a Friesian herd on a local Duke's estate. But judgement was reserved until we saw other well grown Friesian heifers.

Eventually we went to another farm in Devon; the farm was in Barnstable, and we purchased 38 in calf heifers. They arrived on 5th July to be put into the Lord Banks dairy herds, and four had calved before they arrived. They were a nice bunch.

Whilst I have mentioned Lord Banks, I made an appointment to meet him at his farm office, for the purpose of being show his grassland that could be used for sheep keep through the winter. Well, I arrived a the appointed time, we greeted each other, then away we went in his four-wheel drive vehicle. While we were looking round, he was talking about the fencing his son was having done, and was making a very good pheasant shoot there. He was a very pleasant man, and seemed full of life, and then a few months after that meeting I heard the tragic news he had put himself under a train, committing suicide. He seemed a man that loved life, and I can tell you it was quite a shock to me because, not only meeting him at that particular time, I met him once before in the farm office to discuss purchasing in calf dairy heifers. It goes to show, one can never tell the minds of different people.

Then on the 1st July, 1986, I first meet David Patch, a farmer who farmed on the outskirts of a seaside town, about four miles from where I lived at Dove Cottage.

The farming system was buying in mostly calves at about ten days old, and bringing them up on powdered milk, which was contained in large plastic barrels with rubber teats around the sides. He made a very successful job of it. He also purchased a few three month old calves to make up numbers. He also grew three hundred acres of corn.

He became a customer of mine until he retired, also a very good friend. We have kept up to this very day, and hopefully for many years to come.

I used to go to David Patch's farm to pick out fat cattle for a local abattoir. I used to enjoy it very much when he used to take me down to the brook ground in the summer, to select the cattle that were ready to go to the abattoir. I used to walk round with him, looking at these cattle. All of a sudden I would say, "that one is ready to go." David would get out his pencil and paper, and read the ear number on that particular beast. It was a job sometimes, but he succeeded. He was a very good customer.

Sadly, on 9th July, 1986, Richard Ruskin's father, Fred, had a stroke and it left him paralysed in his legs. Therefore, he was wheel-chair bound. Fred and Richard Ruskin were my neighbouring farmers when I was at Coleman's Farm. The gentleman, when I first met him and called him Mr. Ruskin, stuck his head through the open window of the Land Rover, and said "I am Fred." He must have been nearing eighty years of age then. "If you want Mr. Ruskin, you go along the road." Of course, that was his brother who was getting pretty close to ninety, and lived on the east side of Coleman's Farm. Extraordinary! He was settled in a nursing home in a nearby seaside town, where in January 1997 we moved to live in a bungalow only a quarter of a mile from this nursing home. Every time I go by this home, I think of Fred. While he was at this home I used to go and see him. I seem to remember I used to take him Maltesers as he liked them so much. Of course, he liked talking about the old days in farming. He was quite a character. I did enjoy going to see him. Where I live now, near this nursing home, it is only about two miles away from the farm that David Patch farmed.

On 27th July, 1986, I made an appointment to meet Jim Patch on his dairy and corn farm, very near a large seaside town, which he rented from the town's corporation. I was given his phone number by his brother, David. Of course, I went there to meet him as he produced beef from his very nice Friesian dairy herd. I remember he was rowing up grass ready for the baler to pick up, to make round bale silage. He was, like his brother, a very nice gentleman, and he became my customer from then on until they, being brothers, both retired from farming. I have been friendly with them ever since, playing golf with them once a week, and David I used to play snooker, until my right hip stopped me playing either game.

I had the operation for a hip replacement but it has not gone so well. It did not help things as after I had been out of hospital for eleven days, it dislocated, and the surgeon had rather a job to get it back in. At the time of writing, 19 March, 1998, it has been six and a half months since I had this hip operation and it is not right now, and I am told to see the surgeon in six months time. So it means I have not played golf for seventeen months as I had to pack up that game as my hip got so bad a the beginning of December 1996, and since that operation on 28th August, 1997, I have not played snooker. I am hoping to play snooker within a couple of months, but goodness knows when I shall ever play golf, or garden.

On 11th September, 1987 I went up to the North with Dick Longden to sheep sales, as he wanted to purchase well grown shearlings for two or three large estates in West Sussex. Dick went up to these sales quite a few times, and always stayed at the same hotel. Very nice it was too. It was a great experience for me, and what an eye opener. We went to a sale on 12th and 13th which was Friday and Saturday, having arrived at our destination on Thursday at 2.00 pm. On the Saturday I should have gone to the Findon sheep sales to purchase fifty shearling ewes for Messrs. Ruskin, but Dick said, "I will organise with a friend I know up north to show you fifty Scotch half bred shearling ewes, then you can come up with me to the sheep sales." He was as good as his word, and I purchased the shearlings as they were a nice bunch, so it left me free to go to the sales with him.

As I said, what an experience! I had never seen so many first class sheep. Some had been dipped to put a bit of colour into them. I suppose like a woman putting powder, rouge and lipstick on to attract the onlooker. Some even had thin ribbons expertly attached to them. I suppose, if they were put in with rams, the rams would be amazed and wonder what the heck was going on, so would it make them keener!

By the time of the end of the second sale, Dick had purchased over one thousand shearlings. Of course the farmers and auctioneers knew him very well. As soon as Dick made his last bid, all he said was "Longden," and the sheep were his. I remember, he never bought one sheep until the sales were three parts over, but he managed to get as many as he wanted.

Each lot he purchased very soon after he shouted out his name, Longden. All of a sudden there would be a farmer come up between the rows of seats, and say, "Mr. Longden," and he would acknowledge him, and the farmer would give him what is called luck money. Sometimes two or three lots that Dick had purchased were from the same farmer. However, in those two days, he collected over two hundred pounds in luck money. Some were Scotch five pound notes, the first I had ever seen, and in those two days he had spent over sixty thousand pounds. He certainly was in a big way of that kind of business.

It was in October, 1986, as Pat, my wife, recorded all incoming and outgoings financially in our small business, she looked across at me and said: "What are we going to do?" I said: "We have just got to carry on, as this is the only work I know with confidence," and within a month or two, the business started to proceed fairly well. Pat, bless her, would not worry me unless anything was very serious.

I see by my diary on the 10th October, 1986 I put two hundred lambs out from a Kent farmer to keep for the winter on a fruit farm, not far away from the Biggin Hill Aerodrome. That year it snowed quite heavily, but the sheep did very well, as if they could not get to the grass through the snow, they were fed hay. It was very sheltered for them in the orchards.

I used to go to look at these sheep once a month, as I did all other sheep I had out to keep. When going by this aerodrome, I often thought of the pilots that got airborne to save us from the German fighters and bombers, and the poor chaps who never returned. I see that on 20th October, 1986 in the Pevensey area, I went to a dairy farm run by a family to look at seven nice young cross cattle from their dairy herd, and purchased them, but the extraordinary thing was I used to manage for a short while the next dairy farm down the road in 1956. The eldest brother, a very nice gentleman, alas, died recently in –1997 at the age of sixty-two. Going back to what my dear old mother would say "Ah, my boy, it was to be!"

Then, in November 1986, I got into the three month old calf business. I got to know a lady and gentleman who bought calves about ten days old, brought them up to three months, and sold them to different farmers. So my first order for fifteen black Hereford cross Friesian steers came from David Patch, and, of course, these calves came from the lady and gentleman I mentioned who had been in this business for some years. Also I bought from a young chap who started in the business of three month old calves. He did the job very well. These steer calves were purchased at £203 at 100 kilos, and at 65p per kilo above the 100 kilos. Also in November, I see I put twenty seven Southdown ram lambs through F.M.C. from Messrs. David and John Wade's farm.

On my birthday, the 15th, I played golf with my son at a local golf course, but never played at all well, and of course, to my son's delight, he won. Well, as I look at golf it is like life, it has its ups and downs.

On 8th December 1986, it was the Fatstock Show Dinner, held at the local town Hall, whereby Geoff Badle invited me to sit at this table with a few other farmers, which he did every year. It was very pleasant indeed.

I see on 17th December, I sold fifty Oldenberg cross Scotch Black Face ewes to a farmer, and thirty-five to a local contractor and farmer. They were full mouthed ewes and looked pretty good. I had not come across this breed before.

On 6th January, 1987 I went and looked at six in-calf heifers from a local farmer I had known for about nine or ten years, and from that I got another livestock buyer to look at these heifers, and he purchased them. When I sent this particular farmer a bill for selling them off one and a half percent for each £400 heifer, he said he did not think I would charge him for this service, and I may add, they were very big dairy and corn farmers. I asked him how did he think I would stay in business if I did not charge anything for this service. I could not believe my ears. He knew I had been made redundant recently and was starting this new business up to make a living from scratch. My goodness, there is a difference in people.

He used to be in the NFU. of our local branch, so he knew what had happened to me. I sometimes wondered how I was voted in to be vice-chairman and then chairman of the local NFU. branch, as I was not an owner-occupier or tenant farmer, or one of their sons. I was a mere farm manager. There were some very big farmers in the local branch but the different attitude some of them had was amazing.

I remember one such farmer. He had a lovely bunch of well grown in-calf heifers from his Friesian herd he wanted to sell for five hundred pounds per head, so I phoned him up, made arrangements to see these heifers, but I could not be there on that particular day. He said, "That is OK, Ken, send the buyer along. I'll see him." In actual fact the buyer was another dairy farmer, very close to the seller's dairy farm, and they knew each other quite well. Well, this particular buyer purchased six of these heifers. As soon as the buyer got home, he phoned me and said "Very nice heifers, Ken. But the seller has told me that I have got to pay half the one and a half percent you charge for a sale." Well, I could not believe it. Here was a man who had been very friendly with Mrs. Berry over the years, and, of course, knew me and that I had just started this small business. It made me feel as though three or four of these farmers did not want me to succeed, and the others I knew helped me as much as possible.

I remember one particular farmer, who knew Mrs. Berry very well indeed. Mrs. Berry told me one day when his name came up, "I have been told a thing or two about his attitude to his employees." "I cannot believe it," I answered, "but you do not have to work for him!"

I also found when I started going to different farms locally, I had to be careful in what I said, as most of them were related in some way or other.

On 7th January, I judged silage on farms that were members of the Sussex Grassland Society, and belonged to the Beef and Sheep Group. This particular farm was managed by a young man, Alan Day. His farm fattened beef as well as running a flock of breeding ewes for fat lamb production. He had a particularly good clamp of silage for sheep, and I judged that as first prize, and through the years he became very successful, especially with his breeding flock of ewes.

I see by my diary on 14th January 1987, a load of fat cattle had to be cancelled from going to F.M.C. Canterbury owing to snowy roads, some not possible to travel on.

Then on 21ˢᵗ January, 1987 we went to my wife's Auntie's funeral in a very large cemetery at Westcliffe-on-Sea, Southend. I remember the snow still hanging on the trees, also quite a large amount on the different gravestones. It was a very unusual sight.

I had a short period with A.T.B., i.e. Agriculture Training Board, talking about the fat class of cattle before and after they were killed.

I remember having a meeting on 24ᵗʰ February, 1987 and getting different people to feel the cattle, and get as near as they could to the fat class of the particular animal, then the next day go to see the same cattle hung up dead. Very interesting. Of course, I had shown them and explained where to look on the different parts of the animal. The meeting was held at a local private abattoir. It was very kind of the owners to let us do this. I do hope it helped the people concerned.

I used to buy small batches of cattle for different farmers, as I did on 23ʳᵈ February, 1987: ten Hereford Friesians, black steers, eight 425 to 430 kilos, purchased for £422. But I have always said, after purchasing different batches of cattle or sheep that they were right for what they wanted to do with them, but I could not vouch for the management of this particular livestock once out of my control. I shall come to one or two of these cases as I go further into this journal.

As I have said, I used to put sheep out to keep on different farms for Kent farmers. I was very lucky to put sheep out to keep on a farm very near to where I lived at Dove Cottage, about two and a half miles away, on the Southdowns, leading down to Haven River, which is quite a beauty spot for the public, so I never had far to go when looking a these sheep, as I did all other sheep out to keep once per month.

On 11ᵗʰ May, 1987 I purchased twelve Black Hereford cross Friesian steers about twelve months old, nice cattle, but wanted worm drenching as soon as possible the next

227

day. Of course the job was left for about three weeks, and dashed if one died after looking unwell. The vet was called and diagnosed lung worms, and, of course, these cattle were wormed immediately. It was like shutting the stable door after the horse had bolted. This particular gentleman was my customer for the rest of my time in business, but always worm drenched my newly purchased cattle next day, and there was no further trouble. These cattle that were kept until fat did very well.

Most of the store cattle I purchased were from Haywards Heath Market which, alas, is no more, being a site for a large super market.

I remember the beginning of June 1987, I had a call from a farm manager, who managed a farm at the far end of Surrey, enquiring about purchasing young black Hereford cross Friesian steers, about twelve to fourteen months old.

I went to see this farm set up; He was doing the producing of fat cattle well. I sold him about twenty young cattle, from the Woburn Abbey area, also some older ones later on.

This farm was owned by a business man, and a young lady was the farm secretary. She knew nothing about farming, and the ridiculous ideas she had about running this farm, and I may add, over-riding the farm manager, I could hardly believe, as the chap was doing a good job. What a set up! I do not think it lasted long.

Also in May of this year, Richard Ruskin decided to increase his herd of single sucklers from fifty to eighty cows, and I was given the job of purchasing these replacements which I completed on 30th June, 1987. I went to Sheep 1987 on Newbury Show Ground. Dick Longden had a marquee there, in which he entertained his customers, as he was in the farm supply business as well as livestock buying and selling. Farmers from all over the country attended this gathering. I tried my hand at selling one or two sheep hay racks, and a sheep handling pen, and there I was explaining about these items, and one farmer said to me: "Have you always done this sort of job?" I said, "No, I was a farm manager, then I had to start my own business in livestock." He looked at me and said: "Well, all I can say is you have been in the wrong job." I do not know exactly what he meant by that. However, it was quite an experience, which I had never had before.

On 14ᵗʰ July, 1987 I took a farmer to a farm in Wiltshire to look at Friesian dairy cows from a very good herd. Lactation's were good, longevity of the herd was excellent, and we purchased eleven cows for five hundred pounds per cow.

Then on 20ᵗʰ July 1987, I introduced Peter Ellington to the lady and gentleman from whom I purchased three month old calves. Previously Peter had said to me, "We have quite a lot of grass to graze, and the corn job does not seem to be all that good." I said, "Are you going back to single sucklers like you had some years before?" "No," he said, "We would have to have a hundred at least, that means another man for the job." I mentioned sheep, and he said, "I do not like them," so I suggested having three month old steer cross calves, like Hereford, Simmetal Limo crosses. So that is how the Ellingtons became customers for these three month old calves. He always liked me to go with him to see if there were any I did not like, and they started having two hundred a year. I knew they would be managed right, as they had the right buildings for the job and, above all, they were stockmen.

Also, from the Ellington's farms I started having fat cattle for F.M.C. I remember selecting twenty nine steers from yards. I used to mark them with a dab of white paint. Well, this particular day I was quite satisfied with the cattle I had selected, but the next day Peter came to me and said: "My father is not happy with one you have marked." I said: "OK., I'll come down now with you and have a look." Well, we arrived at these yards, and the steer in question was pointed out to me, and my answer was: "he will be alright, he will grade." Well, he was sent with the others, and by gosh! he killed out Q quality steer, so I never heard anymore about it.

As I am writing, on 31 March, 1998, there was the funeral held of Jack and Joe Barnham's father to which we went. Always a sad occasion for the family concerned, but what a good innings Mr. Barnham Senior had. He was ninety three years of age. The funeral was held at their local church, and Joe, the youngest son, read a tribute to his father about his life from a boy, very well done, I thought. We went back for refreshments to the restaurant on the farm, which they use for the general public, as they have a bluebell walk there with the Meriden line running right through it, and, of course, they have to cater for coach parties. The restaurant was closed to the public on that day, and there were a lot of people came back from the funeral. It all went very well.

There were men there that I had not met for twenty-eight years. I looked at them and thought, well, I have seen that face before, but I could not put a name to that particular face until they came and introduced themselves. By gosh! that brought back memories.

One gentleman came up to me and just before I shook hands with him, I recognised him, and said, "John Bowles" and he said, "That is right," and the last time I saw him was twenty-two years previously. John was from a local land agents and valuers, and I used to meet him every spring at the house where Mr. Barnham Senior lived. John and I used to go through the valuation of livestock etc. As soon as I shook hands with him, I said, "John Bowles, how nice to see you. I always remember when I used to meet you once a year for valuation purposes, you wrote every detail down and I mentioned at the time 'by gosh! that's a lot of writing you are doing John', to which you replied, "yes, I always write everything down, then if for some reason over tax purposes, one had to go to court, one had the details in black and white, and there could be no argument about it," to which he replied, "Yes, and that same thing stands today."

As Joe Barnham mentioned in his tribute to his father, in the days when his father was younger, rabbits were prevalent everywhere on farming land, and his father used to shoot with his sixteen bore shot gun, very often shooting twenty-five rabbits with twenty-five shots, and sell them in the local big town to help pay for the rent. As I have mentioned before, Mr. Barnham Senior was marvellous shooting with a shot gun. It reminded me of my dear father. I do not think there would be very much difference in accurate shooting. The only difference would be my father shot with a B.S.A. pistol grip, thirty inch double barrelled shot gun, opposed to Mr. Barnham Senior's sixteen bore, double barrelled shot gun, apparently the gun his father gave him.

Now going back to 1987, I must mention I used to play golf once or twice a week, always once a week with two old friends and, of course, with my son, Nicholas, at different weekends. Of course, Nicholas was working as I have mentioned before, and living in Portsmouth where he belonged to the local golf club. We often now talk about the first time I played golf on his course, and with the handicap I was allowed, dashed if an old hacker like me won, and he has never forgotten it. It was only once, mind you, and it made me feel good, as he plays pretty well.

On 26th September 1987 Nicholas, my son, changed his Alegro Estate car for a Maestro M.G. 1.6. Of course that was on a Saturday, and to try a new second-hand car out, he always drove us to Tunbridge Wells, having tea there, and then back home again, to try the vehicle out. He has done this each time he changes a car.

On the night of 15th October, 1987, the big hurricane came. In the morning of 16th all electric lights were out of

231

action, also phones, except two at the other end of the village. Trees were down on all three roads to the village, so that no traffic could move. So Messrs. Ellington and sons, the local farmers, got their staff with motor saws, and their big Matbro, which is a hydraulic loader, very powerful, and eventually cleared the roads. That same morning I went down the steps from Dove Cottage, as I had three appointments to look at cattle, but I had to go back up the steps to fetch a saw, as a bough was across the gate, and I just could not go anywhere. When I got up to the Ellington's farm yard where I kept my car, I was told by the farm staff: "Well, you are not going anywhere as the roads are blocked." So that was that, until the next day or two.

On 17th October, 1987 I had arranged to meet a young farmer, his name, Michael Apton. He had managed to buy a small dairy farm within a fifteen mile radius to where I lived at Dove Cottage.

He was going to farm it with breeding sheep and arable. That is how I became involved: he wanted me to purchase one hundred Kent Shearlings and a couple of rams. I had already purchased two Texal rams for him.

I remember meeting him to take him to meet a farmer at Bethersden near Ashford, Kent. I picked him up at 8.25 am. When we arrived we were shown a lovely bunch of Kent Shearlings. There were two hundred in all in this field. The farmer said: "You can have the best of those at £63.25 per head, and I will get them as even as I can." We looked through them, and I advised Michael Apton to purchase the hundred at the stated price, the cheque to be written out the same day. We were also told by the farmer, "If I am not in the house, just put the cheque through the letter box," which we duly did, and all concerned were happy with the purchase.

As I had been with breeding sheep for thirteen years, and lambing them amongst other duties as a working manager, I advised young Michael Apton on the management of these sheep, especially with the lovely buildings he had on the farm he had recently purchased. A very lucky young man, I thought. I would have loved to have had that chance at his age, but I can hear my dear mother saying "Ah, it wasn't to be my boy!"

I see that on 14th October, 1987 there were sixteen Limosin cross young steers delivered into a local farmer, from a seller in the Woburn Abbey area. I have mentioned this as first, to prove this was one of several batches of cattle I purchased for different farmers.

On 16th October, 1987 I see by my diary six hundred Kent lambs went out to keep on a farm I had previously okayed for this purpose in Wiltshire, near the Pusey Valley. A retired farm manager was allowed to set up a business of having sheep in to keep. His name was David Otter, and it seemed that he had to have miles of electric fencing as there were not any fences at all. There were acres of ground on these downs, and he used to manage it in blocks of about 80 or more acres in a block. Nearby, the Army had a vast area for tanks and firing ranges, so David Otter had to have an area in reserve, ready for when the Red Flag was hoisted, as that meant tank firing was in progress. David had to shift the nearest block of sheep from the firing range to the reserved block. At that time I had over a thousand sheep out to keep there, but eventually the price of the keep went up more than I could pay, and I just had to discontinue the operation there. I certainly wasn't going all that way to lose money, once a month.

On 18th October, 1987 all electric for cooking was knocked out after the great gale. My wife, Pat, and I went to Eastbourne to Sunday lunch at a restaurant called Shades, where at odd times on a Saturday we used to go in the morning for coffee and their special cheese scone and butter. It was the very first time in our married life we had been out to lunch on a Sunday.

233

I see by my diary, 20th October, 1987 the electric was at last on low power, lovely! and on 25th at 2.10 pm. the phone connected. That was a relief, I can tell you. On 9th December 1987 fifty in lamb full mouthed ewes, mostly cross cluns, arrived that I purchased from Dick Longden, and put out to keep on a farm about fifteen miles away to keep for the winter. Through the winter I used to go to Jim Patch's farm about every two weeks to pick out fat cattle for F.M.C. I remember when, in the first September, Jim took me in his four-wheel drive vehicle to look at his cross steers and heifers. They certainly were some lovely cattle. Some were from his small suckler herd, the rest from his British Friesian dairy herd. We were driving up on the hilly part of his farm, and as we drove through some of the cattle I said to him, "We had better stop. I will get out and have a good look at these animals, especially the heifers," which I did, and when I got back to Jim and got into the vehicle, I said to him, "Lovely cattle, with lovely confirmation, but two or three of the heifers are over fat." He said he expected they would be, and when they went to F.M.C., the two or three heifers proved to be so, very good confirmation, but being over-fat. It knocked the price down five or six pence per kilo, as for some years before this date, the fat had to be cut off as the young housewife would not buy it, so it was wasted. Also, the older housewife became more against the fat, but in Jim's case we started looking at the cattle a little earlier in the year, and it solved the problem.

Going back to fat on meat, this tale is quite true. A lady in her sixties went into her local butchers, and asked for a nice beef joint. The butcher brought out a lovely joint, but as soon as the lady in question looked at it, she said "I do not want that joint as there is too much fat on it." The butcher replied: "But madam, it is an ideal joint for cooking." Her reply was: "I do not want it. I have got to have a much leaner piece as my husband has recently had a heart attack!" So the butcher brought out a very lean piece, where one could see the meat through a very thin covering of fat. The lady immediately said: "That is the piece I want please, and now I want a piece of fat to cook it with! "

On 28th December 1987 one of our in lamb ewes died, and I look it to the local hunt kennels. It was a bit of a blow to me, but I had enough experience to know these things happen from time to time.

On 20th January, 1988 I went to a new customer. The appointment was at 2.00 pm. I went there to see how much grass land he had, and what kind of buildings were available, as he wanted to start a sheep flock. It was a farm near East Grinstead. The gentleman in question knew nothing about farming. He had purchased this small dairy farm, lovely buildings to house sheep at lambing time. However, as he could not be there himself, I met his wife at the lovely farm house, and we talked about what her husband wanted to do. Then she directed me in the direction of a young chap, who they took on to manage the place for them. He lived on the farm in a large caravan with his girl friend. I caught up with him up at the farm buildings, introduced myself, and he told me he had come from Kent, and that he was used to lambing sheep. I thought that will be a good start, so I got him to show me all the grassland that they had got. We discussed what was happening to the farthest grassland, and he said that it was for bagged silage, and after that a neighbouring farmer was renting it for some of his single suckler cows. I thought, well, that sounded right. Then we looked at the rest of the grassland which was near the farm buildings. I noted the acreage, said goodbye to this young manager, and home I went. In that same evening, I phoned the owner of this particular farm and told him I had looked at the acreage of his farm, and leaving out the acreage of the ground where the neighbouring farmers single sucklers were going to graze,

I would advise him to start with fifty maiden ewes, see how he got on, then go to a hundred the following year. It was agreed I should purchase these ewes, so I went to look at a batch of Mule cross Suffolk ewes on 30th January. They were very well grown. I took along with me the young manager and we picked out fifty lovely young ewes, and they were delivered to Charring Farm where the young manager worked.

I discussed the management of these sheep, and told him: six weeks before they lamb, feed them concentrates, but as soon as they were on the farm, worm drench them as soon as possible. I also advised him and the owner's wife, as they had never owned sheep before, that as soon as these ewes had lambed, and the last lamb was a month or five weeks old, then worm drench the ewes and the lambs, then proceed with drenching the lambs every month, and I mean strictly every month. After that I thought, well, I have done all I can at the moment, and went away happy.

Then on 1st February 1988 I was taking David Wade to West Sussex to look at fifty ewes. We were travelling up a very long and straight piece of road. I overtook a car as it was safe to do so, and as I was overtaking, a taxi that seemed to be in a great hurry came out of a road on my off side, did not stop to look, and came half head on at me. I could not do anything about it, only brake. We collided with a great bang. Thank goodness we had seat belts on, or else I could visualise David Wade going through the windscreen. But thankfully no one was hurt. But my first white Granada estate car, which we called Snowy, was a write off. So Shades garage I dealt with towed poor Snowy away and hired me out a Fiat Strada, mileage on the clock, 44,700. It was a basic car but went very well. I got in it straight away and drove it home to Dove Cottage. It was a bit like the fighter pilots in the war, after having had a crash, got in the cockpit of another plane straight away and started flying. I had three appointments the next day. When I started next morning, driving this Strada, I was half afraid to do more than fifty miles an hour with it for fear of a motor coming out of a turning on my off side, but after a couple of days I got used to it, and happily to say, David Wade went to West Sussex under his own steam, and purchased the fifty ewes.

It certainly shakes one up, an accident like I experienced, and that same evening I said to my wife, Pat, "Now it looks as though I am going to be the first one of us two to be taken off this earth, and if this happens, I do not mind what you do when I am gone, as long as you are happy on this earth." If you love a person, you wish them to be happy for the rest of their life, and Pat deserved all the happiness one could possibly have.

On 14th February 1988 I sold the forty-nine in-lamb ewes we first owned. One was not so good as the others, so I gave the buyer that one to help pay for the carriage, but after paying for the keep, I still made twelve pounds per head. I must say, business was going quite well, and I remember a farmer he was a German, seemed a nice man. Who wanted to purchase forty in-lamb ewes. Dick Longden knew of a farmer selling part of his flock, so we met the German gentleman on a farm in West Sussex on 14th January, 1988. The ewes were a nice batch of crossed Mules, and eventually I sold him forty of these ewes and shook hands on the purchase. Well, the sheep were delivered to his farm, and the next evening I had a phone call from him, saying he had changed his mind, to which I replied: "But they are very good ewes for the price you paid, and besides you shook hands on the deal and I quite thought you were a man of your word." So that was the end of that conversation. So I immediately phoned Dick Longden, and he said, "I will phone him right now." After about half an hour Dick phoned back and told me, "It is OK, Ken, he is keeping to the deal." I said, "What did you say to him?" "Well, amongst other things

I said, I thought German gentlemen like himself were very honourable people. I must say the situation was rather worrying at the time."

On 12th March, 1988 I picked up a Ford Granada estate car No. PYO319Y with fifty-two thousand, two hundred miles on the speedometer, metallic dark blue, from Shades Garage, in place of Snowy. I wrote off the first Granada Estate I had owned.

I was lucky, for as soon as I wrote off the white Ford Granada estate, I asked Shades to get me a second-hand 2.3 Granada estate. Well, as the period went on after my accident, they had occasion to M.O.T. a person's 2.3 blue metallic Ford estate car, six cylinder. The same as the first one, only a different colour. Well, they were so impressed with this car that they asked the owner whether he had thought of selling it, and his reply was, "I have already advertised it in a paper." So Shades made a deal with him, and I purchased the same. It had electric front windows, also electric sliding roof, and being a sliding roof, that made a difference of two inches head room, the result being I tended to put my head a little on the side when driving, and people I know used to say when they saw me, "look out, here comes Ken," but it proved to do me very well.

On 18th March, I went to visit Michael Apton, to see how he was getting on lambing the one hundred Kent ewes I had purchased for him. He seemed to have managed them very well, and the lambing was progressing well, all under cover, so that was satisfying.

From time to time, as I have mentioned, I played golf with my son. Most times he won.

I see on Thursday, 31st March, Nicholas, my son, and his cousin, Michael, that is my sister's son, arrived at Dove Cottage. All three of us played golf at the Lewes course on the Friday. We went round twice, thirty-six holes. Of course, the young chaps won. I am what I call an old hacker, and play off twenty-eight handicap, and came up with a score of 102 and 108. Got tired I suppose. I could not do two rounds now.

On the Saturday we played golf at Seaford Head, one round, the same results. On the Sunday, we played again at Seaford Head, self 103, Nicholas 84 and Michael 79. There was one thing that did amuse me and that was when I used to win a hole or two while playing, the look on these young chaps' faces, as though to say, How did the old man do that? I would love to have had a cine camera and taken the expressions on their faces. Of course, Nicholas was a ten handicapper, and Michael a nine handicapper. But playing golf three days running, especially two rounds on the first day, I wondered whether these young chaps were trying to do me in. That was ten years ago. I must have been fitter then than I am now!

Another little upset I had in my business was I purchased nine Simmital x Friesian heifers at £378, delivered in to a new customer. They arrived at his farm, he must have weighed them, as he rang me back and said they were not heavy enough for him. In my opinion they were just right for single sucklers later on, but the customer has the last say. I thought I had got them on my hands, and nowhere to put them, so I phoned another customer of mine, explained the situation, and he took them without hesitation, so that was a relief.

Then on 12th July. 1988, my old friend Peter and I stayed at an hotel at Petworth, West Sussex, for the purpose of judging farms in the Petworth area the next day. It was quite an experience. Very good farming, most of them had lovely soil, coming from the soil Peter and I managed, we called it boys ground. This is where we had the experience of seeing polo ponies being shod on a farm where the farmer let his stables out for the purpose of stabling these ponies. My goodness! these ponies, they seemed to be very pointed on,

I think they call it, the withers, just over the shoulders, in front of the saddle area. They looked very fit, just bone and muscle. They had to be for speed. Something different from the cart horses I worked with through the war years. When I asked how much these ponies cost to purchase, I could hardly believe my ears when told five thousand to twenty thousand pounds a piece. They came from the Argentine country. I read a book of Jilly Cooper's about the polo game, and by gosh! it was not just playing polo they got their fun from.

On 30th July, myself, my wife and my son went to Corpusty in Norfolk. I must not forget

the black Labrador dog named Max that always came with us. We rented a self-contained semi-detached house for a week. The lawn ran to a lovely clear stream at the bottom, and ducks used to come waddling on the lawn for pieces of bread my son used to feed them. We had never been to Norfolk before for a holiday. We travelled about, went on the Broads, and had a lovely time. Different scenery to Shropshire, Wales and the surrounding views.

On 15th August, 1988 I met Michael Apton at the farm to look at the grass situation on the farm, as he wanted me to purchase three hundred more Kent ewes, making his flock up to four hundred. I would have loved to have purchased three hundred more Kent ewes, but I thought he might be over stepping the mark with his grass for grazing situation. He was the same gentleman I had purchased his first one hundred Kent ewes in the previous year. But looking at the farm's grass situation, I advised him to let me purchase just two hundred Kent ewes later on, so that was the agreement.

On 11th October, 1988 I looked at John Barnham's bull beef with Jack Drummond, the gentleman who was in charge of selling all livestock for the partnership. As you may remember, this was the Barnham partnership whom I worked for as working manager for five years. I was asked by John to look at these bulls, and the gradings and price per kilo they had got from another abattoir. I could see that it was a lower price than they would get from Borthwicks, where I suggested they should go, and it was a better price; also, they used to take them five or six at a time in their Williams trailer, and I had that custom until they gave up bull beef. It is extraordinary how life is: when I farmed with John Barnham, I never dreamed that his name and friendship would come up in the rest of my farming life or, as a matter of fact, his brother George. It is like my dear old mother would say "Ah my boy, it was to be!"

Then on 13ᵗʰ October, 1988 I went to Ashford Market shearling and ewe sale, to purchase two hundred Kent shearling ewes for Michael Apton. There were certainly lovely runs of Kent shearlings, and I was able to purchase the two hundred I wanted. After the purchase of these shearlings, I went to the café for lunch, and while sitting eating my lunch, a gentleman came up to me and asked me whether I was the man who had purchased two hundred Kent shearling ewes that day. I said I was, to which he replied: "Well, you are a lucky man, as they are all ten pounds cheaper than they were last week." The gentleman in question was one of the top Kent breeders in the Romney Marsh, so my customer was a very fortunate young man.

On 9ᵗʰ November, 1988 I purchased from Dick Longden fifty-six Border Leicester cross Mules, which were grazed on the same farm as Dick Longden's ewes he had out to keep. The Suffolk Rams went in with these fifty six ewes on 14ᵗʰ November, 1988.

On 8ᵗʰ December, 1988 I met Dick Longden, and worm drenched Dick's and my sheep. Twenty-six Border Leicester shearlings with one Suffolk ram, I sent to one customer's farm and thirty and a Suffolk ram to another customer's farm, out to keep for the winter.

On 19ᵗʰ December, 1988 I paid my usual visit to my old friend in the village of my school days, whom I worked with on my uncle's farm during the war, and also on to my other old friend I knew from my school days, and took them a bottle of drink for Christmas, and had of course, a lovely talk, mostly about the past years.

On 28th January, 1989 I sold and loaded up twenty six Border Leicester shearlings with a Suffolk ram, that I had put out to keep on my own, and paid for sheep keep.

On 23rd February, 1989 I sold the remaining thirty Border Leicester shearlings and a Suffolk ram that I had purchased the previous autumn, and paid for the keep. I managed to make fifteen pounds per head on the fifty six shearlings, and two rams.

I remember in March 1989 a lady customer whom I was taking fat cattle from for F.M.C. I had marked out a batch – they were black Hereford cross Friesian steers – and dashed if she took two of the marked steers to Ashford Market, to see I suppose if they would make more there. Well, I thought she could have told me, but that is the sort of thing that can happen. My wife said to me, "Don't have any more from her," but I did and carried on as usual, picking them out for F.M.C., but it was rather upsetting at the time.

On 13th march, 1989 Dick Longden sold fifty full mouthed in-lamb ewes that I had purchased from him, but they never made any more money per head than I had paid for them, so I lost money on these, which amounted to the cheque I had to pay for their keep. So that was my little venture on purchasing my own sheep.

On that same day was Mr. Fred Ruskin's funeral, the very good neighbour I had while I was at Coleman's Farm. He had had a very good innings as he was getting on for ninety.

On 23rd March, 1989, fifty Limosin cross, three months old steers were purchased by one of my fat cattle customers.

On 31st march, 1989 my son Nicholas's cousin, Michael, and his girlfriend, came to stay for the weekend. As Nicholas, my son, was staying the weekend, we were worried where

242

we were going to sleep Michael, so my wife and I went and purchased a very nice camp bed, and put it in my office. We had never met Liz before. A very nice girl she was too.

We need not have worried, as when they were going back on the Sunday, Michael said to me: "Uncle Ken, Liz and I are going to buy a house and live together!" I said, "Well, very nice, too," but at the same time thought, "as you are young it would be nice to marry." But they certainly had their heads screwed on alright, as they lived together for five years, then got married, and now have two sons.

I know at the time Michael's eldest sister said, "Uncle Ken, they might just as well live together the way they are going on."

Michael is my sister's son, and six months older than my son, Nicholas, and apparently he came down to see his mother and father, purposely to tell them that they, Liz and himself, were going to live together, Because he could not bring himself to tell her, he went back and wrote to his mother that Liz and himself were going to live together. My goodness! my sister was so upset to think that her son was going to live with Liz without marrying her, but when my sister and my brother-in-law were invited to visit Liz's parents, Liz's mother took my sister aside and said, "Don't worry, my dear, my other daughter did exactly the same." So it seemed as though that remark settled things a little, but I remember my brother-in-law told my sister, as my sister was so upset, "Don't worry love, things are very different from the days when we first met, no doubt we most likely would have done the same if it was in these times." I would not like to know the answer my sister gave him. No doubt it would be, "Oh no, we would not have lived together!" but I wonder!

At the time of writing, 15th May, 1998, I attended a funeral of my friend Bill Skye. I had known him and his wife, Peg, for thirty years. He was a farm manager, farming about twenty-five miles from where I was farming. We kept in touch and visited each other once or twice per year. He always kept a lovely flock of Scotch half bred breeding ewes on the farm. I had met him on different occasions at Findon Fair. As I told Peg, we were always made very welcome when we visited them, and I always remember her lovely cooking. Anyway, the funeral went off very well. Bill said when he passed away that he wanted the bagpipes, as, of course, they came from Scotland in 1946. That was the first time I had seen bagpipes played at a funeral. The piper himself was very tall and smart in his lovely appropriate uniform, and Bill requested he play Amazing Grace, which he did, and it was very nice. I'm afraid that time affected me emotionally, so I had to pull myself together. The other thing he requested was a special bottle of whisky he had saved be opened after the funeral. The family made sure that all was in operation that Bill had requested. He had had a good innings, as my dear father would have said, as he lived to the age of 87.

On 10th May, 1989, I was asked to speak to a Women's Guild on farming. They got in touch with me through the NFU. It was held at the Saltdean Lido, and I believe they have all sorts of functions there. Well, I was introduced to these ladies, and I spoke about the experiences I had through the farming year when I was a farm manager. There were two things that I was sure would come up at question time. They were, free range eggs around the farm yard, and the lovely warm milk straight from the cow. They were talking about fifty and sixty years previously, so my answer was, "I am glad I am at the age I am, as I have experienced both. Take the egg situation. If there were not the hen battery plants producing eggs that are just as good as any other egg, and by the way, the brown shell egg that some housewives class as the best eggs, it is all a fallacy, and the quality of the egg is just as good - it is all psychological.

244

When I was a boy we used to collect the eggs around the hay stacks, as my father was a farmer, and my mother had several chickens running around the farm yard. Some laid their eggs in the houses they roosted in, but many more laid them at the bottom of the hay and corn stacks, also in stinging nettles etc., so looking at the subject of fresh eggs, as you ladies believe, sometimes one would come across a nest with five or six eggs in, and of course, they were mixed with the rest, and the week's eggs that were not used were sold in the shops, and another thing, the egg companies like Stonegate, they collected eggs each week in packing cases, so it looks as though eggs can keep quite a while before deteriorating. The other thing I must mention is in those days, before the second world war, and during it, many farms had cows milked and wintered in cowsheds, and at that time, abortion in herds was prevalent, and, of course, the cows were housed for the winter in the cowsheds, and these sheds were cleaned out twice per day by wheelbarrow from the gutters behind the cows. Well, all the juices and urine were all mixed in the dung, wheeled out to the dung heap on planks to build the heap. As one got to the end of the last plank, one just tipped the wheelbarrow of dung each time until it came level at the top, and then put another plank down to wheel the barrow on to extend the length of the heap. Now, where did the chickens go? On the dung heap, scratching about and devouring all sorts of unsavoury food ! That is after they had been fed wheat for breakfast. I think, if people knew about this at the time, they would most likely think differently than they do today!"

The next question was milk. Why cannot we have the lovely fresh milk straight from the cow? Well, I used to hand milk cows during the war and I can tell you if you saw what went into the buckets before it went through a strainer, you would not drink a drop of milk from that day to this. Very often the cows' udders were not washed, and the milkers never washed their hands from one cow to the next, and sometimes to make it easier for milking, one used to squirt a little milk on ones hands, and sometimes a coloured drop or two used to fall into the bucket. Today's milk is all through machines, very sterilized, untouched by hand, straight from cow to refrigerated bulk tank, taken away each day by refrigerated tanker. Also a sample is taken for hygiene and quality of the milk, and herds are tuberculosis and abortion free, which they certainly were not in those days we have been talking about. There was going to be a scheme set up before the 1939-45 war for all cows to be tested for tuberculosis as there were so many of the population in this country becoming ill, and dying from this terrible disease. But the war came and the scheme was scrapped, so the milk you drink nowadays is the most hygienic milk that has ever been produced."

So with that they thanked me and asked me how much they owed me, and I said, as the NFU. was asked for someone to speak on farming, I would not charge, but another time I would.

Well, there was another time I was asked to speak to them again, but this time I told them it would be a pleasure, but I would charge £25. The reply came back they could not afford it, so that was that, end of that episode.

On 13th May, 1989 I played golf at the Royal Eastbourne Golf Club with Nicholas, his friend and his friend's father. In my opinion the course itself did not live up to its name, especially when I was playing a member of the club. On one hole I was just going to play third shoot to the green, I got hold of an iron, saw how far it was from the green, changed my mind, got another iron out of the bag, and before I hit the ball, two chaps on the tee behind me shouted "Get on with it!" I said to the member of the club that I was playing, "My goodness, I have never been shouted at on a golf course before, and I think it is very bad manners," to which he replied, "I have never heard anyone shout like that before. Whether they were members or visitors, I do not know."

On 17th June, 1989 Nicholas, my son, changed his car to another MG Maestro EFI 2 litre. It was black, so we named it Black Beauty. Being 2 litres, it took fewer seconds to reach 60 m.p.h.. It was another grade up from his other Maestro.

Also on that day, a purchaser picked up four in-calf Friesian heifers I had sold him for £720 per head from Mr. Ellington's British Friesian herd, and lovely heifers they were. I always reckoned theirs was a first class herd. This herd had been established over the last fifty to sixty years.

On 19th June, we had to take Nicholas's Maestro to a firm in Seaford as it had a cracked windscreen and had to be renewed. While that was being seen to Nicholas and I played golf at Seaford Head. Nicholas was getting quite a good golfer by that time, and went round in 77. I being a 26 handicapper, went round in 100. I call myself a golf hacker, but enjoy playing.

On 24th June, 1989, I played golf at Nicholas's Portsmouth Golf Club, where he was a member. It shows one how golf is up and down. Nicholas went round in 81, and myself 94, and, of course, I won. I do not think he has ever forgotten that, especially as it was my first time playing that particular course.

From time to time I still purchase a certain amount of cattle through the summer for F.M.C. and Borthwicks.

On 8th July, 1989, all three of us went to North Yorkshire for a week's holiday. We rented a bungalow on a cattle and horse farm. The owners had the pantechnicon for taking very valuable race horses all over the country. The farm was situated about eight miles from Thirsk. There was a race course at Thirsk. Well, on the journey up to North Yorkshire,

I had a Ford Granada estate car 2.3 litres, the second one I had as the first one I had an accident with, and it was written off. However, as the journey was 300 miles, Nicholas took over driving half way, when we stopped as we wanted to relieve ourselves of water pressure. We were just getting out of this ditch, and I noticed water running from under the front of the car. We lifted the bonnet up, and sure enough, the water pump was leaking, It was just lucky enough our dog, Max, was with us, and we always had a bottle of water for him. So we filled the water tank up and stopped several times to refill again until we got to our destination. Once we got to this bungalow I called the AA. and he was out there within two hours. He said: "Well, it certainly is the water pump. I will phone to see if I can get one of that type, and if so I can put it on for you." The extraordinary thing was the garage he phoned, they had just put the last one on a Granada, so they said if I was there on Monday morning at 9.00 am. they would get one and fit it. So we arranged that. Come the next morning, Sunday it was, I said to my wife and son "What about going down to Thirsk for coffee, because if I filled the water tank on the Granada, of course the radiator took quite a lot of water as it leaked over night, but it would allow us to go to Thirsk and back. So off we went. We picked out a lovely hotel to have our coffee in. It was lovely coffee. While we were there I got in conversation with an elderly couple, and remarked on the quality of the coffee, and they said they had retired and lived 25 miles away, but always came to this hotel for coffee on Sunday mornings.

Then I asked them about where Herriot, the vet, lived about this area, and to our surprise they said, "If you go out of this hotel, turn left, then the first road on the right, that is where his surgery is, and his surname is White really, and, of course, instead of the surgery being in Darrowby, it was

Thirsk." Neither of us could believe that his vet's practice was Thirsk and not Darrowby.

Well, Monday morning came and I was at this particular garage to have a water pump put on. They had told me that the job would take two hours, which it did, and they made a lovely job of it. Then came paying for it. I had taken my cheque book with me, also a Nat West Access card, which I only took on holidays. The amount to pay was £72. I offered my credit card, and to my surprise they told me they did not deal in those. So I had to write out two cheques as they were a family firm and they had not got around to credit cards. But they certainly made a first class job of the water pump.

I will always remember what a lovely holiday we had.

Pat and Nicholas took the dog, Max, for quite hilly walks. As soon as Nicholas saw quite a hilly part of the area, he wanted to walk, and he did.

We went for a drive and on the right side of the road there was quite a steep part of the country side. Of course, we stopped. Nicholas, his mother and Max went to tackle, as I call it, this little mountain. I was invited to go, but declined, and stayed in the car. But eventually I walked back along the road to a very open area, and in this area I saw quite a few separate walled built places with no roof on them, so as I could not recall the purpose of these places, I walked over to them. There was quite a lot of heather about the place, and as I looked into them it dawned on me what they were. Butts for grouse shooting. That was quite an experience, as I had never set foot in one before, or had seen the real thing, only in shooting magazines. While I was in one, I imagined my father being in one when these grouse were coming over these butts, as he was a quick and excellent shot. I bet he would have raised a few eyebrows. It was a lovely holiday, and the weather was good. I did not realise Yorkshire was so vast.

However, we made our way home safely on Saturday, 15th. As soon as I opened the door into our home, I said, "Lovely to go away for a few days, but how lovely to be back home again."

On Sunday 16th Nicholas and I played golf at Seaford Head, and with my 26 handicap, I won. Nicholas went round in 80 and myself in 92. So that was a nice end to the holiday.

I had been thinking of changing my Granada estate as it had 75,000 miles on the clock, also I asked the engineering firm whom I always dealt with, what the difference would be if I changed it now, or waited until next year. I was told I would drop £1,000, so I asked them to look out for me a 2.3 litre estate, preferably a Volvo.

Well, they eventually got hold of one, a three year old estate, the top model, a Turbo 760 with leather seats, air conditioning, and as I am very tall, it was just right for me to drive and sit in comfortably. The other great thing was it was automatic, and after driving that car with automatic, I would never go back to manual gear change again.

But the price was £12,500, and it was beyond what I could afford in my small business. In exchange they gave me £3,500 for the Granada, and that meant I had still got to find £9,000. Well, I talked it over with my wife, Pat, and said that my business would not warrant £9,000, but her answer was: "You have always wanted a Volvo, so have it. We can purchase it with money my Auntie left me." So on 17th, at 9.00 am., Pat and I went to look at this Volvo, and drove it up the road, came back to the garage, and Pat liked it straight away, so that is how we became the owners of the Volvo 760 Turbo Estate 2.316 cc, manufactured 1.6.86, C897WLP. We named it Phoenix, as when I looked up in a car magazine, it was described so, as it is a biggish car, does not look fast, but when the Turbo comes in, it is just like something shooting out of the ashes. I remember when an engineer brought it back from a service, he said to me, "My goodness, that estate car of yours is the most impressive estate car I have ever driven."

On Saturday 22nd, Nicholas drove Phoenix and we all three went to Rye, had tea there, then onto Fairlight, near the church where nowadays there are car parks, and so the general public can walk the Fire Hills, as they are called, in that area, and just to mention and my dear sister was married at Fairlight Church. Then we went on to Crowhurst and had a drink at the pub there. Of course, Crowhurst is where I was a manager on a farm for 20 months, and Nicholas went to Crowhurst School. While we were sitting having a drink in the pub, we were talking about Nicholas's school days at the school, and he said: "Just down the road from here is the football pitch. I used to look forward so much to the day in the week we used to go down there and practise, so hopefully we were good enough to play other teams." I think they were quite successful in those days. He was mad about football, but eventually, when he went to a bigger school after he was eleven years old, there was rugger there, and then he forgot the football, and went rugger mad.

I remember when I was managing a farm, at the time Nicholas was at the larger school, there used to be a maintenance man come to see to the diesel heating boiler. One day we were talking while he was washing his hands, and he said, "My son goes to the same school as yours does, and do you know what his nick name is?" I said, "No, I don't," and he said, "Well, at rugger they call him E.Q." "Oh," I said, "Why?" "It means Earth Quake" he said. Well, that was the first we had heard of it!

On 24th July, 1989 I see I purchased 7 bulls from the farm my old friend Peter Braden managed, and the same day, 80 lambs for F.M.C. The lambs came from a customer; I always had his fat cattle. I finished up with having the rest of his fat lambs. A very tragic thing happened to this young man. His father still worked for an oil company, and one weekend where his mother and father were being driven home, they were involved in a motor accident, and both his mother and father were killed. I suppose, when one thinks about it, the only lovely thing about it was they both went together. That same day, I sent 20 fat cattle to Borthwicks, from David Patch's farm, the beginning of his fat cattle off grass.

On 28th July, my old friend Peter Braden took me to the game fair, which was held at Reading. It was very enjoyable.

On 5th August, Pat and I picked a few pounds of black currants at a local fruit farm, and had lunch at the Golden Galleon, which, being situated on the Seaford side of the Haven River, obviously is Seaford, what a co-incidence, as I now live at Seaford.

But little did I know of the tragic thing was to happen by the end of that month that changed my life. It is a good thing we do not know what is ahead of us sometimes. I see on 8th August I had another 14 fat cattle for Borthwicks from David Patch's farm.

Now, going back to 1979 year, when I was managing Coleman's Farm and fat cattle, where the cash flow came from. I remember just coming back from Haywards Heath store sale after purchasing several good pens of cattle, young Ray, who worked for us, met me as soon as I was back, and said, "You had better come down to the brooks," which was the farthest end of the farm. On the way down he explained that when he was putting nitrogen on, a steer, all of a sudden, put its head up from grazing, tore across the smaller field which joined the 50 acre field which was the biggest field on the farm, where also we had not long ago had a fence erected by the same gentleman and his sons that picked our straw bales up and stacked them. It was a lovely fence, stock wire netting and two strands of barbed wire at the top. He could not believe his eyes: this steer kept going at race horse speed, hit the fence and somersaulted on top of the fence, fell the other side and went off grazing with the others. One soon saw the damage it had done to the fence. As soon as I saw the steer it was grazing with the other as if nothing had happened, but I noticed switches of the ears from time to time, and thought, "that will have to be shot!"

We went straight back and I phoned the knacker man, told him the situation, and he said he'd be there in an hour, and he was as good as his word. He, and his top man with a 22 calibre rifle. I always remember it, he edged up in his Land Rover within 25 yards of this steer that was standing between two other steers. I said, "Don't shoot one of the others" as they seemed to be standing very close together. I ought to have know different. This rifleman raised the rifle, aimed, pulled the trigger, and the steer fell down like a log, dead.

The bullet had hit it dead centre of his forehead.

I was 53 years of age at the time, and with all my experience with dairy cows, single sucklers and fat cattle, I had never experienced this situation before. When I asked the knacker man if he had come across this thing before, he said yes, and recalled a time when he was called to shoot a lovely Charilais steer. As soon as they got out in the field, it charged the Land Rover. They had difficulty with it but shot it in the end, and the cause was an abscess on the brain! and the steer they shot of ours had exactly the same trouble. Happily I did not have another occurrence for the rest of the years I was managing that farm.

In that same year, I was looking at the younger steers, which in numbers I had 120, and was in a batch of them when I noticed two black limo steers could hardly walk, and they were from the batch I had recently purchased. They were so bad, we had to take our old cattle tractor-drawn trailer to get them in, so we could get them up to the yard. I called the vet. He examined them, looked at me and said, "Well, Ken, they have lamenitis." I looked at him and said,

"They cannot have, horses have that." "Ah, he said, "so do cattle." Well, that is another thing I had never seen before in cattle, but with the prescribed treatment, they soon got well.

On 11th August, 1989 I went to look at sheep keep out at Folkestone, enough for 300 lambs through the winter, purchased it, and had it for two years, just right for a customer that farmed near Tenterden.

I remember as soon as I kept appointments on farms and, of course, drove there in our Volvo estate car, I soon got quite a lot of stick, such as, "My goodness, Ken, there must be a lot of money in this beef job." Eventually I got fed up with it, and told each farmer remarking on those lines, "Ah, young man, the bank owns the car," meaning it was purchased on borrowed money but, of course, it wasn't, but it stopped these remarks.

On 29th August, 1989 I took my wife, Pat, to the doctors as she was below par. He came up with gall bladder trouble, gave her some pills to take, and said come back in a week's time. Well, on 30th at lunch time, Pat could not eat anything and she felt sick. I said, "You go and lie down, as I have got to go to the bank, and I'll be back in about an hour's time." I went to the bank, got back to Dove Cottage, unlocked the front door, and shouted out, "I am back," which I always did when I got back from different farms. There was no answer, so I went up to the bedroom and there was Pat, sitting on the edge of the bed in agony. Pat was the kind of person who would not complain about pain if she could help it, and kept it to herself too much. So I phoned the doctor. It happened to be his half day off as he said, but I told him,, "It was only yesterday at 5.35 pm. she came to see you," and that he had given her pills. He said, "I'll be there as soon as possible," and he was. He arrived in the family estate car with his three boys and his wife. He went up to see Pat and within a few minutes he phoned for an ambulance. He was most efficient, wrote out a note for the ambulance, also

254

gave me a phone number so that if the ambulance wasn't there in twenty minutes, to phone them on that number, which I had to, but they were on their way, and before he left he said to me: "I am not supposed to, but I could see the pain in her eyes, so I injected her immediately." I said: "Thank God for that."

The doctors at the hospital did not know really what it was, until 31st, then said she was seriously ill with inflammation of the pancreas. On 1st September, when I was there, she was in intensive care and her kidneys failed. They had not got a dialysis machine and they were going to transfer her to Brighton, but there was some scare of some bug that was running riot there, so they had to transfer her to Guy's Hospital in London. Thank goodness, before I left that day I told her our son had won a cup at golf, and that I loved her. When I got home I phoned to see when she was going. A male nurse answered and said Pat was just going, being put in the ambulance for her journey to Guy's Hospital, and what I thought so marvellous was, he said, "Hold on and I will get her on the phone for you," which he did, and I was able to have a word with her and told her Nicholas and I would see her that evening. How thoughtful that male nurse was. Eastbourne Hospital is the most marvellous hospital to be in when one is ill.

So Nicholas, Max the dog and I went to stay at my sister's in Seal, Sevenoaks, as it was much closer to Guy's Hospital. Then late that evening, I had a phone call from Guy's, telling me Pat was much worse than they were led to believe, and was in intensive care and was on one of their breathing apparatuses, and that it was best for us to come as soon as we could. Good job my son had a car, and he drove us up there, as I could not. Well, we arrived, they gave us a pot of tea and toast and were very kind, and from then on we stayed at Pat's bedside, but, of course, she was not conscious, and this breathing apparatus was not nice to see as it pushed her head up as it worked. We just sat there, holding her hand, and talking to her as we were told she may hear what we were saying, and at 3.30 am. they said we had better stay. So they found a bed in the nurses' home, and I slept in the bed and Nicholas slept on the floor. At 8.30 am. we were ready to go and see Pat. As we were going up the steps to the intensive care unit, Nicholas said, he is a very quiet voiced chap, like his mother, "You go in, I cannot." I could tell he was upset and I said, "That is OK, my boy," and I can tell you now, I had a hell of a job to go in there without breaking down. Well, it was decided that we go back home to my sister's and they phoned us before the end. Nicholas and me sat on a seat outside the hospital. Being in the farming world, my goodness, I have been very, very tired at times, but nothing like I was at that moment. I was so tired I could have easily fallen flat on my face if I had not sat down.

Anyhow, we went back to my sister's, that would be 2nd September, but on the Sunday, 3rd, we had a phone call to go to Guy's as soon as possible. My sister, Sylvia, and her husband Peter, came as well, and at 2.30 pm. my darling Pat passed away. That was the most horrendous time of my life.

People are very kind. Pat's cousin from Shropshire came to stay with Nicholas and I to show us how to cook, and help at the funeral as we had never cooked in our lives before, only a boiled egg or fried bacon and eggs.

On 15th September the funeral went off very well, with my sister and her husband, Peter, also their two daughters and son. Then came the terrible time of living without Pat.

On the weekend after his mother's funeral, Nicholas, my son, said to me, "I am going to leave Ferrantis at Portsmouth, and get a job in Brighton, as you are not going to live on your own." My answer was: "It is a lovely thought, my boy, thank you, but you are not going to ruin your life for me." I would not be happy, as I knew as he had been at Ferrantis for four years, he had made a lot of friends, especially through the golf club he belonged to at Portsmouth, and golf he loved.

So immediately he said: "Well then, I am coming home every weekend from Friday night to Sunday night," which he did, and all his golfing at Portsmouth was forgotten for a whole year. Odd times we had a game at Seaford Head Golf Course, for I realised what he had given up for me.

I have always thought that Nicholas saved me that year, as I felt like shooting myself, and the other thing that helped was, I had a son like Nicholas, thank God for him. I could not understand how I used to breakdown every day and cry, a big chap like me. It was a good job I had my little business to run. But farmers and their wives were very kind to me. I remember going to one particular farmer, he had just done the milking and had his breakfast, but as I arrived he said, "Come in, Ken, sit down," this was in the farm house kitchen, "while I have a wash and shave." His wife immediately said, "Have a coffee, Ken?" and I said, "Yes, please," and this lovely cup of coffee was put in front of me, made with Guernsey hot milk. I looked at the cup of coffee, tasted it, and said to the farmer's wife, "What a lovely cup of coffee, it reminds me of the coffee my mother used to make." It was lovely. I was at that particular farm for the purpose of picking out fat cattle for F.M.C. (Fatstock Marketing Corporation). The farmer's wife said to me. "It is best to talk about a bereavement, Ken." We did, and she was quite right.

That particular farmer certainly knew how to fatten cattle. These cattle were from Guernsey cows, with a Charalais bull on the cows, and a Sussex bull on the heifers. The Sussex cross steers were OK, but the heifers tended to get over fat if one did not watch it, and of lower weights, but these Charalais crosses, they were excellent. I told them at the

257

timc to keep to the same AI. nominated bulls, as they were no doubt right on that herd. This farmer and his brother's Guernsey herds were the first Guernsey herds I had ever selected fat cattle from, and my goodness, I could hardly believe how good they were. Oh, AI. stands for Artificial Insemination.

On 23rd September, 1989, my old friend Peter Braden and I were invited to judge ploughing out in the Henfield area. The ploughing to be judged was at West Grinstead in Sussex. Very enjoyable day. Peter, of course, picked me up to go to this particular area.

On 3rd October, 1989 I went to Ashford to the Kent Ram and Ewe Sales and purchased thirty-five Kent ewe tegs and one Kent ram for Michael Apton, the same young farmer that I started his first flock of Kent ewes, and built it up to 300 Kent ewes.

On 13th October, 1989, my old friend Peter Braden picked me up at 6.00 pm. and drove me to the annual West Grinstead District Ploughing and Agriculture Society dinner, held at 7.00 pm. in Henfield Village Hall. That was an enjoyable evening.

On 21st October I attended a party, a farewell one, for a Bishop, such a lovely man. If a tramp came along he would speak to him, and as my old friend Peter said, a more religious man he had never met. I always said that is how a Bishop should be. He went on to become Bishop of a big cathedral, and also, a boy spilled the beans on him. It just goes to show we all have failings. A little like when my mother, in her young days, was a devout church goer, and attended a church for years. The vicar was such a lovely orator, and when preaching, he preached so that the ordinary layman could understand, and could hold his congregation so much that one would not mind sitting there listening to him until 12.00 at night. But, then my mother learnt that he was an atheist! And my dear old mum told us that it nearly broke her faith. To think he was an atheist and to stand up in that pulpit and preach the word of God! Well, it was a shock to her, especially being in the Victorian era.

Going hack to the present day, 15th June, 1998, our very dear friend Ann was buried today. It was such a shock to Olive, my partner, and myself, as Ann was only 60 years old, and a very special person to us. Poor girl, she died of a very sudden heart attack. I always remember when I first introduced Ann to Olive. They got on the first moment they met. It just goes back to my dear old mum's saying, "Ah, my boy, we have all got an allotted time on this earth, and when the good Lord calls, you have got to go." Of course, we only pass by once in this life time. There is no second chance.

On 23rd October, 1989. I looked at a couple of batches of Hereford steers for a customer ready to fatten in yards, and purchased 36, 24 at £438 and 12 at £420. They were the right price at the time, especially being delivered free of charge, but alas, the following spring, B.S.E. hit the beef industry hard, and spelt disaster in the beef world.

On 29th October, I fetched my sister from Seal, Sevenoaks, for the weekend. She was very kind to me after my dear Pat passed away. Many weekends I would fetch her and then her husband, Peter, would come down to stay with their old friend Mr. King. It was all a great help to me at that period of my life.

On 13th November, 1989 I went to a farm in Pett, Sussex. Sale accepted price of 20 Red Hereford steers at £320, also I see I had an order of 20 three month old Limo bull calves for March 1990 from a large farmer who farmed in Aldington, Kent. They farmed, I believe, four square miles of land, the biggest farmers I had as customers. I also put sheep out to keep for them, so in my small business I had customers further afield than I thought.

On 1st December, 1989, I purchased 25 male cross Suffolk lambs, dagged, injected and worm drenched, and put them out to keep on one of my first customers' farms.

I see on 8th December I had a rest from the business and played golf at Lullington Golf Course in Kent, close to Iford. I played with Nicholas, and David, David being my sister's eldest daughter's husband. Ah, yes it looks as though I lost! The score Nicholas 84, David 103 and myself 105. But we enjoyed it, and also had a lovely meal at my niece's home. She is a very good cook, so that put the icing on the cake, as they say.

On 12th December, 1989 I went to a shoot on an estate in West Sussex, by invitation from Dick Longdon. I had a few misses at pheasants that my dear old dad would have brought down if he had been there. Then at 2.00 pm. I went to lunch at a local pub, all especially laid on by Dick, and what a marvellous lunch it was. He certainly did us well. This estate was around the Lodsworth area.

25th January, 1990, I sold seven Hereford cross Friesian heifers to start a single suckler herd. The gentleman had not done this sort of thing before. I just hoped they were going to be well managed as they came from the very good British Friesian dairy herd of Messrs. Ellington. Also that day, the youngest son of Mr. Ellington ordered 40 three month old steer calves per month for five months from July onwards.

On 30th January, 1990 I went to a rough pheasant shoot on the land my old friend, Peter Braden managed. I was invited once a year about that time of year. Quite a number of fat cattle were coming off different farms. I purchased for F. M.C. and Borthwicks.

On 20th March, 1990 a customer of mine, David Patch, started playing snooker at a club in Eastbourne, and kept it up over the years, especially when our weekly golf day was put off owing to rain.

I remember a couple of years earlier, Nicholas and I were coming home after playing snooker at the Eastbourne club. It was March, and migration time for toads. As we turned off the main road, there was a sign telling one about this happening at the beginning of the road that ran between a dyke on one side and a large wooded area on the opposite side of the road. This particular evening must have been at the height of the migration of these toads, and ahead of us we saw the lights of a car ambling along with a person holding a torch walking in front of this car. Of course we were going at a snail's pace after we passed the sign. All of a sudden, our head lights picked up these toads crossing the road. Then we realised why the car coming towards us was going so slowly, and a person walking in front with a torch. I had never seen such a sight in my life time. There were a few dead ones that had been run over, but we counted them as we drove very slowly along this mile and a half of road, avoiding running over them as much as possible. We were very successful and counted 132 live ones. I said to Nicholas I would doubt if he would ever see anything like it again in his lifetime. It was a most marvellous experience!

On 6th April I had an appointment with a manager of a farm regarding fat cattle. Being a new customer, I looked at these cattle and remarked at the time who purchased the store cattle, and was told a relative of the farmer, to which I remarked, "Well, many of these cattle have not got the confirmation they should have and, therefore, when they are the right fat class they will not grade," which proved to be right.

They eventually started a single suckler herd of Friesian cross Hereford heifers with a Limosine bull put to them, and that was certainly a different tale with regard to grading those cattle when ready. Up to this particular farm there was a flint lane, and when I came down it and just about got home, I had a flat tyre, and dash me, a flint had cut right into the tyre and the result was a new tyre! It made it a very expensive trip. Thank goodness, I purchased several more cattle from that farm at the time.

On 19th April, 1990, I played golf for the East Sussex Golfing Society at Willingdon Golf Course. I used to play two or three times a year for this Society; sometimes I used to win three to six golf balls an odd time or two, but never the cup, until one year I did. It was not available to be presented, and I never did get this cup. My son, Nicholas, was able to play that competition, and that year he would have won it, but as he was a guest it was not allowed, so he had some other present. But I always enjoyed playing with the other guys. We had some jolly good laughs, and the dinner at night was always good.

On 26th April, 1990 my old friend Peter Braden picked me up at 11.40 am. and took me to Seaford Head Golf Course for our weekly game. On 1st May, 1990 I went to the Grassland Society's spring visit, which was held yearly. I went to some very interesting farms, generally my old friend Peter was there.

On 11 May, 1990 a new Electra Tumble Drier arrived at 7.00 am. which I had purchased new. At that time I was on my own, and Nicholas used to bring his weekly washing home, so that was a great boon. If one got the shirts out as soon as it finished drying, all one had to do was to iron the collars and cuffs, and the shirt was finished. That was just up Nicholas's street, as he had to do the ironing. It is still going strong after eight years.

On 25th May, 1990 Peggy, my late wife's school friend and her husband came at 12.00 noon, and we went to lunch at the local pub.

On 7th June, 1990, I was selecting a few fat cattle to F.M.C., 12 from a local farm. And on 16th June, Nicholas and I started ten days holiday. We went to my late wife's cousins in Ludlow, Shropshire. Joan was an excellent cook, and they always made us very welcome. A lovely base to start off in the morning and come back to about 7.00 pm. Nicholas and I played on four or five golf courses. I remember, on one, part of the course was in Shropshire and the other part was in Wales, and when one was on the highest part of the course one could see two or three counties, marvellous views.

There was some very good farming there. Some parts were poorer ground, only fit for cattle and sheep, and the better ground was cereals and dairy, also some black currants at places. That was on a very big estate. One must remember the land was very undulating, and around that area and Wales there were thousands of sheep and, of course, when you got on the border of Shropshire and Hereford, there were some nice hop gardens, and very good grade ground.

Nicholas and I came back from Ludlow after a lovely holiday on 25th June, and the same day played golf at Haywards Heath, a course we had never played. My score was 108 and Nicholas's 84. Then on the 26th, was the first time we played golf at Lewes, and the first time we hired an electric buggy. Score, self 98, Nicholas 83.

On 29th June, 1990 I went to Neville and Peggy's in Dorchester for three days.

On 2nd July I had interview with Jim Patch regarding cattle.

3rd July I ordered 30 Continental steer calves, three months old at £230 per head for Jim Patch. The same day eight cat cattle went to Borthwicks from his brother David's farm. And on 4th July, I had forgotten about it, but in my diary I see I played golf at Lewes Golf Course for the first time with Jim Patch. We enjoyed it, no doubt, as we always did in the future, but I never put the scores down for that day so I assume they were not very good!

On 6th July, 1990 I went to the Herstmonceux Farmers Club which I belonged to, to their Centenary Buffet Super, an excellent meal, and of course met different farmers and their wives. Had a very nice time.

On 12th July I was picked up by a neighbouring farmer to go and judge oats and spring barley on different farms for the Herstmonceux Farmers Club, and on 13th July, David patch ordered 40 Black Hereford cross Friesian three month old steers at £210.

On 15th July, I played golf with Nicholas, my son, at Seaford Head, but he had one of his off days at golf and at last, a rare occasion, I won - self 97, Nicholas 90.

In July cattle started coming fat off grass more frequently, hence my visits to David Patch's brook ground he fattened cattle from. That I enjoyed very much, especially watching him reading the numbers in the ears of the cattle I selected for fat.

On 18th July, 1990 I played golf for the East Sussex NFU Golfing Society summer meeting at Eastbourne Downs Golf Course. It was a lovely day.

Then on 30th July I had an appointment with Peter Bowles on a farming estate near Haywards Heath to look at Friesian bull beef, and he became another customer for Borthwicks, as they paid a better price for good bull beef.

On 13th August, I met Nicholas at Hindhead golf course in Surrey for a round of golf; score was self 107, Nicholas 84. Very interesting course. This was where Nicholas got a hole in one on a 175 yards 3 par, when playing in a competition, and it cost him £60 in drinks that day. He said, "I hope I don't have the luck to do it again!"

On 14th July Jim Patch ordered 20 more Continental three month old steer calves at £230 for 100 kilos in weight.

On 20th August I had an appointment with the stock manager of Messrs. Barnhams, the same family I was working manager for, lasting five years. The purpose was to look at Friesian bull beef and a few Hereford cross Friesian heifers, and there on I looked at the Friesian bull and selected those that were ready to go fat every month, and continued that business until they gave up bull beef and went into the storage of caravans.

On 28th September, 1990 I had an appointment with Messrs. Barnhams stock manager at 2.30 pm. to pick out 15 twelve month old Friesian cross Hereford steers for a customer out of about 50 very nice young cattle. It seems extraordinary how Messrs. Barnham's name comes up, the farmers I worked for over a five year period. The family started in Haywards Heath area on a 125 acre farm, which six Ayrshire milking cows which they purchased from Haywards Heath cattle market, then graded them up to a Friesian herd. Now, at this date of writing they have a herd of 260 cows and several more acres of land. What an achievement!

On 13th October I purchased a Sussex bull with a bit of Limosin in him from an estate in the Petworth area for the well-known Messrs. Wade's farming concern.

Then on 30th October I picked up my friend and customer, David Patch, for a game of snooker at an Eastbourne club. I joined with Nicholas, my son.

On 9th November, Peter Ellington ordered 40 Friesian cross Hereford three month old black steer calves at £178 per head.

I went to the usual Fatstock Show dinner on 3rd December by invitation of Geoff Baden, my bank manager. I always had a very pleasant time there.

On 7th December I took the two sons of a very good customer to see round the F.M.C. abattoir at Canterbury. They were shown the different fat classes of the animals hanging up. A most interesting day. On the way back they treated me to lunch at Tenterden.

On 16th December several fat cattle coming off farms out of yards and I see that Limosin three month old steer calves are £228 per head.

On 23rd December my son, Nicholas, and I went to my sister's at Seal, Sevenoaks for Christmas, then on 13th January, 1991 I went to lunch with John and Margaret Barnham at 12.45 pm. and we certainly talked a lot about old times when I worked for them.

I went with Peter Ellington and purchased 20 three month old steer calves on 19th January, and on 23rd January I met Dick Langton to look at heifers on a farm, and purchased 27. I travelled quite a bit with Dick, looking at different livestock.

Sadly, on 1st February, my accountant had a heart attack, so no longer could attempt accountancy any more, so I had to go to his home and pick up any files from a Mrs. Brenda Ascot, a friend of his.

I went to a memorial service on 6th February for my cousin Joyce. She was the eldest daughter of my father's sister. Always a sad occasion, but I went back to her son's place where there was a very cheerful gathering.

On 11th February, 1991 I had an appointment with Paul Gent, an accountant, to see if he would take on my accounts. I may add, he was recommended by my bank manager. Well, as soon as we met we got on straight away. We greeted each other by Christian names and shook hands, then I said, looking round his office with the leather studded chairs, "I hope you are not going to charge me an arm and a leg for your services," mentioning the chairs, and he said very quickly "Oh, but they are all on hire purchase." He has been my accountant ever since. We play golf two or three times a year with each other, and try to take some money off each other, and have a jolly good laugh! He is about 54 years old, I call him my boy and he calls me Uncle Ken, so we have been friends every since.

On 20th February, 1991, several fat cattle coming from different farms this month, including Messrs. Wades that I was selecting this morning. I will explain how I select these cattle in different yards. I have a stick about one a half inches thick and about four and a half feet long, and a pot of white paint, I dip the end of the stick in the white paint and I was ready to mark a fat animal. I must admit this particular yard was very long, and the particular ones I wanted to mark came by me at break-neck speed at times, but I managed to mark them alright but, by golly, one had to be quick. I did say to David Wade one day, "Are you sure these cattle in this yard are going to be ready?" and his reply was "Oh, I think so, but don't spoil your reputation!" he did not say what reputation. There was a great advantage to me regards to picking out fat cattle for two abattoirs. I had the experience of selecting fat cattle for a few years when managing a farm where I was responsible for buying the cattle to fatten, and selling them at the right fat class. As I mentioned earlier in this manuscript, I just looked at them and I knew they were ready for the abattoir, except one with a small lump on its side, which I did feel on different parts of its body, decided it was just ready, sent it with the others, and happily it graded out a quality steer. It was the same when I bought cattle at auction. I just watched a particular pen of steers as they went around the action ring while the bidding was going on, and if I thought these cattle were right for our system, I would start bidding before the last bid was accepted. I expect anyone reading this may thing I am big headed, but it was successful, and remember, I was responsible for the outcome!

27th February, 1991, a very sad day. Edmund, a very good dairy farmer who used to play golf with my old friend Peter and myself at Seaford Head Golf Course, it was his funeral on this day. To look at Edmund, he seemed healthy enough. He was a year or two younger than myself. He became ill and within three months he was gone from this world. It comes to mind my dear mother's saying "Ah, my boy, it was to be."

I remember, about a month after his funeral, my old friend Peter and I were playing golf on the same golf course as we three always did once a week, and as Peter and I got on to the 13th fairway, I could see Edmund on my left as clear as though he was there, just going to his golf ball to make another shot. It shows how the mind plays tricks on one sometimes.

My sister Sylvia and her husband Peter came for the weekend on 1st March. As I mentioned before, they came periodically, which was a great help to me.

On 6th March, our friends Bill and Peg Skye came to visit. Lovely to see them and, of course, the main topic was farming, especially about sheep.

I made an appointment with Dick Langden on 12th March 1991 to go to a farm in Hurstpierpoint, regarding cattle, and purchased several. Very good day, and when the lady farmer paid my commission, she thanked me for making the purchase. Nicholas, my son, came for the weekend. I played golf with him, and what a rare occasion, we tied the scores.

On 12th April, I played golf at Willingdon for the NFU. golf society. Best I ever played, 36 points, 18 holes.

On 17th April Dick Langden and I met a customer regarding continental in-calf heifers, made the deal, and replaced same with empty heifers.

On 23rd April I went to the Mid Surrey Farmers' Drag Hunt dinner at the Meridian Hall in East Grinstead at 7.30 pm. Always an excellent dinner. That is where I heard the joke after dinner told by a QC. He began: "Now gentlemen, as, of course, there are only gentlemen attending, we all know about the pearly gates in the sky, and that there are some marriages not so faithful as others. Well, this is the part of heaven where married couples are interrogated as to how faithful they have been in their married life. It came the day the first gentleman was asked had he ever been unfaithful to his wife. His answer was No. So, for getting about in this special place, he was allotted a Rolls Royce car. The second gentleman was asked the same question. 'Well, I did once succumb,' so he was allotted a Serrier Ford car; then came the third gentleman and his answer was, 'I did a couple of times' so he was allotted a Ford Anglia. Well, it came to pass the gentleman with the Rolls Royce was driving along and came to traffic lights which showed red. He stopped immediately, and while waiting a lady on a bicycle came to a halt next to him. When he looked at her, to his great shock it was his wife! So one must assume that his wife had been unfaithful a few times! I came to be invited to these yearly Drag Hunt dinners because whilst waiting I was in the barbers in a nearby market town, I noticed a gentleman reading the paper, and all of a sudden he lowered the paper, and to my surprise, I recognised him as a QC., a friend of my last employer. We got talking, and in the course of conversation I mentioned I had lost my wife. He immediately expressed condolences and said. "Let me have your address, and I will send you an invitation to our Drag Hunt dinner." It was very kind of him, as every year I have an invitation. To those who wonder what a drag hunt is, it is similar to the fox hunt, but instead of hunting the fox, they get someone to lay a scent over different farms so the hounds follows the scent, and no kill at the end of it, and the dinner is held for farmers whose land they have permission to hunt over each year.

On 16th May, I went to stay in Dorchester for three days at the home of my late wife's old school friend and her husband. They always made me welcome, and it made a nice change as I was on my own.

On 22nd May I went to visit, Rosie, my Aunt's niece. Uncle Harry and Aunty Flo owned the 68 acre farm at Bankhurst where I worked during the second world war. Rosie who never married, had a bungalow built in Ore, Hastings, where she lives today, this day of writing 19 August, 1998, being the age of 76 years old. Always have a lovely tea with her, and in recent years have to go about a week before Christmas to have a Christmas dinner with her, always lovely chicken and the trimmings and afterwards, Christmas pudding. She has joy in doing this, very nice. At this time in my life I belonged to Date-Line, as I was determined I would not be on my own if I could help it. On 1st June 1991, I met a very nice lady, Ann Bennett and we spent a very nice afternoon together. We told each other about ourselves, and we eventually went together four or five times. Although we were fond of each other, we parted amicably, and really she became my agony aunt, and kept friends until she died this year, 1998. As my dear mother would say, "Ah, my boy, it was not to be."

On 8th June, 1991 I went to my Aunty Win's party. This lady was my mother's young cousin whom I had not seen for many years. It was a most emotional experience, but we all had a marvellous time.

On 12th June, Nicholas was home on antibiotics from Portsmouth. His doctor told him he had got to be away from work for a week in bed. I quite enjoyed looking after him. His doctor did not tell him what it was he had actually got, so I got a second opinion from my doctor, and it was diagnosed as chicken pox.

On 1st July, Nicholas had to have another week off work owing to this chicken pox.

On 13th July, Messrs. Barnham's stock manager came to tea. During July a few more cattle were coming off grass from different farms, and on 16th July I went on holiday with Nicholas to my late wife's cousin and her husband John in Ludlow. During that time we booked bed and breakfast on a farm in the Manchester area, purposely to see the British 120th Open at The Royal Birkdale Golf Course. My goodness, what a lovely experience. As we had to have our evening meal out, we were half way through our meal, and

Nicholas said, "What about a trip to Blackpool?" Nice experience, but neither of us was very impressed. We were hoping to see the Blackpool lights, but were told we were a fortnight too early, so that was rather disappointing. We ended our holiday in Ludlow on 26th July.

On 12th August, I purchased 14 fat heifers from Messrs. Barnham for F.M.C. and 11 Friesian bulls from another customer for Borthwicks. On 19th August I met Messrs. Barnham's stock manager regarding Friesian bulls for Borthwicks. I always enjoyed selecting cattle. On 4th September I went to a dairy cows sale to purchase five of the best cows for my golf friend's son, which we selected from the catalogue. On the way back from this sale I called into a pub to have some lunch, and well, sitting there on the next table was Jimmy Hill, the football commentator, also a keen golfer. I spoke to him and said, "I saw you at the golf celebrity match at Stoke Poges Golf Course." "Yes, you did, what a coincidence."

On 7th September I went to West Sussex where a couple had just started farming, and they wanted 50 Lieyn breeding ewes, and two rams of the same breed. I took them to a Lieyn breeder of sheep, selected 50 ewes out, and two rams. They were a nice couple. I went and had coffee with them before looking at these sheep, and I got paid my commission on the spot, which was very nice. Then, about three days after the purchase, the young lady farmer phone me and said that a man they had employed to help them with the farm said one of the rams had front hooves not quite right. I said, "I cannot recall that, but if you are not satisfied, the seller will change the ram." I have had many years experience with sheep, so it was quite a puzzle to me. How much their man knew about sheep I do not know.

On 8th September I umpired a fun cricket match between two villages. I had not played cricket for 50 years, but I got on better than I thought. Quite an experience!

I went to dinner with Jim Patch and his wife on 10th
September, and what a lovely spread they provided. VIP.
treatment. I remember during the meal, Jim asked me if I
would like another glass of wine to which I said, "Yes,
please" and with that I got hold of my empty glass, put it
further towards Jim, and must have put it down harder than
I should, as to my surprise and embarrassment the stem came
clean away from the bottom of the glass. I offered to buy a
new glass, but they would have none of it, and said it wasn't
their best glasses, as they had not unpacked the best ones
yet. They were very kind, but I often wonder about it. On
14th September I went to Bexhill cemetery to scrub my late
mother-in-law's grave.

On 25th September I attended the local ploughing match
and met different farmers. I remember going to one in a
previous year and was introduced by a well-known farmer
to two young gentlemen. They had very smart suits on, and
I thought they do not look like farmers, and I said, "What
sort of work do you do, young men?" and they said, "We
are accountants." Of course, as soon as I knew that, I put
both my hands out palms flat, and said, "What about a sub,"
and told them I always put two hands out to accountants,
that made them laugh. My philosophy is if you can make
someone smile or laugh, you are doing a tremendous lot of
good each day of your life. With all the television and paper
talk of today we do not see half the misery in this country
alone that there is.

On 1st October, 1991, Peter Ellington picked me up at
1.30 pm. to meet Messrs. Barnham's stock manager on one
of their farms to look through a bunch of young store cattle,
Friesian crosses, mostly Hereford crosses, store, meaning
fair condition, not fat, to grow them on, ready eventually to
sell fat. He purchased 32 of them for £9,280. As I have said
before, it is extraordinary how many times Messrs.

Barnham's name crops up from time to time, as I was employed by them at a period in my life and it used to bring back memories when I used to go back to their farms I had quite a lot to do with.

On 2nd October, 1991 I met Dick Langden at Stag Park on a large estate in West Sussex, purchased a Sussex bull for a customer, and on 6th October went to see Barbara, my niece, that would be my sister's middle daughter. I visited her at a cottage she had purchased some time before. I took Max, our Labrador dog we had at the time. The cottage was very nice. It was situated in a little village just off the M11, Saffron Walden, Essex. She is certainly a lovely girl, and if I was not her uncle, and was her age and not married, I would certainly try to date her, of course, allowing that I was not too shy. Barbara made me so welcome, and cooked me a lovely Sunday lunch. It made my day.

On 11th October, 1991 I went to the Herstmonceux and District Agriculture Society Harvest Supper, which I generally went to if possible. Had a very nice evening.

On 17th October at 7.30 am. I played golf at Lewes with my friend and accountant, Paul Gent and beat him on strokes, lost on points 32 to 35.

I went to Ashford Sheep Sale on 24th October and purchased 50 Kent shearling ewes and one Kent ram for Michael Apton, the same young farmer I started his Kent flock for.

On 26th October Peter Ellington purchased 30 Hereford cross Friesian heifers from Messrs. Barnham at £270 per head.

On 2nd November I played golf with Nicholas, my son, at Lewes, for a little trophy we had between us. At that time Nicholas held it, but to my surprise I won it back, the score myself 97 and Nicholas 87. November 15th was my 65th birthday. Nicholas, my son, gave me a gold Parker pen. I have always treasured that; then the following evening we went out to a lovely dinner.

On 28th November fat cattle coming out of yards quite well. Today, played golf for NFU. Golfing Society at Bexhill Highwood golf course. It was one I always wanted to play. When visiting my late mother-in-law's grave, one could look right down on this golf course, and I always thought I would love to play that course. Little did I think I would.

Nicholas and I went to my sister and brother-in-law's on 24th December for Christmas. Always had a lovely time.

January 1992, beginning of another year. Cattle flowing from yards fairly well. On 14th January I met a lady from Date Line, I mentioned before, after meeting others that did not materialise. This lady was with me when I had my left hip operation and looked after me very well indeed. But alas, after two years it ended, all amicably thank goodness! On 15th February Nicholas came home. At that time he was waiting for another second hand car as he had written off Black Beauty, the M.G., and had a lucky get off. No one else was involved. He was coming round a roundabout and the front tyre burst. He went up a bank and over the M.G. turned onto the driver's side. Well, two days before he was home I went to look at a Saloon Audi 80E 1984cc, registration March 1990. It was a lovely car, so on the morning the 16th, Nicholas purchased this car and how right that proved to be. On 28th February I attended a well-known farmer's funeral. I knew him pretty well in the NFU. He became chairman to the local branch. I suppose, it was unusual as he was a farm worker before he farmed himself. His name was Tom Flaxton. Anything he was asked to do in the NFU. he would do if possible. I suppose a little like myself. As a farm manager I was voted in as chairman of the local NFU. branch. Generally it was farmers and farmers' sons.

On 28th February 1992 I went to see 15 Friesian cross Hereford 14 month old steers at £375 delivered, and 14 Limo cross much younger at £360 per head, delivered to a farmer which I had purchased. Then on 4th March Peter Ellington picked me up to go to Arundel to look at store cattle, and I purchased all but two.

On 16th April, 1992 I had my left hip replaced at the Horder Centre and on 31st August Geoff Badle and his wife Pam came to dinner. He was my bank manager friend now. Of course, he is retired. We had a very nice evening and they thought I had got a soul mate for life, but as my dear mother used to say, "Ah, my boy, it was not to be!"

Jim Patch and his wife came to dinner on 29th September and we did our best to welcome them and enjoyed a lovely evening. On 31st October, Mike and Liz stayed the weekend. They are my sister's son and his wife. Nicholas, Mike and I played golf at Lewes. I hired a buggy and Mike was chauffeur. That was a laugh! However, I got permission from the Horder Centre doctor. He told me as long as I did not fall about, I would be alright. I can tell you what a relief that was. I completed the 18 holes with a five iron all the time, as my son said, "If you get hold of a three wood you will try too hard." He was right, so we ended up with a lovely weekend, and from there on I played golf in a buggy once a month for six months, so that I did not over do it, and then walked it with an electric bag trolley.

I went to tea with David Patch and his wife on 27th November. That was when they were farming.

I had to go to the doctor's surgery for blood tests as I had thrombosis after my hip operation, and he put me on Warfrin for six months, and after that I was alright, thank goodness. On 9th December I went to lunch with John and Margaret Barnham. A lovely lunch and, of course, lovely talking over old times.

In December of 1992 very few cattle going fat. B.S.E. was really getting hold of the cattle industry. For example, eventually where I purchased three month old calves, overnight they had cancellations and were stuck with many calves on their hands, which, in the end, finished their business. The gentleman in question got a job as a green keeper on a golf course, and his wife started a business in house cleaning. That was only one business gone, but there must have been many more over the country. A very sad time.

On 28th January, 1993, owing to the disaster in the beef industry, I closed my business operation before I started losing money. Rather a sad time, as I would have like to have carried on, but as my dear mother would say, "Ah, my boy, it was not to be!"

I went to the funeral of Johnny Johnson on 5th February. He was a rep for Boots on the farming side and I had been a customer of his for many years. One could not wish for a more genuine and honest man for the job. At last I was able to come off taking Warfrin tablets.

On 27th February I had a rather traumatic experience. Coming up a hill at 6.15 pm., all of a sudden my Volvo 760 Turbo engine made a heck of a bang, and a hole appeared in the side of the block. This engine had only done 82,000 miles, never used any oil, and no one seemed to know the cause. So I had to have a reconditioned engine put in at over £2,000 cost, so that was quite a blow. The new engine has done 49,000 miles and seems quite alright at the time of writing, 25th August, 1998.

Going back to my business, I recall I looked at some Friesian steers for a farmer and his son that I knew a few years. They were not satisfied with the local market. I may add that it was at the time when the B.S.E. was hitting the beef industry hard, and they knew I had had to start my business from scratch, and also knew the circumstances why.

Well, I selected a lorry load of these steers, and sent them to F.M.C. Canterbury. The farmer's son told the hauliers they were not going to pay for cartage, and as all customers of the two abattoirs I dealt with paid their own cartage, I phoned this farmer's son and spoke to him about it. He said, "We are not going to pay," so I said, "What does your father say about this?" and he said, "He agrees with me." With that I said "Well, I'll never do any more business with you," and I never did. It seemed to me that some farmers did not want me to succeed. Sometimes I wondered if it was jealousy, but I do not know why.

Well, following that little episode I had occasion just before the Christmas of that year, to go to visit the senior partner of the cattle haulage firm, Alec Teal. Just before each Christmas I would have a phone call from Alec. The conversation would be like this, he never mixed words, and, may I add, was a very genuine man. "Well, you better come up to see me, I have got a turkey for you," and I said thank you and arranged the evening. I arrived that evening, was greeted by Alec and his wife, and after the greetings I got out my cheque book and Alec said, "What have you got that out for?" I said, "I owe you £84 that a certain farmer did not pay you for haulage to F.M.C. Canterbury." Alec: "You put that away. You are not paying anything." Myself: "Well, the son in question said he would not pay you." Alec: "Ha, that son has always been a shit, and always will be!" Myself: "Well, even his father agreed with him." With that Mrs.Teal said, "But his father is such a gentleman." Alec: "I do not bloody think so," and also added, "don't you worry, we will get it out of them as we do all their work," and with that he said "Here is your turkey," and it was beautifully dressed etc., and with that he went to a cupboard, pulled out a bottle of whisky and said: "You'd better have this with Christmas greetings." As I said, Alec never wasted words, and what he thought he would say. I always remember him when I used to buy many store cattle from Haywards Heath Market. I would be sitting around the ring just before the sale started. I could see Alec out of the corner of my eye coming up to me, and before he could get to me I knew what he was going to say, as it was the same every time. Alec: "How many cattle do you want then?" Myself: "I do not know, Alec, until they come through those pens." Alec: "Eh." He knew. It did not matter how many I purchased, he would have the job of taking them back to the farm.

Going back to my business, just before I closed it down, F.M.C. and Borthwicks closed down, so that was two thirds of my business really gone, so it was no good carrying on.

On 5th April, 1993, Nicholas, my son, left Ferrantis in Portsmouth and started a new job in Epsom, working for a computer firm that was employed by Bacon and Woodrow, the pension firm. He was lucky to rent a flat where he could park his car in the private grounds of the flats, avoiding parking in the street. The flat is only four minutes from his offices, seven minutes from the leisure centre and eight minutes from the shops, and his golf club about half an hour away at Slinfold, where he spends a fair bit of time at weekends. So he is very lucky, and thank goodness he is still there at the time of writing, 25th August, 1998. Of course, now I am retired, the financial side is much lower but my living expenses are the same, but still I shall survive, I expect.

On 22nd April, 1998, what a surprise, my sister Sylvia and her husband Peter came down at 12.30 pm. We went to see a school friend of Sylvia's in Seaford, and then had a meal at Hill Pub Langley, a lovely afternoon and evening we certainly had.

I collected our dog, Max, from the vets on 23rd April after the removal of two lumps, a wart and a dew claw. Max seemed quite alright. Little did we know what was to come for him in a year's time.

On 28ᵗʰ April Bob and June Longley came to tea. A very nice couple. I met him when I had my first hip operation at the Horder Centre at Crowborough Arthritic Centre. Unluckily his went wrong, and today he has no hip at all, and that leg is one and a half inches shorter than the other one. But he walks with a stick and he tells me he can get up a ladder, also umpires stoolball, as his wife and daughter are very keen on this sport. I can hardly believe he walks on it let alone climb a ladder.

Nicholas and I played golf at Lewes on 1ˢᵗ May, 1993. Nicholas went round with a score of 80 so that meant I lost. Nicholas borrowed my Volvo on 8ᵗʰ May to move his bits and pieces from Portsmouth to his flat in Epsom. On 14ᵗʰ May I played golf with Paul Gent at Lewes, on point system, very frustrating for him. He had a bad day, 21 points, but myself the best I have played since my hip operation, 33 points. I do not know how I actually achieved it, but it was a lovely feeling. We certainly had a laugh about it.

On 29ᵗʰ May I played golf with Nicholas and I had a bad round. Nicholas went round in 80, so I lost, which is general when I play him.

On 2ⁿᵈ June I went to the Congress Theatre in Eastbourne to see the show, Barnham, which was very good, and the following week I took my friend David Patch to the golf practice ground at Horam. I played golf at Lewes on 15ᵗʰ June with my friends David and Jim Patch. David had never played the game, and Jim, he used to play three or four times per year. Both these brothers have been farming all their lives. Jim is just over 60 years old and David is just under 60 years of age. Well, when they first started playing golf with me, they swung through the ball like 20 year old's. I was amazed. There I was, 66 years old, and I had an injured shoulder through a farm accident 34 years before, preventing me from swinging right through the ball, and had not long had a hip replacement. Well, I could see they had a very good chance of playing good golf at their age. But when they came up with scores of 120 and 140, they got very despondent, but I said to them, "I came up with scores like that when I started playing at just over 50 years old," and they just did not believe me, and said, "But you are so consistent." My answer was "So will you be one day." I predicted David, before the year was out, would break the 100 mark, and he said he would not, and so I bet him £5 he would, and that was the middle of this particular year. Well, just before the end of this year, I played golf with him one day. We put our golf trolleys and clubs in my estate car, and David totted up the scores. All of a sudden he got out his purse and gave me £5. I said "What is that for?" and he said, "Well, you bet me that I would break the 100 mark before the year was out, so here is £5 as I have at last broken the 100 score." Well, I was absolutely delighted for him. David and his brother start beating me now, which is very delightful. I know one day when I was playing golf with David at Lewes, he scored a hole in one on a three par 165 yard hole. He was so excited he jumped about all over the place. I was so pleased for him, as it was more than I had ever achieved.

On 16th June, I went to tea to my old friend Peter Braden and his wife and had a very pleasant afternoon.

On 25th June I went up to Birmingham to stay with my nephew and his wife. Nicholas, my son, came about 8.40 pm. Mike, my nephew said, "I bet if Nicholas is here at 8.40, I will buy the wine, Uncle Ken. So all of a sudden a car drew up and it was Nicholas. Mike could not believe it, and he said, "Uncle Ken, I reckon Nicholas was waiting up the road ready to pounce on us at 8.40 pm. He has never forgotten it, and, of course, when I pull his leg about it, we have a good laugh. All three of us played golf at Edgbaston, and to my surprise I came up with a score of 35 points. I would loved to have had a camera, and taken a photo of the expression on Michael's and Nicholas's faces, much as to say, "How did the old man come with 35 points on this course?" It was very enjoyable and of course I was highly delighted, and as Liz and Mike made us so welcome. It was a lovely weekend.

On 14th July I met a farmer customer of mine when in business, went to a particular farm with a view to purchasing, as he had become a millionaire over night by selling five acres of land for building and was looking for a farm where he could see the South Downs from. I told him such a farm would not be in this particular area, as, where there were, the farming families would hold on to them. Hence, looking at this farm land and not the buildings, I advised him it was ideal if he had building permission to erect buildings and a house on the higher ground of this land. Well, eventually he purchased the land and erected the buildings, but as far as I know, has not built the farm house yet. Not knowing a lot about farming, he is making a very successful job of it. He has about 400 acres, mostly cereals and a few beef stores for fattening. He was lucky the following year, Brussels set the farming year prices at around paying out £47 for growing an acre of cereals, as they thought cereal prices would come down form £100 per tonne to £70 a tonne, but it did not happen like that. The selling price of cereal still remained at £100 per tonne, and the price of growing an acre of cereals had risen to £100 per acre before the bubble burst this year of writing, 1998, when at last it has come down to £70 per tonne. Well, I recall talking about these farm prices, and he said: "Well, I am going to make hay while the sun shines, because within two years time the bubble will burst, and cereals will come down to £70 per tonne," and by gosh, he was right. The farm building are situated in a position where he can see the South Downs, so it was very fortunate he was able to acquire this land.

28th July, 1993, going to Bob and June Longleys for tea at 3.00 pm. A very nice couple. I met Bob when he had a hip operation about the same time as I had my hip replacement, and having been farm managers in our farming life, we had a lot to talk about.

On 29th July, my old friend Peter Braden and his wife came to tea, and we always had a lot to say about farming, as usual.

Went to Geoff Badle and his wife's house for supper on July 30th. My friendly bank manager as I call him. The supper was superb, and they made us most welcome. It was always a pleasure to go there.

On 7th August, Rosie, my Uncle Harry and Auntie Flo's niece came. It was her niece she brought up from five years of age. They farmed at Bankhurst Farm where I worked for four and a half years through the war. Anyway, Rosie wanted to look over the farm house again, so I arrange to take Rosie with the permission of the owner at 3.30 pm. John and Margaret, the owners, made us so welcome and, of course, Rosie was in her element. It brought back memories to me, for the old cowshed that was built of wood and corrugated tin where I used to hand milk seven days a week, half of it had fallen down. After the owners took over in 1947 with a jersey herd and machine milking in a parlour, the old cowshed was only used for calves. The owner used to do the milking until he had serious back trouble, and they gave up milking. In the house they had spent quite a lot of money, and made it more modern without spoiling the character of the place. I was very impressed. Biggest picture came to my mind, seeing myself sitting on a stool with my head stuck hard against a cow, milking her, and in the summer, when the flies were about, her tail swishing about, and catching me across the face, and by gosh, didn't it hurt! Anyway, they gave us a lovely tea, and, of course, we were asked questions about the war years when we lived there. It was a lovely experience.

On 13th August 1993, as my friendly bank manager suggested one day when I was talking to him about golf, he said that he went with a foursome to Chartham Park Golf Course, East Grinstead, so we phoned the club and arranged to tee off at 10.30 am. at £23 per round. Nicholas and I thought it was the best course we had played together. There was something about it we liked so much. Nicholas went round in 80 and myself, 104. At that time they were operating from a put- you-up wooden club house, but it was not long before they built a lovely club. Nicholas and I have played the course since the new club house was built, and they have made a lovely job of it. I believe the course was designed by Neil Coles. The next day, we played Lewes Golf Course, tee off time 2.30 pm. also hired a buggy. Nicholas 80 and myself 103, so we did not get any better at the job in hand.

On 16th August, Paul Gent and I played golf at Lewes, tee off time 3.00 pm. Paul Giles 84, myself 96. The best weather and game of golf I had ever played at Lewes.

On 30th August I played golf at Lewes, teed off at 10.15 am. and Nicholas, my son, scored 75, the best ever for him at Lewes, and I was the worst with a score of 113.

6th September: I had always thought the country I would like to go to was Canada, so my partner at that time, and I went to my sister, who lived in Seal, Sevenoaks, Kent for the night and my brother-in-law, Peter, took us to Gatwick Airport on Tuesday, 7th, getting to the airport at 11.00 am. We flew out of Gatwick at 1.30 pm. on time for Toronto, flying at 560 miles per hour at the height of 32,000 feet until we got to the Canadian Zone, and then we were flying at 37,000 feet. Now, my late wife had distant relatives in the Ottawa area, so we stayed two weeks with them, and two weeks with my partner's relations in the Toronto area.

It was a great experience for me as I had never flown in a big jet plane before. The most marvellous thing about it was when flying at 32,000 feet, one looked out of the window and it seemed as though one could get out and walk on the wing. It just seemed as though we were only travelling at five miles per hour. The other great experience for me was flying from Toronto to Ottawa, and afterwards, after a fortnight's stay, flying back to Toronto. These planes were smaller and flew around 20,000 feet, and when landing this did not affect my ear drums. But the planes coming down from 37,000 feet did. While we were there in Canada, we went to the Thousand Islands, also the Niagra Falls, then by the kindness of my partner's daughter in law, we were taken to the big Opera House in Toronto to see 'Carmen'. It was excellent, and a jolly big place. Also we were taken to dinner one Friday night to a large hotel. Part of the hotel seemed to be built on big blocks, so that gave space for car parking, then one walked up several wide steps through the doors into a lovely foyer, then into a lovely dining room with quite a few swivel chairs to sit on. After dinner I saw the reason. I had never been in such a large dining place. There was the largest buffet I had ever seen with all kinds of lovely food. One just helped oneself, until it closed at 8.00 pm. Then at an appropriate time after the meal, in one corner of this building, on a stage, and a very nice play was acted. I had never experienced anything like it.

The son-in-law took me to a large stadium to see American football. The stadium held 52,000 people. What an experience. When one came to sit down you went along to your seat, it nearly made one giddy, as you looked down it seemed as though the seats were built on a roof of a house. It was so steep and either end there was a great television screen, so that you could see what was going on in the game of this American football. Another experience in my life. As it was, previous to that, my partner and I went to lunch at the top of the C.N. Tower in Toronto, the whole dining area revolves, and it is so high. When we were there low cloud came down and one would think one was flying in an aircraft. A great experience.

Going back to the Ottawa area, and my late wife's relations, Jack and Sue, they had built up a quality business in computers, and eventually each of the 220 staff had a share in the business. Well, at the time of a bit of farming depression, when Canada was affected as well as England, they were looking for a house to buy, and they came across sale boards of an 160 acre farm for sale in Carp Koa Ilo. They were not looking to buy a farm, anyhow, they drove down this long drive and when they got to the house and buildings, it was secluded from the road with a lovely lot of trees, and also there was a small bungalow in the grounds, and the farm house was built in 1850, and that is old in Canada. They just fell in love with the property, and purchased it for nearly half the price it was a year or two before, owing to the farm depression.

They had no intention of farming, but gave it a try, buying machinery, etc. But Jack said there was no money in this farming, and so the young chap who ran it for them, he became their tenant for one dollar per year. Now, from the business they had built up, Jack sold 70% of his shares and had to stay on for about six months, but eighteen months before that he started another computer business not too far away, so they still had a business. I may add, the computer business they ran was top quality. They were in defence for the Canadian Government and they had a compartment in the offices. He sold his shares with computers belonging to the Canadian Government, and these computers were twice the size of the upright freezers we have now. What an experience again. Their objective on the farm was to modernise and extend the farm house. Well, they built on a big sitting room, a room for a picture gallery and a very large library with beautiful mahogany looking wood panels all around the walls. In the library was a new fireplace to take three feet logs, and the surround was some kind of stone being carved by hand. The panels came in sections. Outside, between the pond and the house, a lovely patio was built, lovely stone to match the house. I asked Sue, Jack's wife, how much the patio and the library fireplace cost, and she told me $60,000, well, in Canada at that time this would be about £30,000. There had to be another staircase put in and, of course, floors, and they were all maple wood; also, a jolly great □– it looked like a treble – garage, with electrically operated doors.

While they were waiting for these alterations, they stayed at another house they owned. This job should have been finished by May of this year, but they still had not finished it by September when we were there. While staying with Jack and Sue, we were taken to the Reader Club that Jack belonged to. What a marvellous place: in earlier years it was two blocks away, but got burnt down, but was shifted to its present destination six floors up, but as soon as you come to the entrance, you go through these large beautiful mahogany double doors. They are the original doors that were saved from the fire, and you can see burn marks at the bottom of these doors. As one came into the foyer, there was mahogany everywhere with a desk behind which a gentleman sat to book people in. As soon as Jack and Sue walked in, they were recognised immediately and we just walked into the large lounge with chairs all mahogany, with leather backs and seats studded with the appropriate studs. It was, I thought, 1900 English with great character. Oh, by the way, the foyer had a beautiful very large chandelier hanging from the centre of the ceiling. It was all a matching style, and when it came for the time for us to go into the dining room for dinner, the dining room was of the same style and character, and the food was first class. This is where with starter, Jack ordered white wine. I said to him: "Well, I've never had wine with a starter before," and he said, "Try it," and I did, so that was another experience for me. Then one day Sue said, "Jack cannot make it, but would you like to go to dinner at a Japanese Restaurant?" We said with pleasure, so the Friday night came and off we went to this restaurant in Ottawa, picking up a lady friend of Sue's on the way. She was about eighty years old, a very nice lady, who had a false leg. Well, when we walked in the door of this restaurant the management knew Sue immediately and the manager was showing us a part of the restaurant where one walked up three steps and you were on a different floor. The tables were very low and you sat down on the floor part and dangled your legs under the low table giving the impression you were squatting at the table like the Japanese do. But our lady guest said, no thank you, I cannot sit there," and I said also "nor can I with the hip operation I had last year." So we sat in the area with ordinary chairs and tables. I was asked if I would like a Japanese beer, which I accepted. I am not really a drinker, mostly a shandy man, but this beer was absolutely marvellous, and very cold, just how I like a drink. Then the food I chose sort of a beef stew, was perfect. Sue also ordered, along with her family different food on a large plate. I believe some were raw fish pieces, and also there was Sacky. I thought, I am not going to be beaten, so I tried a piece of this raw fish and Sacky, but was not fond of it, but, I thought, it is another experience. Then came the time when there was a small round ball I was told was horse radish. No one else wanted it, so it was offered to me, so I took it. As it was the size of a small golf ball I put it straight in my mouth and started chewing. Well, that was a bad mistake. My goodness, it was so hot, it nearly choked me. There I was, throwing my arms about, trying not to shout out, my eyes streaming, and of course the rest of the party could not help laughing at the antics I was performing.

However, I succeeded in containing myself, but what a different experience, I shall never forget it.

At, the next lunch at the farm house, we were just going to start lunch, and on the table was some very hot red sauce. I put some on my plate with other food, and all of a sudden the youngest son got up and told me to stop. He was about nine or ten years old and he went over to the cupboard, reached up, brought out a glass, went over to the cold tap, filled the glass, brought it to me and said, "Now you can start, Ken." He had not forgotten the fiasco of the previous evening at the Japanese restaurant, and then his father appeared, just going to sit down to lunch, and said, "Well, Ken, I hear that I should have been at the Japanese restaurant last night with a camera." I said, "You certainly should have," and with that we had a jolly good laugh. I must say both homes we went to we experienced such a welcome. I like that part of Canada very much.

On 6th October, 1993 we arrived back from Canada, flew into Gatwick airport and were picked up by my brother-in-law, Peter, taken back to Peter and Sylvia's home to rest for about three hours, and home to Dove Cottage, but I must add, we told him we would arrive on the 5th October, so the poor chap had a lost journey, getting messed with the different hours change. Well, what can one expect from an old farm boy! But I achieved at last to go to Canada.

On 16th October, I played my son, Nicholas, golf at Lewes. He had a score of 84, and I had a terrible round and went up to 114. On 22nd November I played golf at Lewes with Jim and David Paul and their friend. I went round in 103, so that was better than previously. David and I were just beaten by John Brown, Jim's friend, by him pitching up on to the green and the ball going straight in the hole. What luck!

On 29th November I met one of my previous customers and went to Hailsham and purchased 15 very good store cattle. On 11th December, 1993, I went on my usual journey before Christmas to see my two old friends of the past with a bottle of drink and a good old chat with the older gentleman with whom I worked in the war on my uncle's farm, that chat would be about farming, and with the other gentleman, it would be about shotgun shooting.

On 14th December, 1993 I played David Patch at snooker at an Eastbourne club, and David won all three games. All I could say to him at that time was, "You just wait until I get you on that golf course!"

On 26th December 1993 I went to my sister and brother-in-law's for the day and had a lovely time.

31st December, the end of another year.

On 16th January, 1994 the chimney caught fire at Dove Cottage at 6.20 pm. My goodness, the smoke was like a fog. The fire brigade came very quickly to put it out and made a very clean job of it. The chimney stack walls were very warm - a good start to the New Year!

Went to tea with Brian and Win, his wife, on 18th January. I had known Brian for years; he was a rep for an agriculture feed firm, and he was the gentleman who was responsible for letting me know about the farm manager's job at Coleman's Farm, which eventually I got. We had a very pleasant time and were made very welcome.

I played golf on 21st January with my son and Michael Maplesden, my mother's cousin's son. We were playing for the Memorial Cup in memory of his late father. We enjoyed it very much. Before the dinner at night, Nicholas and I played snooker against Michael and Peter. It was very close; we managed to lose on a black.

Nicholas had to be up at 3.00 am. on 4th February to get his connections for the journey to France to go skiing. I am so pleased he is enjoying these sort of sports while he can.

On 7th February I took Max to the vet at 9.10 am. to see David Lang. I had known him for years, very good vet. There was a very hard lump on Max's side near his back leg, not very good news. Had to have an operation on Tuesday, 15th. 50/50 chance.

On 15th February Max, our dog, was operated on for two cancerous growths and seven bad teeth extracted. It did not look very hopeful.

On 2nd March, 1994 Max, our dog, had to be put to sleep. A tumour in his bowels had formed which was not there when he was operated on before. He was a lovely dog, and we certainly missed him, especially Nicholas when coming home at weekends, as he took Max for very long walks. But as my dear mother would say, "Ah, my boy, it was to be."

I went to D.B. Autos on 8th April for a trim to be fitted to my Volvo after repairing damage that was sustained in a car park at Eastbourne. Good job it was an insurance job, as it cost over £600, and I paid £50. Very unfortunate, but they certainly made an excellent job of it.

I played golf with David Patch at Lewes on 13th April, the gentleman who had never played golf before. Myself 118, David 152. He was quite despondent, but I told him that within the year he would break 100, as when I started I had had that sort of score. He said, "How you play now I do not believe it," but happily that was the case.

On 23rd April I played golf with Nicholas at Lewes. Nicholas 32, self 25. It was one of those games we call a bit of a nightmare. However, that is golf. That same day I purchased a new putter for £23. Whether it has improved my putting I do not really know, but on the next day we played there again, Nicholas 78, 39 points and myself 100 and 35 points, so we both felt better that day.

On 11th May I played golf at Lewes with David and Jim Patch, David 130, Jim 118, self 102. Then Nicholas and I played there again on 14th May with Mike Maplesden and his son-in-law. We managed to win on points.

We went to Shropshire to Joan and John's on 25th May, for a fortnight, our usual place where we were always welcome.

I played golf with Paul Gent at Blatchington Seaford course on 17th June. A lovely course, Paul 28 points, self 30 points. Just managed to win, very rare against Paul. Then on 22nd June, 1994 I played golf at Wellshurst, Horam, a new course, with two friends, Ken 117, Les 103 and myself 97. I can see Les saying when counting the score up, "I don't know! Ken has never played this course before and yet has gone around in 97." It was my lucky day.

As you can see, I played a lot of golf, in between looking after the lawn and flower and vegetable gardens and, of course, going to visit different people and a theatre or two.

On 30th June, 1994 my lady partner and I parted after two years three months. We parted amicably and, thank goodness, she went to live with her youngest son, but it was very upsetting.

On 2nd July Nicholas came down and we played golf at Lewes. Nicholas 83, 35 points and self 105 and 33 points.

I went to Peter and Sylvia's, my sister and brother-in-law's, on 3rd July, 1994. I arrived there at 8.05 am., had breakfast then, of course, talked about the parting of my partner and myself. They could not believe it. Anyhow, it was nice to talk about it, and I didn't leave there until 8.12 pm. Had a lovely day.

As I have said before, I had no intention at all to be on my own for the rest of my life, so I got a Date Line magazine and wrote to two ladies looking for a gentleman. All of a sudden I received a phone call from one of the ladies. Her name was Olive. From that we met for lunch at the Birch Hotel in Haywards Heath on 31st July, 1994. A lovely lady, and from that meeting Olive has been my partner for four years, and Olive gets on so well with my son, Nicholas, which is a bonus. To me 31st July was the most fortunate day of my life for the last five years. Olive also has two lovely daughters that I get on well with. So, as I have said previously, we lived at Dove cottage. Olive eventually sold her house and purchased a bungalow in a nearby seaside town, into which we moved on 27th January, 1997. We are very happy here, but since living here we have had health problems, Olive having a back operation, myself a replacement hip operation that has not gone right. So at the time of writing, 3rd September, 1998, I go back in hospital to have another operation on my hip that I had first operated on a year ago. I do hope it is successful this time. When I look back at 1996, Olive was going to the chiropractor, acupuncture etc. to try and avoid an operation, but to no avail, and ended in having the operation in May 1997. So 1996 was not a good year, neither was 1997, and this year, 1998, is proving to be as bad, so I hope it can only get better for both of us.

Looking back over my life, I have been pretty lucky, and one high light is in having a very caring son. Also I have enjoyed my farming life, although I had to struggle to get where I wanted to in my farming career, and also had to set up a small business, involving farm livestock, but I succeeded, thank goodness. I can see my dear mother saying, "Ah, my boy, it was to be!" The two things I pray for are that Olive and I have better health in the future, and that once again I can play golf.

As I have said, the operation on my hip that I had on 28th August, 1997 was not a success. It became loose and eventually I could hardly bare to walk on it. In the end they had to carry me out to the ambulance, get me to hospital, carry me in and put me into a wheel chair to have an X-ray and be taken into the consulting room to see a nice young locum as my surgeon was on holiday. This was on 28th August, 1998. He looked at the X-ray and said, "I believe you have an infection on the femur bone," and I nearly fell out of the chair with shock. Then he proceeded to say, "Do you feel alright in yourself?" and I said, "Yes, I feel very strong, but it is my hip that is giving me hell, and when this happens it generally affects your whole being." He said he'd ask his colleague to come in, as he was a well known surgeon. He looked at the X-ray and agreed on the diagnosis. I said, "Well, something will have to be done as I cannot go on like this." He said "Now, I will go in, take the hip out, scrape the bone, so the scraping's go on a culture to identify the infection, so that we then will pump you with antibiotics for this particular infection. You will be hobbling about on crutches for three weeks in hospital, and also a few weeks at home without a hip. He also said: "I will try to operate on 7th September." He went away for a few minutes, came back and said: "Yes, you be in here on 6th and I will operate on the 7th." Well, with that the ambulance men carried me into the bungalow and then I had verification that I was to be admitted to Eastbourne Hospital on 6th September, and operated on the next day.

So, on the Sunday, I was carried off to hospital on the 6th September 1998, operated on the 7th. The hip was taken out and the hard work came. I was given a special tall zimmer frame with two small wheels on the front part, and had to use it, hopping on my good leg and keeping my operated leg off the ground. I could not believe the energy that took. I never hopped more than 30 feet and then 30 feet back to the bed, and I was exhausted, as though I had been chasing 20 bullocks around a 20 acre field for a two hour period. I just could not believe it. But the sister in the ward said to me "You must remember, Ken, you have had a major operation and lost a lot of blood, which has made you weaker than normal." The other thing I remember is hopping on one leg with that zimmer takes much more energy, something like fifteen times as much. However, my arms ached so much, I thought the muscles were going to give out on me, but gradually I became more used to it and, of course, I was getting stronger, thank goodness. I was walking like that for eleven days, then on a Monday morning, a young physio chap came to me and said: "Are you walking on your one hip leg yet?" I said, "no and I am not going to until you people say I can," and with that he looked at his book and said you can, and with that he took me off the zimmer and straight on crutches, and by golly, I had to concentrate so much to keep upright. I could only look four or five feet in front of me, for fear of falling over. Gradually it got better, and I remember saying to a physio young lady just before I came out of hospital, while I was using my crutches hobbling along with her in attendance, "Even if a lovely young lady walked across the corridor naked, I could not look more than ten feet ahead of me, so if she was further than that distance and I looked up, I would soon be on the floor." "Oh," she said, "don't for goodness sake do that."

I was three weeks in hospital and during that time, the scraping's from my femur were put on a culture and nothing came up. So the surgeon sent me home without a hip, and wanted me back in six to eight weeks time to put the hip back in. So I am hobbling about without a hip at home. What a game it is. If I lay flat in bed it hurts too much, and so I sit up in bed with six pillows behind me, but then I cannot sleep and after two hours that leg starts hurting, so I just sit on the side of the bed to ease the pain. After a while I sit up in bed again, and after another couple of hours I get up. The time is about four am. I hobble down to my high chair in the sitting room, put my feet up, and Olive covers me up like a little baby, and that is where I stay until breakfast time. The first procedure is a bowl of hot water and flannel, shaving gear, then I wash and shave at the table, sitting down, as I cannot, after being out of hospital for three weeks, stand at the wash basin to wash and shave, and I can tell you, I would not wish a hip being taken out on my worse enemy, not as I know I have got any enemies.

When I first came out of hospital, I phoned Mr. and Mrs. Barnham to say that I was out of hospital, as they had kindly come to see me in hospital, and that was a lovely surprise. As I said, I always got on with them well. In the course of conversation they said they had been for a week's holiday over to the Isle of Wight to his late mother and father's bungalow. He said they had spent a lot of money on the bungalow to bring it up to good repair. And then, to my great surprise, they said, "As soon as you are able, you can have a week's holiday in the bungalow with Olive and Nicholas, free of charge, as you have done enough for the Barnhams in the past." What a lovely gesture!

22nd October, 1998 at last I have got two appointments at the local hospital, one for a pre-med on 13th November, and one for the 25th November to put my hip back in again. I do hope my new hip will be successful this time, and that I will eventually be able to do things, for at the moment I cannot do a damn thing, only read and write and dress myself. On 13th November I went to the hospital for a pre-med, and have been told they want me to go into hospital on 24th November so that I have two days in hospital before my operation, owing to me being on Warfrin tablets, so that they can stop the Warfrin tablets and put me onto some other procedure before I am operated on to put my metal hip back in, so that I do not bleed too freely. I do hope this time it is going to be a success.

After my hip was put back in, I had some infection that caused some trouble, but a doctor in the field of that kind of trouble gave instructions to inject me three times a day with antibiotics, going for the "big infection" as he called it. I had a week of injections, then they were stopped, and then the oozing stopped after another week, and I was allowed to go home, just before Christmas 1998. I had been in hospital for three and a half weeks - how nice to be home for Christmas.

It is marvellous how it all healed up, and I have not had any more trouble with it. I had to be on crutches for two months, keeping my weight of seventy per cent off the operated hip. Then after two months, I saw this excellent surgeon on the 28th January, 1999, and he allowed me to be on two sticks for two months, then on 1st April, I had an appointment to see him. I was x-rayed on my operated hip, and afterwards I saw this same surgeon who operated on me, putting in a special longer hip in which the femur bone grows to the metal, no cement. He looked at the x-ray and said, "All OK." I said, "Well it should be. I have kept to all the rules." He said "Good, now you can go onto one stick." I said "What about driving?" and he said, "Yes," so I said, "Can I go back to a normal life?" "Go by how you feel," he said, "and in everything go very steady. I will want to see you again on 2nd December, and then I will x-ray both hips. The reason for that is, as the opposite hip was operated on seven years ago at the Horder Centre, by putting in a metal hip it now takes so much pressure.

To date, I am getting on very well. How lovely to drive, and have a shower at last. So it looks a great success after such a long time, thanks to the excellent surgeon.

This manuscript is actually what happened in my life.